LAMAR
HUNT

the gentle giant
who revolutionized
professional sports

David A.F. Sweet

TRIUMPH
B O O K S

Library of Congress Cataloging-in-Publication Data

Sweet, David, 1963–
  Lamar Hunt : the gentle giant who revolutionized professional sports / David Sweet.
     p. cm.
  Includes bibliographical references.
  ISBN 978-1-60078-374-6
  1. Hunt, Lamar, 1932-2006. 2. Football team owners—United States—Biography.
3. Kansas City Chiefs (Football team) 4. American Football League. I. Title.
  GV939.H86S84 2010
  796.332092—dc22
                                 2010030236

This book is available in quantity at special discounts for your group or organization. For further information, contact:
  Triumph Books
  542 South Dearborn Street
  Suite 750
  Chicago, Illinois 60605
  (312) 939–3330
  Fax (312) 663–3557
  www.triumphbooks.com

Printed in U.S.A.
ISBN: 978-1-60078-374-6
Design by Patricia Frey
Photos courtesy of AP Images unless otherwise indicated

To Tricia

CONTENTS

ACKNOWLEDGMENTS

THE DOZENS OF PEOPLE I SPOKE WITH for this book—from NFL principals such as former commissioner Paul Tagliabue, Buffalo Bills owner Ralph Wilson, and former Kansas City Chiefs coach Marty Schottenheimer, to soccer impresarios such as U.S. Soccer Federation head and New England Revolution president Sunil Gulati, to the pro tennis executives who ran Lamar Hunt's World Championship Tennis for nearly every one of its 23 years, Owen Williams and Mike Davies—all were unfailingly friendly and giving of their time and memories. Being able to speak with many of Hunt's executives and employees—especially on the soccer and tennis side, where his story has been little told—was a blessing.

Aside from those mentioned above, interviews were conducted either in person or via telephone with, in alphabetical order: Ernie Accorsi (former general manager of the Baltimore Colts, Cleveland Browns, and New York Giants); Rob Baade (president of the International Association of Sports Economists); Bill Bartholomay (chairman emeritus of the Atlanta Braves who helped found Atlanta's NASL team); Raymond Berry (Hall of Fame wide receiver and Hunt's teammate at Southern Methodist University); Andrew Brandt (National Football Post president and Wharton School of Business professor); Butch Buchholz (member of the Handsome Eight and founder of the Sony Ericsson

Open); Bud Collins (former NBC announcer and author of numerous tennis books); Lester Crown (Chicago Bulls investor and former chairman of General Dynamics); Rick Gosselin (*Dallas Morning News* sportswriter and former *Kansas City Star* sportswriter); Forrest Gregg (Hall of Fame offensive tackle and Hunt's teammate at Southern Methodist University); Bob Harlan (chairman emeritus of the Green Bay Packers); Bob Hermann (former owner of pro soccer's St. Louis Stars and chairman of the NASL's executive committee); Rick Holton (whose father helped sponsor Hunt's tennis ventures); Ted Howard (former NASL executive); Rod Humphries (former COO of WCT among other WCT positions); Don Maynard (played in every AFL season for New York Jets); Patrick McCaskey (Chicago Bears executive); Andy McKenna (former chairman of the Chicago White Sox and the Chicago Cubs); Thom Meredith (Hunt's onetime administrative assistant who also worked for the Dallas Tornado and WCT); Bobby Moffat (longtime Dallas Tornado player); Murray Olderman (former nationally syndicated columnist who drew Hunt's portrait for the Pro Football Hall of Fame); Don Pierson (former president of Pro Football Writers Association); Temple Pouncey (former *Dallas Morning News* sportswriter who covered soccer and tennis); Marty Rotberg (former NASL and WCT executive); Gale Sayers (drafted No. 1 by the AFL Kansas City Chiefs); Jim Schaaf (Kansas City Chiefs general manager from 1976 to 1988); Hank Steinbrecher (former secretary general of the U.S. Soccer Federation); R. Gerald Turner (Southern Methodist University president); and Pat Williams (former Chicago Bulls general manager and present Orlando Magic senior vice president). Almost all are quoted in the book, and their information is also used to support other material. Some were able to share important letters from Hunt to executives such as Pete Rozelle and from fans to Hunt. I thank each of them for their valuable insights and help.

Research materials are also essential, and I owe a debt of gratitude to scores of books, magazines (especially the superbly written *Sports Illustrated* articles of the 1960s and 1970s), newspapers (a tip of the hat to the *Dallas Morning News*), trade publications, documentaries, and other sources of information. Even *Cigar Aficionado* lent a hand (and not because Hunt smoked cigars).

Looking back, had I not sat in Deerfield Academy teacher Bryce Lambert's English class as a sophomore in 1978, this book never would have happened. Mr. Lambert's was the only class I ever took that I looked forward to attending, because of his entertaining, eccentric style and disciplined mien. Mr. Lambert at one point assigned all of us a thesis, and mine was on Henry Wadsworth Longfellow. I remember spending many winter nights during Christmas break at home, reading Longfellow's works and writing notes on the 3 x 5 cards Mr. Lambert insisted upon—and enjoying it immensely.

The research skills and discipline he imparted, along with demanding precision in writing (to emphasize its lack of impact he cut out the word *very* every time it was used) were essential to what I'm doing today. So I salute Mr. Lambert, who died a few years ago but whose spirit endures.

I've been blessed to enjoy many excellent bosses in sports journalism. Jeff Prugh hired me for my first full-time sports job, as executive sports editor of the daily *Glendale News-Press* and two biweekly papers in Southern California. The former *Los Angeles Times* sportswriter was unfailingly helpful and gracious, and he died far too young last year at 69. Will Springer guided me at the *Wall Street Journal* Online and shepherded the weekly "Nothing but Net" column into publication on the web and often in the paper. His unflappable demeanor and quiet humor were always appreciated. And Jerry Kavanagh, retired New York bureau chief at *SportsBusiness Journal*, has been immensely kind and supportive throughout the years. His contacts for this book especially have been invaluable.

I would be remiss not to thank Frank Ward, former coach at Lake Forest Country Day School, who nurtured my enthusiasm for sports for years on the playing fields and who has imparted great wisdom ever since.

Of course, none of this would have been possible without my parents, Nancy and Philip Sweet, who have been supportive and complimentary of my writing always and also uncovered a few key people to speak with. My brother Kirk and sister Sandy have also been encouraging. Finally, my wife, Tricia, has been unfailingly positive about this project from its inception.

INTRODUCTION

THE FIRST TIME I SPOKE WITH LAMAR HUNT, he surprised me in a couple of ways.

He was probably the easiest executive in pro sports to get in contact with. When I talked with him after securing an interview with a simple call to his Dallas office, he spoke calmly and seemed to have as much time as I needed. This was stunning coming from someone so deeply involved in interests ranging from the National Football League to Major League Soccer, which happened to be our topic for the day.

Also, his honesty was striking. He pointed out problems with MLS at the beginning of the new century in his even-toned voice, refusing to sugarcoat the fact that expenses far exceeded revenues. Not that he would give up on pro soccer; he harbored great hopes for the game. This was the man, after all, who in the 1960s had introduced the North American Soccer League's Tornado franchise to Dallas—a city where soccer balls were as rare as blizzards.

After talking about MLS a few more times, we later touched base for a football story on one of his favorite topics: the two-point conversion. After joining the NFL in 1970, the Kansas City Chiefs owner proposed that teams be allowed to get twice as many points after a touchdown, an opportunity afforded in the American Football League he had launched. Turned down time and again ("The most difficult obstacle was the coaches," Hunt told me, "because they didn't want to think about the possibility of losing a game on a two-pointer"), the owners finally relented—nearly a quarter-century after Hunt first proposed the measure.

For what seemed to be as long ago as Hunt's initial quest for the two-point conversion, I had written a simple subject line in a Microsoft Word document on my home computer in 2002: "book—lamar hunt." First typed on 70th Street in New York City and buttressed with perhaps 250 words of background information, the file sat dormant for years, surviving a move to the Chicago area and the arrival of three children who love banging away at the keyboard and somehow missed opening it.

During the summer of 2009, I scoured some old files for book ideas. I was itching to write a sports book. I emailed Scott Rowan of Triumph Books, noting I would like to submit a few proposals and asking how I should go about it. Though we hadn't been in touch for seven years, he emailed back immediately. Since our last conversation, he had moved from public relations at Triumph to acquisitions. He ushered the process along and—thanks to Scott, Adam Motin, Laine Morreau, Tom Bast, and many others at Triumph—the end result of a once-light file rests in your hands.

CHAPTER 1

A LIFE-CHANGING DECISION

TWO DAYS BEFORE CHRISTMAS IN 1962, 20-mile-per-hour winds lashed the faces of Bostonians. Temperatures in Chicago and Denver sank into the teens. Snowflakes drifted onto New York City's endless pavement.

On that December 23, a Sunday, many stores were closed because of state blue laws, which restricted commerce during days of worship (in Connecticut, for instance, only Jewish-owned businesses could open on the Sabbath). Across the country, three television channels—CBS, NBC, and ABC—ruled broadcasting. No matter how one altered one's rooftop antenna, choices of what to watch were limited. Lifetime, AMC, and hundreds of other cable channels had not been created; VCR and DVD players were no more than a dream.

As morning passed and early afternoon rolled around, parents reminded children they couldn't open Christmas presents yet. With little else going on, it was truly a day of rest. Given the absence of activity combined with the wearisome weather in much of the country, many flicked on their black-and-white television sets and turned the knob to ABC, where a football game was being played in Houston.

There, the best teams in the upstart American Football League—the Western Division Dallas Texans (11–3) and the Eastern Division Houston

Oilers (11–3)—faced off for the championship. The difference between the title game that day and how pro football runs the Super Bowl in the 21st century is staggering.

For starters, Houston played host to the game at Jeppesen Stadium—originally constructed as a high school football field—rather than battling the Texans at a neutral site. Only one week separated the game from the regular season's finish. To say a buildup preceded the AFL Championship Game would drain the word of its meaning. Elvis Presley didn't sing at halftime, unlike the Rolling Stones or Bruce Springsteen 45 years later. Millions watched the game on ABC, but the audience pales in comparison to the 93 million U.S. television viewers who are captivated annually by the Super Bowl.

The crowd of 37,981 that packed Jeppesen Stadium would barely fill half of a Super Bowl. The single-level stadium, built before the Japanese bombed Pearl Harbor, lacked luxury suites, and its bare-bones scoreboard showed no replays. The game, which kicked off at 2:00 PM, ended almost at supper time (as it was then known) in the Central time zone, which is about when the Super Bowl begins these days. Winning players received a few thousand dollars for their work; in 2010, the share topped $70,000 apiece. And, perhaps most important, in 1962 the AFL was one of two pro football leagues trying to survive. The other, the National Football League, served as the granddaddy of the game, and its championship game would be held one week later at Yankee Stadium in New York City.

The country, too, would barely be recognized by an American today. The idea of nuclear armageddon rattled citizens. Only two months earlier, the Cuban Missile Crisis—prompted by the Soviet Union building missile bases 90 miles from the Florida Keys—had stunned the nation, as the United States sat one wrong move away from a war of annihilation. Segregation and Jim Crow laws controlled the South. General Motors flourished like no other company; the thought of bankruptcy for such an omnipotent organization was preposterous. Men and women smoked cigarettes, even indoors. *Lawrence of Arabia*—a historical movie set in the Middle East and lacking any of the pyrotechnics prevalent in modern cinematography—captured the Oscar for Best Picture. The Internet, microwave dinners, voice mail, and other advances were unknown (clips of the game couldn't be posted to YouTube, nor could viewers change channels with a remote control). Technological marvels, though, did occur high in the sky, as John Glenn became the first American to orbit Earth. The Beatles? Little discussed outside of Liverpool.

In sports, the National Hockey League counted six franchises, the World Series had never been played at night, no pro soccer leagues existed in the 50 states, and tennis championships—such as the one at Forest Hills in New York—were played solely by amateurs. The start of the tumult of the 1960s—assassinations, riots, and the rest—would begin 11 months later in the Texans' hometown of Dallas, when President John F. Kennedy was shot dead by two sniper bullets.

What links December 23, 1962, to life in the 21st century is the game itself—played on a 100-yard field, featuring two teams in different-colored uniforms, with players engaged in mind-shaking hits and a nearly primal desire to win.

The team new to the championship game resided in Dallas. After a .500 record during their first two seasons, the Texans trampled opponents in 1962. A new quarterback named Leonard Ray Dawson—who had toiled five uneventful seasons for Pittsburgh and Cleveland in the NFL—helped rejuvenate the offense. At 238 pounds, new fullback Curtis McClinton, a star at the University of Kansas, bowled over tacklers, enough to earn AFL Rookie of the Year honors. Abner Haynes, already a star, kept churning out yards as a running back.

The defense, spearheaded by the linebacker corps of E.J. Holub, Walt Corey, and Sherrill Headrick, intimidated opponents. No team had given up fewer yards that season. Combined, the offense and defense boasted the best takeaway/giveaway differential in the league, with 17 more turnovers in their favor.

The Texans entered Houston's home stadium with confidence. Five of their last six games were victories by an average margin of more than two touchdowns, even though their star wide receiver, Chris Burford—who had scored 12 touchdowns in the first 10 games—suffered a season-ending knee injury. Despite the fact that the Oilers (Houston's first major pro sports team, which had riveted the town by signing LSU star Billy Cannon before it had played a down) had captured the first two AFL championships, the Texans believed they would bring a title to Dallas, about 240 miles away. After all, during their last visit to Jeppesen Stadium in the fall, they had crushed the Oilers 31–7, halting their strong offensive attack (the Texans and the Oilers finished as the two top-scoring teams during the regular season).

Roaring into Jeppesen, the Texans gunned for Dallas' first football glory since Southern Methodist University delivered a national championship behind Doak Walker in the 1940s. And in the first 30 minutes, they jumped out so far ahead that spectators wondered whether it was worth staying for the whole game.

Thanks to two touchdowns by 6'1", 200-pound running back Haynes—who earned both Rookie of the Year honors and the league's MVP award in its inaugural 1960 season—Dallas grabbed a 17–0 lead on the windy, overcast day. With a stout defense prepared to finish the job, the Texans entered the locker room believing the AFL trophy could finally be wrested from the biggest city in Texas.

But after their halftime rest, the Oilers battled back. A 15-yard pass from quarterback George Blanda—a 13-year veteran who was cast aside by the Chicago Bears—to receiver Willard Dewveall (another former Bear who was the first player to abandon the NFL for the AFL) resulted in a touchdown. The following extra point, kicked by Blanda, capped a six-play 67-yard drive to cut the margin to 17–7. Kicking toe-first in the style of the day, Blanda lifted a 31-yard field goal through the uprights in the fourth quarter, slicing the lead to 17–10.

With less than six minutes remaining, fullback Charley Tolar—a 5'6", 210-pounder known as "the Human Bowling Ball"—rushed one yard for a touchdown, tying the game at 17 once the extra point sailed through. Soon after another Houston defensive stop, Dallas faced the unthinkable as Blanda prepared for a 42-yard field goal with three minutes left. Given Dallas' inability to muster any offense in the second half—the Texans hadn't advanced past the Oilers' 46 and were bewildered by their opponent's blitz schemes—a historic collapse looked likely. But Headrick threw up a hand and blocked Blanda's attempt. A desperation heave by the Houston quarterback in the waning seconds (as 10 Dallas players defended the pass with one rusher) failed and, for the first time, an AFL Championship Game entered overtime.

Though Haynes had rushed for more than 1,000 yards during the season and excelled during the first 60 minutes of the title game, he fumbled when trying to follow coach Hank Stram's coin-toss instructions. Stram told Haynes to choose to defend the north goal (to benefit from a 14-mile-per-hour wind) if Dallas won the coin toss. That would mean the Texans would kick, which was fine with Stram. Though it may sound bizarre considering the next score would win the game, Stram's defense had allowed a league-low 233 points that season, and his offense had sputtered after the first half. Kicking seemed a small trade-off for getting the wind at the Texans' backs.

As referee Harold Bourne's coin toss tumbled through the air, Haynes called heads. He was correct. Bourne said, "You have your choice, of course, receiving or kicking."

What Haynes said next stunned the national audience, who heard the whole exchange because ABC's Jack Buck stood in a suit at midfield with a lengthy microphone recording the scene.

"We will kick to the clock," Haynes said.

"You're gonna kick?" Bourne questioned.

"Yes," Haynes said.

Bourne put a hand on Haynes' shoulder pad and swung his right leg in a kicking motion.

Since Haynes first said Dallas would kick, Houston was able to choose which goal to defend. The Oilers nabbed the one with the strong wind at their backs. So even though Dallas had won the toss, they lost in both ways possible due to Haynes' mistake.

But Haynes would not become a goat. No one scored in the first overtime. The teams switched sides, giving Dallas the tailwind. The Texans had been outplayed in some respects (by the end of the game, Houston would post 359 net yards compared to 237 for Dallas). But by the beginning of the second overtime—after 75 minutes of tension-packed football—Blanda had tossed four interceptions, while Texans quarterback Dawson, the AFL Player of the Year, had thrown zero. For that reason, Dallas was still fighting to win its first title.

And Blanda's fifth misfire would help give the Texans the crown. With Houston marching into field-goal range, the Texans' Billy Hull grabbed a Blanda pass and returned it to midfield. Aided by fullback Jack Spikes, Dawson drove Dallas into Houston territory, ending up inside their 20-yard line.

Fourth down arrived. Less than three minutes into the second overtime period, Dawson put the snap from center down and pointed the laces toward the goalposts. Tommy Brooker, a 17th-round draft choice who had made only 12 of 22 field goals during his rookie season, struck the ball and kicked a 25-yard field goal into the stands. The longest game in professional-football history—exceeding the Colts-Giants single-overtime championship thriller four years earlier, which had persuaded a young man named Lamar Hunt to focus on buying an NFL team—had ended. Dallas 20, Houston 17.

"We're just proud that we can win the championship and bring it back to Dallas, Texas," Stram told Buck after the game.

Both the head coach and Brooker were carried off the field. They headed toward the Texans' locker room. There they would find their owner, a humble Dallas native who refuted the stereotype of the hail-fellow-well-met Texan. It was Hunt, the man who had failed in his quest to buy an NFL franchise. Unhappy with that setback, the multimillionaire had decided to launch an entire professional football league. His entrepreneurial zeal hadn't guaranteed him the best seats for the championship game—in fact, he sat up near the top of the stadium where the wind wailed. (He had also missed the botched coin-toss decision, having slipped out to the bathroom.)

But now, though he may have looked out of place in his necktie and horn-rimmed glasses among all the helmets and shoulder pads, it was time to enjoy the wild, champagne-soaked locker-room celebration with his players and coaches.

In the next day's paper, *Dallas Morning News* columnist Gary Cartwright wrote that "everyone was watching Hunt, who looked like he had just dog-paddled the Atlantic pulling the Queen Mary with his necktie. They had to cut off his tie that night. He taped it together the following Thursday and wore it to a Spur Club luncheon and nobody laughed.

"'They probably thought it was the only tie I had,' Hunt said."

At age 30—younger than some of his players—Hunt had won his first pro football championship. Invigorated by the historic victory, he celebrated in the dingy locker room surrounded by men amazed at their good fortune that he had created a second pro league.

Yet, despite the thrill of the game, the excitement in the depths of Jeppesen Stadium, and the best early Christmas present he had ever received, Hunt confronted a painful predicament. The Texans, it seemed, could no longer survive in his hometown of Dallas, neither as AFL champions nor as last-place losers.

It wasn't as bleak when Hunt formed the American Football League with seven other owners—who became known as the Foolish Club—in 1959. At that point, when he announced a franchise in Dallas, he owned the market. But the National Football League countered by depositing the expansion Cowboys there in 1960—the same year the Texans kicked off—and it became obvious the city of 700,000 felt crowded trying to support two professional football teams. Luring fans, capturing advertising, and drumming up newspaper coverage became much harder than it was in cities with single franchises, such as Philadelphia and Detroit.

Hunt tried mightily to make the Texans Dallas' team. Aside from Haynes, a North Texas State product, other important players—such as quarterback Cotton Davidson—graduated from Texas schools. Hunt's marketing campaigns oozed pizzazz; in one, women stepped out of Renaults and appeared at the front doors of Dallas homeowners to sell season tickets. At a "Meet the Texans Night," 1,000 orchids were handed out to women spectators and dozens of footballs were kicked into the crowd. Two season tickets filled a number of balloons that rose into the air during an exhibition game.

There was more. Hunt launched the Huddle Club where, for only a buck, children could join the club and gain free admission to each Texans home game. Out in public, the young owner carried a season-ticket order book in hopes of attracting new customers. In an early game against the New York Titans, Hunt proclaimed Barber Day, where wearers of barber smocks were let in free.

"We did every crazy thing we could think of—and a few more—because we knew we had to pull out all the stops. Not that we were any great shakes as salesmen," Hunt said. "We had thousands of those Huddle Club kids. And, if you can believe it, they got a T-shirt to go with it."

Despite the promotions, the Texans sold perhaps 6,500 season tickets (a number which may have been inflated and likely included substantial discounts) for the Cotton Bowl, which held a shade over 75,000 and which also served as the Cowboys' home field. Yet in that inaugural 1960 season, the Texans won the battle against its intracity competitor, starting with the home opener.

On September 24, 1960, 30,000 attended the Cowboys game, a 35–28 loss to the Pittsburgh Steelers, who were led by University of Texas standout Bobby Layne. The next day, the Texans—fresh from a 6–0 preseason—defeated the Los Angeles Chargers 17–0 before a crowd of 42,000. Over the course of the season, the Texans averaged more than 24,000 fans per game at the Cotton Bowl at ticket prices ranging from 90¢ to $4, compared to 21,417 for the Cowboys. Of course, they were more fun to watch—the Texans finished 8–6, and the lowly Cowboys ended their expansion season with a mark of 0–11–1, including 10 straight losses.

Sons of successful oilmen owned both teams. Hunt's father was H.L. Hunt, whose Hunt Oil pumped out tens of thousands of barrels a day, while Clint Murchison Jr., son of the Texas oil magnate, owned 90 percent of the Cowboys. As *Sports Illustrated* reported, despite their millions, the duo faced obstacles prompted by each other's existence:

> For three seasons Dallas saw a sort of civil war, and a lot of businessmen didn't know which way to jump. The Murchisons were a more social family and had a more diverse empire. But it was very dangerous to underestimate the Hunts. One result was that a great many Dallas business firms declared themselves neutral and deprived themselves of football altogether, refusing to buy blocks of tickets to the games of either team.

Hunt presented the Texans as an equal of their NFL counterpart. In 1961, he challenged Murchison to an exhibition game for charity. The Cowboys declined, a smart choice. As running back L.G. Dupre explained, "If we lost, people would run us out of town with a pole."

"We were able to present more wins on the field, but we didn't have a product people respected like they did the NFL," Hunt said later. "While the Cowboys weren't winning, they were playing teams like the Detroit Lions, New York Giants, and Cleveland Browns. We were playing teams no better known than we were."

The attendance told the story. The Texans couldn't build on their successful opening campaign. During their last year in Dallas, in 1962, they averaged just over 10,000 paid fans a game while winning 11 of 14 contests. The Cowboys finished with only five victories (in fact, during their first three seasons, they captured only four home games). Yet the Texans failed to win over Cowboys fans.

The war had created casualties—including Hunt's checkbook. In three seasons, the Texans had lost about $2.5 million, a staggering amount at the time, 100 times more than the purchase price of the franchise in 1959.

Hunt faced the toughest decision of his life. Should he abandon his hometown—where he had lived for nearly a quarter-century, where he had graduated from college, and in whose name he had just won a championship—to try to help the flailing league survive? Or should he stay in his beloved Cotton Bowl—a stadium he first entered as a four-year-old boy—and fight the Cowboys to the death?

Encouraged by Texans general manager Jack Steadman, Hunt began to visit cities without pro football teams, such as Atlanta and Miami. And enticed by friend David Dixon—with whom he would one day start a pro tennis circuit—he looked prepared to venture to New Orleans. He offered Dixon a 2 percent share of the team at no charge if he could secure Tulane Stadium. But the powers that be in that Southern city were more interested in obtaining an NFL franchise (which would happen in 1966 when the Saints were born on All Saints Day), and the New Orleans idea fell apart.

But even before those trips took place, the mayor of Kansas City, H. Roe Bartle—whose nickname was "Chief"—had called Hunt out of the blue and asked him to check out his city on the prairie. Bartle, a renowned public speaker and 300-pound force who often started his days with a morning radio broadcast on the state of Kansas City, was wrapping up his second and last term. Landing the Texans would be the capstone of his political career.

Bartle made a number of promises to Hunt and Steadman. Aside from adding 14,000 seats to Municipal Stadium—a facility built in 1923 that had played host to the Kansas City Monarchs of the Negro League, the minor-league Kansas City Blues, and the city's two original pro football franchises, the short-lived Blues and Cowboys of the 1920s NFL—Bartle guaranteed

Hunt's request to sell 25,000 season tickets by May 15, 1963. Two years of free rent were included if the franchise inked a seven-year lease.

The entreaties were substantial. Bartle told the city council, with Hunt in attendance, "Gentlemen, you have known me a long time and you have never known me to make love to another man, but, Mr. Hunt, I have courted you and wooed you like a princess, have I not?"

Hunt considered his options. To see if he could somehow stay in Dallas, he and Steadman decided to meet with Murchison and Cowboys general manager Tex Schramm.

"I didn't tell them that I had the Kansas City feeler. The theme was, 'Look, we've both lost money for three years. Let's one of us leave town,'" Hunt said. "We came to the conclusion that the Cowboys were not really interested in leaving."

Even though Kansas City had sold only 13,000 season tickets by Hunt's deadline, he was impressed by the enthusiasm and believed the 25,000 mark could be attained before the 1963 season started. Not only that, but the number sold—which raised about $600,000—marked a new record for the young league.

At a news conference on May 22, 1963, Hunt announced the Dallas Texans—who had played their first game as a franchise not even four years earlier—were leaving town and would be playing in Kansas City. That thrilling, double-overtime defeat of the Oilers would be the Texans' last— and only—championship for Dallas.

Some said the decision to abandon Dallas broke Lamar Hunt's heart. Though not demonstrative by nature, Hunt said nearly as much.

"The decision was painfully difficult. It was hard…emotional. I was a Dallas resident since 1938. All I ever wanted was a professional football team for Dallas."

Despite the anguished choice and an inaugural preseason game against the Buffalo Bills in Kansas City that drew fewer than 6,000 fans, Hunt didn't look back. (Neither did the Cowboys, who nearly doubled their per-game attendance to 38,000 during the 1964 season, their second without a competing Texas team.) In fact, after their first season in Kansas City, the newly named Chiefs (after Bartle, though Hunt fought to keep the name Texans) not only stanched their losses but made $35,000. That marked Hunt's first profit in pro sports, but it was far from his last.

By the time he died after a long battle with prostate cancer in 2006, Lamar Hunt had done much more than launch a firebrand league and introduce Kansas City to future Hall of Fame players such as Dawson. Through his high-profile involvement with the National Football League, two pro soccer leagues (the North American Soccer League and Major League Soccer), and pro tennis (World Championship Tennis), he helped revolutionize pro sports. He had a hand in changing the way games are watched by fans in stadiums, the money made by athletes and owners, the rules governing contests and, finally, the overall importance of pro sports in American life. Without Hunt, the NFL might still be plodding along without teams in places such as Buffalo and Denver, be wedded to a dull emphasis on the ground game (surely no two-point conversion would be in play), and be toiling in stadiums where the 20-yard line is washed away by the dirt of a baseball infield. Hunt's money and passion were essential in getting pro soccer off the ground—not once (he estimated he lost $20 million owning the Dallas Tornado of the NASL) but twice. Though the sport still hasn't captivated the American public as it has the rest of the world, it's safe to say it would be struggling even more if Hunt had not been around to insist on soccer-specific stadiums (his Columbus Crew built the first professional one in the U.S.). And perhaps no sport changed as drastically as pro tennis once Hunt arrived in 1967. Run then by the International Lawn Tennis Association, poorly paid pros could not even play in Grand Slam events. Thanks to Hunt, the popularity of tennis soared (along with the dollar amounts of pros' paychecks) as Wimbledon and other major tournaments opened their doors to nonamateurs.

Given Hunt's unassuming demeanor and wealth, some may assume his successes came easily. They didn't. In the 1960s, Hunt was enmeshed in battles with a host of rival leagues in pro football, soccer, and tennis.

Lawsuits and countersuits were common; he even filed one against the organization he would eventually join: the NFL. When Hunt started leagues or circuits, he had to be willing to endure huge losses at the outset. Many versions exist of a story about his father, saying how long Lamar's Texans could last funding million-dollar losses each year. Some claim the oil magnate—the richest man in America and one of the five richest in the world in the 1950s—said 1,000 years; others 250; others 100. As Lamar noted, "I've heard many different numbers—and all of them are overly flattering, by the way."

This is the story of Lamar Hunt, a man who helped rule one of the most violent games on earth but who also enjoyed pruning trees when he found a spare moment. A man who, as a teenager, when asked what he wanted to accomplish in life, didn't share specific dreams but instead told one prep-school classmate, "To do bigger and better things than my dad…no matter what I do, I'll always be H.L. Hunt's son." And a man who, despite the stature of living in a house that looked like Mount Vernon and despite being given more money before he entered kindergarten than the vast majority of Americans earn in a lifetime, refused to spend his childhood bragging about his riches; rather, he made up and played games.

CHAPTER 2

A BOY CALLED "GAMES"

HAROLDSON LAFAYETTE HUNT JR. was born in Illinois in 1889. His father, H.L. Hunt Sr., farmed land in Fayette County in the southern portion of the state. His mother, Ella Rose, reared eight children. H.L. was her baby.

The 19th-century agrarian world Hunt grew up in stood light-years away from 20th-century life in high-rise Dallas, where he eventually settled with not one, not two, but three families (for years, each family knew nothing about the existence of the others). In Fayette County, horses and one's own legs served as the main modes of transportation. Though Thomas Alva Edison had invented the lightbulb a decade before Hunt's birth, candles lit houses at nighttime in the majority of the country. If one wanted news to travel more quickly than letter, he or she strolled to the nearest telegraph office.

A nation at peace greeted the youngest Hunt, although the Civil War remained a vivid memory for many adults. Though Illinois supported the Union and sent thousands of troops to help one of its own, President Abraham Lincoln, the state is bordered by Kentucky and Missouri, and Southern Illinois saw plenty of Confederate sympathizers. Cairo, resting at the bottom tip of the state, was a strategic staging area during the war. Waddy Thorpe Hunt, H.L.'s grandfather, had served as a cavalry leader in the Confederacy and was killed when he opened his farmhouse door to see who had arrived.

By the age of three, H.L. Hunt was able to read, and at five he could beat all family members at checkers. That same year, he began handling scales that weighed livestock and assessed what they were worth.

The years passed with little note in Southern Illinois. By the time he reached his teens, H.L. visited Mississippi and Arkansas at his father's request to trade and buy animals. He did attend Valparaiso College for a short time at age 15, but by the next year he was off to California, where he worked as a dishwasher and tried other odd jobs.

When his father—the richest man in Fayette County—died in 1911, Hunt inherited $5,000. Soon after, he moved to Lake Village, Arkansas, where he bought a 960-acre plantation nearby.

H.L.'s move from Illinois to Arkansas would prove fruitful in many respects. Hunt met Lyda Bunker, and after a quick courtship the 25-year-old Hunt married her on November 26, 1914. Children soon followed, six in all. Hunt—who believed he carried a genius gene—did not stop there. On a business venture in Tampa, Florida, he met Frania Tye. He told her he was Major Franklin Hunt. An affair proceeded, and in 1925—the same year a daughter, named Lyda after her mother, died soon after his first wife gave birth to her—Hunt married Frania in Tampa.

Down the line Hunt denied that he and Frania were formally married, but he admitted he was the father of her children. In 1930 Hunt moved Frania into Highland Park, an exclusive Dallas suburb, while he, Lyda, and their growing family lived in El Dorado, Arkansas, unaware of the other family.

Within a decade of his move to Arkansas, Hunt became known as a major player in the oil fields of Arkansas and east Texas. The legend says he won his first oil well in a poker game. Though he was a notorious gambler, the truth is not as romantic as that. Hunt did win enough poker hands to buy some oil leases. Though he struck oil with his first well, the venture did not succeed. And as he pursued this line of work, he battled against better-funded competitors.

At first, Hunt was called a "poor boy," meaning he drilled his wells with whatever equipment he could muster through begging or borrowing. The sobriquet is quite ironic considering his eventual Midas-like fortune. Relying on unexceptional gear and his own instincts, Hunt forged ahead. And he found immense success. By 1924 Hunt had gathered hundreds of thousands of barrels of oil reserves, whose value approached $600,000.

The core of H.L. Hunt's (and also Lamar's) later worth came from what's known as the Dad Joiner deal. In simple terms, H.L. bought a number of east Texas oil leases from Joiner for about $1.5 million; they would be worth more than 60 times that to Hunt during the next few decades. The east Texas field, considered the world's largest, would, in the next half century, pump out in excess of 4 billion barrels of oil. The Joiner deal featured days of negotiations between the two men in a hotel suite and later prompted hundreds of lawsuits, all of which Hunt settled.

It wasn't as easy as drilling holes. The rush to production in the early 1930s in east Texas decimated the price of oil. Governor Ross S. Sterling—urged in part by Hunt—claimed the oil operators were in "rebellion" because of excess drilling and dispatched more than 1,000 national guard troops to close the wells. Irony abounded; Sterling himself had founded a successful oil company that later became Exxon. Big independents like Hunt and major companies with deep pockets kept drilling new wells during the shutdown, something little operators couldn't afford. When martial law was lifted, Hunt and the big boys tapped those new wells, bringing them new riches, while the smaller operators suffered.

Margaret Hunt Hill, a daughter of H.L. and Lyda's, recounted life at the Hunt El Dorado homestead during this time. A growing success in the oil fields, she said H.L. believed in capitalism as well at home.

"We were questioned on subjects including the presidents of the United States, the Cabinet members, the Bill of Rights, and the preamble to the

Constitution. Daddy paid us a dime for everything we got right—the incentive system," she noted.

Despite the all-American atmosphere H.L. promoted when he enjoyed the comfort of El Dorado, reality dictated he stay away from home for long stretches due to his need to oversee work in the oil fields. Lyda was raising the family, now five strong. Nelson Bunker Hunt recalled her egalitarian nature, saying, "Mother was much the same to everybody, be he the king of England or a hobo at the back door. She treated everyone politely."

And on August 2, 1932, born to a strong entrepreneur and a gentle soul—traits he would display throughout his life—Lamar Hunt arrived.

Around this time, H.L. Hunt bought a mansion—known as the Mayfield House—in Tyler, Texas, a town where nearly three dozen oil companies had established headquarters. The Greek Revival structure boasted servants' quarters and a Texas-sized backyard. His family— which included three teenagers, two youngsters, and the newborn Lamar—moved in to the elegant spot. Black servants helped around the house, though Lyda worked hard in the kitchen and elsewhere. And she allowed the third floor to metamorphose into a sports haven of sorts where roller-skating flourished.

Though Lamar's parents didn't introduce him to sports as early as, say, Tiger Woods', who was playing golf on the *Mike Douglas Show* at age two thanks to the ambitions of his father Earl, suffice to say the youth was enraptured by what he saw. His family brought Lamar to the inaugural Cotton Bowl in Dallas on January 1, 1937, where 17,000 fans watched Texas Christian University topple Marquette University 16–6. The event obviously moved the four-year-old, and he did not miss another Cotton Bowl until the 21st century.

As Lamar got older, he made up games, usually ones that he played by himself. He invented rules and kept records of the contests. His desire was so pronounced and insatiable that it generated a nickname that stuck throughout his life: Games. Decades later, in the 1970s, his penchant for inventing games had not weakened. He said, "When my 15-year-old son

Lamar Jr. and I were on the beach in Hawaii, we scratched a court in the sand and we took a beach ball and we made up a tennis game that we played with our feet, like soccer. I don't know, maybe I have some kind of creative impulse in me. Others paint or write; I make up games. I'm working on a terrific one at home. We have a putting green, and I've worked out four different tees and three water holes, and I'm using four different flags with four different colors on the green. It's a terrific game. Who knows? I might sell franchises!"

During his childhood, Lamar also started noticing attendance figures in box scores, more interested in how many people paid to see each sports event than in which team won it. No doubt this prompted his lifelong desire to make sure his stadiums were packed, a goal he always advocated by engaging himself in season-ticket sales for any team he backed. SMU president R. Gerald Turner was impressed by Hunt's passion to persuade alums to buy season packages for Mustangs home games. He said, "You would think a guy who has all he has to do would not be involved in a run-of-the-mill alumni-support activity."

At age six, Lamar and his family moved to Dallas, into a home that was a replica of George Washington's Mount Vernon in Virginia, though it was a tad larger than the first president's estate. The house, built in 1930, sat on 10 acres and overlooked a lake. Lamar's father paid $69,000, a tiny price for such a sterling property.

Typical of a young boy, Lamar was not awestruck at first by the idyllic home, but he was extremely fond of one of its features. He said, "My first recollection of Dallas is the wonderful laundry chute.... You threw sheets or soiled clothes into it from the second floor and they went straight down to the laundry room in the basement.... We didn't care about how many rooms it had or how many square feet or how good the kitchen was, the 10 acres, the lake. No. The laundry chute."

Despite the charms of shirts and socks tumbling down the dark tunnel, Lamar soon discovered joy outside, playing football in the expansive yard. Even the dogs got involved.

"He loved our dog Whiskers," his sister Caroline Rose Hunt said in a documentary commissioned by the Hunt family. "Whiskers had 12 puppies, and six of them were spotted and six of them were plain. And he tells this story on himself that he would play football, and the spotted ones were on one team and the plain ones were on the other team, and he'd move them around to their different positions."

By age 11, he was mad about football. His brother Bunker even gave him a blocking dummy as a gift one Christmas.

"We did always play football in the backyard," his brother William Herbert Hunt said. "No touch—it was all tackle."

Ironically, H.L. Hunt had not let his namesake, known as Hassie, play high school football, scared he might suffer kidney injuries. It was different for Lamar. As a teenager, he left Texas for the longest stretch of his life. He decided to go to Pennsylvania (later known as a cradle for quarterbacks, thanks to Joe Namath, Joe Montana, and others), where he attended the Hill School in Pottstown. It was not virgin ground for the Hunts, because two of Lamar's brothers had matriculated at the preparatory school.

In his junior year, Hunt played quarterback and fullback, kicked off, and averaged an astounding 39 yards per punt, practically NFL numbers. Teammate and lifelong friend Tom Richey remembered him as first on the field and in the weight room and the last to leave both spots. Proficient in both the T formation and the single wing, the 182-pounder helped Hill achieve its first undefeated season in nearly 30 years.

During his senior year, Hunt was named Hill's team captain. In those days, in the middle of the century, the *New York Times* often covered preparatory-school sports, a rare occurrence today. Box scores even accompanied game stories. The paper of October 1, 1950, looks to be Lamar Hunt's first mention as a game participant in the national press, a home contest in Pottstown. During a 49–6 thrashing of Williamson Trade of Philadelphia, the newspaper reported, "Captain Lamar Hunt's 45-yard pass to Pete Scott gave Hill its fourth touchdown of the [second] quarter."

His enthusiasm for sports delighted classmates. As Richey recalled in a book he wrote about his classmate, "Lamar Hunt ate, slept, and breathed sports, and that's what brought us together. When not in the study hall, we'd go to the library and rifle the magazines for sports pictures of our heroes. Doak Walker and Kyle Rote were the buzz for Lamar. Lamar... loved all of it: football, baseball, golf, tennis, wrestling, prize fighting, and even the fledgling sport of soccer."

The mild-mannered Texan was a big success at the Eastern prep school (where today a dorm is named after him and fellow graduates Bunker and Herbert). He was voted "Most Popular" and "Most Likely to Succeed" and was vice president of the Class of 1951.

During his years at Hill, Hunt also realized the breadth of his father's fortune—and thus got a sense of his own. One day in 1948, his freshman roommate appeared with an issue of *LIFE* magazine, one of the country's most popular publications. Inside, a photo of Lamar's father rested above the caption, "Is this the richest man in the U.S.?"

H.L.'s wealth had grown tremendously since Lamar was born. In fact, the fear of his children being kidnapped, especially in the wake of the Lindbergh baby kidnapping in 1932, was palpable. Lamar found out the hard way. During a trip on a ship in Alaska, eight-year-old Herbert and five-year-old Lamar couldn't be found after they had been left in a locked stateroom. Margaret discovered them after she heard them giggling while hiding. She lit into the brothers, wondering why they'd scare everyone to death and make them worry they'd been kidnapped. She promised their mother would discipline them with a switch. She recounted, "Lamar rushed over to [his] mother.... He threw his arms around her and, half-crying with remorse, said, 'I'm sorry to have scared you, Papoose Mooze [her nickname]. We would never scare you about kidnappers.'"

Unlike many Texans, H.L. Hunt did not flaunt his wealth. Though Lamar understood his family had money, it held no magic for him.

"I knew we lived in a big house, and the yardman or the cook used to drive me to school sometimes in our Plymouth, and I was embarrassed getting out in front of my classmates," he said. "But money was no big deal. If I wanted a little money, I just asked my mother, and generally she'd let me have it. It doesn't sound like I was too well-trained, does it?"

While H.L.'s fortune had soared through the Great Depression and beyond as Lamar was growing up, his private life had also become more complicated. About a year after moving to Tyler, Frania found out from a friend that Franklin Hunt was really H.L. Hunt and hers was not his only family. After confronting Hunt, he moved her to Great Neck, New York, where she gave birth to their fourth child.

She soon tired of New York. Frania moved her four children to Houston in 1939, and as she passed herself off as Mrs. H.L. Hunt, a day of reckoning occurred. Before arriving at a River Oaks tea party, she picked up a phone call. On the other end, a woman's voice announced she knew she was not Mrs. H.L. Hunt and demanded $5,000 to keep the information private. More blackmail calls ensued. Frania confronted H.L. in Dallas. Sensing his secret lives were set to explode into the open, H.L. decided to introduce the two women in his life. Considering the stakes, both emotional and finan-cial, it may seem surprising that they seemed to bond. Frania was amazed at Lyda's kindness; Lamar's mother even offered to adopt Frania's children.

Though just a middle-aged man, H.L. had been starting to think about how to pass on his money to his children. In 1935 he had established a number of trusts for his offspring. The Loyal Trusts were created for his six children with Lyda, including Lamar. The children could not spend the principal but were free to use the income. The money came mainly from Placid Oil Company.

Then, in 1941, Hunt set up trusts for his four children with Frania called the Reliance Trusts, which offered an income of about $6,000 a year.

But Hunt realized something had to be worked out with Frania as well, as Texas law did not allow bigamy. The next year, after much cajoling, Frania inked a deal saying she was not married to Hunt and released him from future claims. In exchange she received a $300,000 settlement and $2,000 a month until she died.

As Frania was paid to be out of the picture, H.L. was beginning a relationship with Ruth Eileen Ray, a secretary at Hunt Oil. H.L. sent her to live in New York City and, in April 1943, they had a child, Ray Lee Wright, only months after Lamar's sister Margaret had given birth to their parents' first grandchild. Soon after, Ruth and her baby moved to Dallas just a two-minute drive from Mount Vernon.

Though Lamar knew none of this at the time, he was aware that his older brother, Hassie or H.L. III, was suffering. The dead ringer for H.L. himself was becoming more troubled. In the army at Camp Beauregard in Louisiana, he was hobbled by paranoid ideas and "went berserk" when he was put out in a firing field. He entered a mental ward of an army hospital and was ultimately discharged.

Afterward, Hassie tore into frequent rages. Not able to control his son, H.L., looking for some sort of cure, set his namesake up for a prefrontal lobotomy. His violent outbursts ended after the operation, but Hassie's conversations made little sense and he faced other challenges. He was sent to a psychiatric institution to receive constant care.

And then, after nearly 60 years of little to no publicity, all of a sudden in 1948 H.L. Hunt was featured in an article in *Fortune*. The magazine reported, "The Hunt Oil properties have been valued at around $237 million and their daily production of crude estimated at 65,000 barrels. At last year's average price of $2.25 a barrel, this would have given him a gross weekly income of more that $1 million."

Soon after, Hunt moved to ensure the economic future of his family with Ruth Ray Wright (so named because of a fictitious marriage concocted with one "Raymond Wright"), though his decision didn't quite compare to his first-family munificence. He set up the Secure Trusts, which were said to be worth $1 million.

Like Lamar, H.L. was also entranced by football—though in a different way. He bet Jimmy "the Greek" Snyder $50,000 per game (usually three per weekend) played in college football's Southeastern Conference.

Around this time, Lamar was trying to figure out where to go to college. He considered Washington and Lee, an all-male school in Lexington, Virginia. But the truth was, he missed Texas, and the prestigious Southern Methodist University—which was becoming a football powerhouse—sat in his hometown of Dallas. His father insisted he go there. And, even though brother Herbert had gone to W&L, Lamar chose SMU, mainly because Heisman Trophy winner Doak Walker had played there (at Hill, Hunt wore No. 37, just like Walker).

SMU boasted a strong history in college football. In 1935 the Mustangs were crowned national champions, finishing 12–0 while scoring 288 points and allowing 39. Eight wins were shutouts.

But the biggest boost to the program occurred when the 5'11", 165-pound Walker enrolled in 1945. Almost single-handedly, the football renaissance man who could run, pass, and kick reenergized a failing program. By 1947 the team moved a home game against the University of Texas from the on-campus Ownby Stadium (capacity around 20,000) to the Cotton Bowl, which then seated 46,000, to satisfy ticket demand. About 50,000 showed up and watched a 14–13 Mustangs victory, a game Walker later considered his highlight in sports.

SMU made the Cotton Bowl its home in 1948, when the stadium was enlarged to accommodate 67,000 fans. That fall, Walker appeared on the cover of *LIFE* magazine and became known by millions—the same year, ironically enough, that H.L. Hunt entered the nation's consciousness thanks to a photo in the magazine. In Walker's senior season, the Cotton Bowl again expanded, this time to seat 75,000. And the Mustangs sold out games against Notre Dame and others in what became known as "the House That Doak Built."

Walker's presence and performance—he won the Heisman Trophy in 1948—began to make SMU the go-to school for Texas high schoolers. By the time Hunt arrived there in 1951, dozens of top prospects were dying to earn playing time. After Hunt played on the freshman football team, where he started and earned a letter, he moved up to the varsity to play end. Ahead of him on coach Rusty Russell's squad were three players who would be drafted by the NFL: Doyle Nix, Ed Bernet, and Raymond Berry.

Berry, a future NFL Hall of Famer, didn't go straight to SMU. After graduating from Paris High School, he attended Schreiner Junior College. He then received a one-year scholarship to the Dallas school.

During his sophomore and junior years, the end wouldn't be confused as a Doak Walker–type playmaker. He caught five passes in 1952 and 11 the next season. Yet Berry was held in such esteem that he was elected as a cocaptain for his final season. He made 16 catches and was named an All-Southwestern Conference player as the team ended up 6–3–1.

Even though Walker's exploits had caused the university to switch home games to the Cotton Bowl, the Mustangs still practiced at Ownby Stadium, a two-minute walk from the athletic dormitory where the players lived. Berry and Hunt blocked dummies on the practice field, attended team meetings, and dressed in the locker room for three seasons together.

Berry remembered Hunt in a way many have never thought of him, despite his life in sports: as a solid athlete.

"He was very quick," Berry said. "He could very easily have been a halfback. He could catch the football and he could run. His physique was compact. He wasn't an oversized guy, nor was he necessarily small.

"Lamar was competing with the same group I was. But the rules had changed. The NCAA wanted to reduce scholarships, cut costs. They instituted rules that brought back one-platoon football [in 1954], and you needed to play both offense and defense. The guys who played most in that era were the guys who could play defense. Lamar was not a necessarily gifted defensive player [as a defensive back]. He would not have been helped by that rule change."

Forrest Gregg, who would become a star offensive lineman and respected head coach in the NFL, matriculated at SMU a year after Lamar. He remembered his teammate's tenacity during practice.

"He was a tough guy. He wouldn't back off from anything. We used to have these drills called the Oklahoma Drill: one offensive lineman with a running back behind him and one defensive lineman. We'd line up between blocking dummies. I remember going up against Lamar in these drills. I was quite a bit bigger. Sometimes he was offense, sometimes he was defense. I would always beat him. I said later if I had known I was going to be a pro football coach and knew he'd become an owner, I'd have let him beat me a few times."

Gregg said he and Hunt dressed similarly—blue jeans, penny T-shirts, and "SMU T-shirts we had stolen." He was shocked when he discovered his teammate's background.

"I went home one weekend as a freshman to Sulphur Springs. When I got back, I asked my roommate what he had done over the weekend. He said, 'Went to Lamar Hunt's and went swimming.' I said, 'Lamar who?' He said, 'Lamar Hunt.' I said, 'Lamar Hunt's family has a swimming pool?' He said, 'Boy, where you been?'

"He was just another football player. I had no idea of his family situation," Gregg said. "After you knew what Lamar's circumstances were, you knew he didn't have to play football. He didn't have to be there in August when it was 105 degrees, taking all that pounding. The fact that he did made him special to me. He loved football and being an SMU Mustang."

Hunt could have deflected his athletic and academic shortcomings with braggadocio about his father's pile of money; after all, Texans boast about far less. But Berry said Hunt was as humble as could be, despite H.L.'s extraordinary riches.

"I never really knew anything about the wealth that he came from. That was one of his great characteristics. He never talked about it. He fit in. He was very team-oriented. If you had to pick someone for your sister to marry, you couldn't come up with a better guy than Lamar Hunt. He was an outstanding young man."

Others, though, said Hunt's background was known, even if he himself never bragged about it. According to *Sports Illustrated*, "Like all the other SMU scrubs, Hunt took a pounding. One day he was thrown all the way off the field, across the cinder track, and into a concrete curb on two successive plays. On the second hit, 250-pound Willard Dewveall picked him up and said, 'Poor boy, you better get Popsie to cover that curb with foam rubber!'"

To train for football, Lamar would run alongside a car driven by Bunker at a manageable speed of 10 mph. But once he jumped from the freshman squad to the varsity, where he wore No. 80, he was no more than a third-string benchwarmer. During his senior season, Lamar spent about 20 minutes on the field and made little impact. Bunker began driving for his younger brother in another sense. As Lamar told his sister Margaret, "Bunker used to bring my mother out to the Cotton Bowl an hour before kickoff because the only way she'd get to see me play was when I was out there with everyone else warming up."

Lamar's academic record mirrored his football career there. "I was such a mediocre student, it's embarrassing," he said.

Off the football field, many important events were happening in the young man's life. In 1954, he married Rosemary Carr; they had known each other since high school. The next year, on May 6, Lamar's mother, Lyda, died at 66. Her interest in the family home was handed to her youngest son.

Yet Mount Vernon—Lamar's home for nearly his entire life—soon would change drastically. After Lyda's funeral, Ruth Ray Wright began to appear there often, children in tow.

According to *Texas Rich: The Hunt Dynasty from the Early Oil Days Through the Silver Crash,* "Ruth would fuss over the old man and look after the wifely responsibilities of the household. When Hunt got depressed, she would send her daughters over to serenade him with happy songs. The children even began to have their birthday parties at Mount Vernon. Though Ruth and her children still maintained residence at the house on Meadow Lane Avenue, they practically lived at Mount Vernon."

In 1957, two years after Lyda's death, H.L. married Ruth. Neither Lamar nor any of his siblings attended the ceremony, since they didn't know about it. They found out the worst way possible: through the next day's newspaper. Even Ruth's mother, who was contacted by the Associated Press, said she had no idea her daughter had gotten married.

His sense of security shaken as his father welcomed a new bride and his half-siblings took over Mount Vernon, Lamar—who had graduated from SMU with a bachelor's degree in geology in 1956—looked to find a purpose in his life. After working briefly at Hunt Oil Co., he realized his passion lay elsewhere.

"He never really had any interest in geology," said Jack Steadman, who worked at H.L. Hunt's Penrod Drilling before becoming general manager of the Dallas Texans. "He was just always working on games."

Hunt began to travel and speak with people about sports franchises, discovering the best way to finance football and baseball teams.

In early 1958, he called NFL commissioner Bert Bell, whose modest offices lay just outside of Philadelphia, to inquire about procuring an NFL expansion franchise. Though the league had formed an expansion committee, the likelihood of a new team among the dozen hidebound franchises was minuscule. Washington Redskins owner George Preston Marshall, for one, would have none of it. "There's no excuse for expansion in the National Football League.... Expansion can only weaken the personnel," he said in an interview around that time.

Bell told Hunt to check with the owners of the Chicago Cardinals, the only NFL team likely to sell, since expansion was not an option at that point.

Over the course of a year, Lamar talked with Walter Wolfner. The Cardinals were owned by his wife, Violet. In the past decade, the Wolfners, it was estimated, had lost about $1 million on their team, which shared Chicago with the older and more popular Bears. Two teams meant not only a lack of sellouts but a dearth of television coverage, given the NFL's policy of refusing to televise any game for an area audience if a local team played at home. Comiskey Park on the South Side served as the Cardinals' home, and crowds were unimpressive. When they tried to move to the bigger and better situated Dyche Stadium at Northwestern University in Evanston, Chicago Bears owner George Halas pulled out a decades-old agreement saying the Cardinals could not play north of Madison Street in Chicago, which would cut into the Bears' crowds at Wrigley Field.

In 1958 the Cardinals even tested the Buffalo market, playing a few exhibition games and their home opener there. But crowds around 20,000 didn't qualify as a stampede for the Cardinals to relocate.

Compared to others, Walter Wolfner came late to the NFL. His wife was previously married to Charles Bidwell, a sports enthusiast who had died in the spring of 1947 before the team finished 9–3 and captured the NFL championship (the Cardinals waited more than 60 years and two moves to challenge for the title again in the Super Bowl). Only two years after Bidwell's passing, Wolfner married Violet and helped run the team.

Described as abrupt and pugnacious, Wolfner had lambasted both Bell and Halas, among others, at various times. (Only a few years later, in 1962, he would challenge his wife's will upon her death, and the team history section of the Cardinals website at www.azcardinals.com ignores him entirely.)

Now he had a 25-year-old rich kid interested in his team, and he moved slowly, despite the Cardinals' never-ending losses. As the months went on, Hunt also decided to meet with the legendary Branch Rickey, who had run the Brooklyn Dodgers and was talking about starting a new baseball league, including placing a franchise around Dallas. But nothing came of Lamar's interest. Soon after that, he dismissed baseball and focused on football, prompted by a game that galvanized America: the 1958 NFL championship between the Baltimore Colts and the New York Giants at Yankee Stadium in New York.

Unlike most Americans, Hunt could point to the television screen that December day and recognize players he had suited up with. One was fellow SMU graduate Berry. Here he ran before tens of millions of TV viewers, catching a championship-record 12 passes for 178 yards.

As the epic game captivated a country (except in New York, where it was blacked out as part of the league's policy), Hunt watched closely. The thrilling overtime battle, won by the Colts 23–17, had sold the football fan in Texas.

"The '58 Colts-Giants game, sort of in my mind, made me say, 'Well, that's it. This sport really has everything. And it televises well,'" he later told author Michael MacCambridge.

Buoyed by his insight, in February 1959, Hunt flew to Miami to visit the Wolfners and try again to buy the Chicago Cardinals and move them to Dallas. Given that he had given up on a pro baseball team and that the Cardinals were the only pro football team even close to being on the market, it seemed to be a do-or-die affair.

Again, Walter Wolfner wasn't budging. But he mentioned a name to Hunt that would change football history.

"Do you know Bud Adams?" Wolfner said.

Hunt didn't.

Adams, a Houston millionaire, was among a handful of other suitors who had approached him, Wolfner said, but he turned them all down. And Hunt was no closer to buying the team from him than any of the others.

Hunt left the Wolfner house and grabbed a cab to the Miami airport. He had dedicated a good part of a year to buying either a football or a baseball franchise. And he had failed.

As he faced a long flight home to Dallas, Lamar Hunt was little more than a 26-year-old dilettante, a jobless college graduate who had wasted hundreds of days on a quixotic quest to own a sports team. What would he do now?

By the time he stepped off the American Airlines plane, an inspiration had hit that would end up transforming not only his own life but pro football itself.

CHAPTER 3

FASTEN YOUR SEAT BELTS

IN AN AGE BEFORE JETS DOMINATED THE SKIES (only a few weeks before Hunt's return to Dallas, American Airlines had introduced transcontinental service with a flight from Los Angeles to Idlewild, New York), the wannabe owner had plenty of time to think during his four-hour sojourn on a propeller plane.

As he headed west, a brainstorm struck. He later described the eureka moment as being like a lightbulb going on over his head: Why not start a pro football league? Why couldn't a new league succeed? Why not speak with those men Wolfner had mentioned to see if they'd be interested?

After requesting American Airlines in-flight stationery from a stewardess, he wrote these words at the top: "Original 6: FIRST YEARS OPERATIONS." He then jotted specific ideas, such as three exhibition games and an unbalanced 15-game schedule (where three teams would play eight home games and the three others would play seven). He decided the net gate should be split 60–40 in favor of the home team, with visitors choosing to receive the larger of 40 percent or $35,000. Each club, he wrote, should have the right to two territorial draft choices.

A month later, Hunt called Bell again to inquire about the possibility of an expansion franchise. Nothing would happen, he was told, before the league could figure out what to do with the woebegone Cardinals. Hunt contacted Halas, who was chairman of what operated as an expansion committee in name only. Halas brushed off the Texan, believing their similarities stopped at their horn-rimmed glasses, and denied his request to visit him. In neither instance did Hunt mention the idea of a new pro football league.

Hunt started to call upon Wolfner's contacts, such as Kenneth S. "Bud" Adams, an oilman down in Houston. They enjoyed dinner together at the Charcoal Inn, which Adams owned. When Hunt finally mentioned the idea of starting a pro league well after dessert, Adams enthusiastically agreed to own a team. During trips to Denver and Minnesota, Hunt also landed potential investors. One of his selling points seemed to be elementary in its simplicity: tracing paper and map in hand, he would show how nearly all of the 12 NFL franchises existed in a tiny region smaller than Texas itself. Given the size of the country and the burgeoning fascination over pro football, why couldn't there be more teams?

Unsurprisingly, considering his detail-oriented nature, ambition, and sense of loyalty to those who had listened politely to his ideas, Hunt returned to see Bell that June. During lunch, Hunt again raised the possibility of an expansion franchise in Dallas (but nothing about a new league). Bell said he not only doubted the owners would put a team there, but he suspected that they would never add another team *anywhere* in the United States.

In July Hunt asked Davy O'Brien, a former Texas Christian University star who was friends with Bell, to tell the NFL commissioner about the new league being formed. The meeting was cordial; most importantly, it set the stage for Bell to break the news about the AFL. Called to testify in Washington, D.C., before a Senate judiciary subcommittee as he looked to clinch antitrust legislation for the league, Bell needed ammunition to prove the NFL was no monopoly. On July 28, he told senators that a new league was being formed and would likely field six football teams during the 1960 season, including one in New York, and that none of the 12 NFL owners objected. Among those in the room listening to Bell's comments was Hunt. Asked by reporters to describe the people launching the circuit, Bell didn't give names but said, "I know they don't need money."

"Bell Tells Congressional Hearing New Pro Football League Is Being Formed" announced the headline in the *New York Times* the next morning. The public relations for the incipient AFL was priceless. As Hunt later said, "That was a lot better than having Lamar Hunt announce a new league."

But six days after Bell's testimony—and the day after Lamar's 27th birthday—that's what Hunt did. During a press conference in Houston, Hunt and Adams announced a Houston franchise would be part of the American Football League (which was often referred to in newspapers as the American Professional Football League at the outset). At that time, only two teams, Dallas and Houston, were revealed, with four others promised soon. "This definitely will not be a rebel league [or] a minor league," Hunt said. "We will be full-time big-league professional football."

In one sense, Hunt was right: it was better for Bell to let the world know about a new league. Inherently quiet and not a proven public speaker, Hunt's introduction to the press was singularly unimpressive. Years later, his meek performance as the head of a new league was recounted in *Sports Illustrated* by a veteran football reporter. He wrote, "We shuddered on his behalf. Here was this poor little rich boy, son of one of the world's richest men, standing up there like he was making a speech in catechism class. He spoke almost in a whisper, without any force or authority. Somebody nudged me and said, 'Wait till George Halas gets ahold of this punk!' It was like watching the first act of a Kabuki play. No matter what else happens, you know the last act's gonna be a beheading."

Though Bell publicly praised the new entity, the NFL's general reaction may have been summed up by Cleveland coach Paul Brown, who himself had been a luminary in the All-America Football Conference, a league that challenged the NFL. His quarterback at the time, eventual Texans star Len Dawson, remembered Brown's dismissal of the upstart entity.

"He said, 'There's a new league starting. Don't worry about it. It's not going to succeed. It's a bunch of sons of rich guys.'"

One of those rich guys, H.L. Hunt, was nearly as pessimistic about the whole venture as Brown.

"Dad felt it was kind of a crazy idea," Lamar Hunt said. "He never told me that explicitly, but I could tell by the way he encouraged me to talk to financial advisors and financial people who worked for the Hunt Oil Company."

Lamar spoke with Jim Breuil, a business associate of H.L's who had been involved in the All-America Football Conference that eventually failed. Breuil told Lamar, "I think it's something you'll really enjoy. There'll be a lot of challenges, and you'll meet a lot of interesting people."

"I'm sure it wasn't the answer my dad had been anticipating," Hunt said. "His attitude was, 'Well, this new football league is your problem, and you're gonna have to learn for yourself.'"

H.L. Hunt even sent a letter to various Dallas newspapers dismissing the Texans and claiming college football would be damaged in Dallas by the pro game. Though it may seem bizarre or even cruel on its face, the goal was to disassociate his son's team from his sports-betting activities, which were so pronounced that Hunt placed a phone in his boardroom solely for calls with his bookie.

Ironically enough, amid the darts thrown at Hunt's venture, a new pro baseball entity had been announced only a week earlier. In July 1959, the Continental Baseball League was officially formed with teams in Houston, Denver, and elsewhere, poised to take on Major League Baseball. Despite high hopes, it withered before playing a game, in part because Major League Baseball responded by announcing its own expansion and even lured Continental's New York franchise backers to join the new Mets.

Rival leagues were nothing new, and Hunt was far from the first to gamble that the American sports public would back a competing pro football league. In fact, he wasn't even the first to launch the American Football League.

Back in 1926, only six years after the founding of the NFL, football star Red Grange's agent, C.C. Pyle, started the original American Football League. Like Hunt more than three decades later, Pyle had tried to nab an NFL franchise (this one in New York) and even procured a lease at Yankee Stadium for potential games. But the New York Giants did not want another team nearby, which would detract from their ticket sales. Pyle's request was refused.

Nine teams played, including three in the New York area: the Yankees, the Newark Bears, and the Brooklyn Horsemen. Problems quickly arose; the baseball Yankees had first dibs on their eponymous stadium, which meant the football franchise couldn't play there until the World Series ended. After Halloween, the Cleveland Panthers rejoined the NFL, and the Brooklyn team merged with the NFL's Lions. Four teams finished the season. While the Yankees, led by Grange, played 15 games, the Horsemen only competed in four.

The AFL fell apart after one season.

A much bigger threat to the NFL appeared near the end of World War II. Arch Ward, the *Chicago Tribune* sports editor who was the brains behind the launch of Major League Baseball's All-Star Game, gathered a number of millionaires in St. Louis to form the All-America Football Conference. In 1945 the league caught a break when Don Topping decided to move his Brooklyn franchise from the NFL to the new league.

The next year, a signing war erupted. About 100 former NFL players joined the upstart league. At the College Football All-Star Game that summer—a game that had been founded by Ward—nearly 75 percent of the players ended up in the AAFC.

More than 60,000 watched Cleveland's first game, a 44–0 blowout. The Browns drew 71,134 later that season, by far a record for a pro football regular-season game. But all was not well across the league, as the struggling Miami franchise quickly moved to Baltimore.

By 1948 the AAFC tottered. Baseball's Branch Rickey, only a year removed from hiring Jackie Robinson to break baseball's color barrier and energize the Brooklyn Dodgers, tried to resuscitate the football Dodgers. He couldn't. The following season, the AAFC welcomed its third commissioner in only four years. The league dwindled to seven teams. And in December 1949, three AAFC teams—Cleveland, San Francisco, and Baltimore—joined the NFL. The AAFC was dead.

The four-year experiment had cost the NFL an estimated $5 million in player signing wars. So in 1959 many NFL owners still had bad memories of battling another league and had no desire to see another one begin.

Deep pockets hadn't helped either the first AFL or the AAFC. What Hunt possessed, which the other leagues had lacked, was timing.

Suburbs were expanding across the country in the 1950s, along with the leisure time of their new residents. Mobility improved as scores of newly built highways let people travel freely. The economy during the Eisenhower administration grew solidly and featured low inflation; after the Korean War ended, the country enjoyed a long stretch of peace. Amid all this, pro football was growing.

The NFL started the 1950s with a dozen teams drawing about 2 million fans. By 1959 a dozen franchises existed still, but the number of spectators neared 3 million. What had changed was the advent of television.

For the first time in 1951, the NFL Championship Game—won by the Los Angeles Rams 24–17—was televised coast-to-coast. The rights to the game cost the DuMont Network $75,000. Four years later, NBC televised the title game, paying 33 percent more than DuMont had. In 1956 CBS broadcast regular-season games to a handful of markets around the country, meaning fans were getting their first glimpses of NFL stars from other cities.

And then the historic championship game riveted American television viewers in 1958, solidifying the NFL's popularity. It can be argued Hunt never would have pursued a career of owning sports teams in the radio era. Watching the 1958 NFL Championship Game prompted him to focus on buying a football team, and seeing the World Cup on television in 1966 spurred him to invest in pro soccer.

Back when the NFL started, news of a game's score could take days to reach parts of America. Now, one could watch games at home, and millions of people were buying televisions. The change was stupefying.

This landscape would ensure the AFL—even if not a huge success—would at least not quickly collapse. During their inaugural 1960 season, each team received more than $100,000 from broadcaster ABC, thanks to a revenue-sharing agreement that Hunt helped usher in. And three crucial changes benefitted the league, according to Robert McChesney's *Media Made Sport*:

1) Videotape, slow-motion, and other innovations were helping viewers enjoy games.
2) The 1961 Sports Broadcasting Act let teams negotiate for TV rights as a cartel, which increased marketing power and revenue.
3) Broadcasters started to understand that sports could be used to sell premium advertising.

The timing extended to Lamar's age. So young at this point in his life, he had only been allowed to vote in one presidential election, President Dwight Eisenhower's second defeat of Illinois senator Adlai Stevenson in 1956. According to the U.S. Constitution, he couldn't run for the senate (minimum age 30) or for president (minimum age 35).

What he could do was follow his passion and start a new pro football league. His youth meant that not only was he unbowed by the prospect of taking on the mighty NFL and fearless about risking millions of dollars, he would also want fresh approaches in football on and off the field. What unfolded was a league that jokingly became known as the All Fun League, whereas the NFL at many junctures was draped with the moniker No Fun League.

The fee to join was reasonable, almost laughingly so in retrospect, given the exponential jump in franchise values since then. At the first official league meeting in Chicago on August 14, 1959, Hunt requested $25,000 from each owner or ownership group—which numbered six at the time—for the league treasury.

On that August day, Hunt confirmed that, aside from Dallas and Houston, four other cities would get franchises in the new league: Denver, Minneapolis–St. Paul, Los Angeles, and New York.

Having named Adams the Houston owner 11 days earlier, he revealed the names of the next four: Barron Hilton, son of hotel magnate Conrad, would run the Los Angeles team; Robert Howsam, aided by his brother, would be in charge of Denver; Max Winter, former owner of the Minneapolis Lakers, and Bill Boyer had signed on for Minneapolis–St. Paul; and famed radio announcer Harry Wismer would be the power behind the Big Apple's entry.

A host of cities competed for the two other franchises slated to join, and only a day later, it looked like Seattle would be one. Hunt sent a wire to Willard Rhodes, leader of the city's effort, saying that if the franchise-to-be could secure a commitment with the University of Washington's football field, it would be accepted into the new league. But that commitment never occurred, and Seattle remained without a pro franchise until the NFL expanded there in 1976.

About one week later, AFL owners, save for the ill Bob Howsam of Denver, gathered at the Statler Hilton in Dallas (no doubt lured by a bargain rate from Barron) for a weekend of meetings. New York's Wismer revealed his showmanship abilities quickly, saying he wanted his team's home games to be played not on Sundays but a day earlier since "[New York]'s the largest city in the world with nothing to do on Saturday afternoons." The head of the league's television-radio committee, Wismer also revealed that all broadcast revenue would be shared equally by the teams, which would become one of the most successful moves in sports.

And that money would help offer the players better salaries. As Hunt's league was being formed, NFL players averaged anywhere from $8,000 to $20,000 per season, with backfield stars enjoying the highest pay. He said the AFL planned to set its minimum salary 10 percent higher than the NFL's $6,500. Even game officials would earn higher pay. Hunt stiffened himself to commit $8 million to his team's operations.

On the last day of the meetings, Hunt announced that all clubs would post a $100,000 performance bond, which would guarantee they would play all games to help appease any worries of stadium operators. When the NFL's Texans played their only ill-fated season in 1952, they eventually were taken over by the league and ended up playing their schedule on the road.

By late August, other cities were fighting to secure a franchise in the new league. Miami representatives hoping to land the Orange Bowl as a home stadium conferred with Hunt and planned to submit a formal application around Labor Day. Kansas City investors had raised the requisite $25,000, and even Louisville, which into the 21st century never hosted a major pro sports franchise, boasted investors with $25,000 to spend.

That was the good news. Less than a month after Hunt held his Houston press conference, the NFL responded to his bomb with a stunner of its own, also originating from Houston. Halas—he who had shown no interest in Hunt or his dream of an NFL expansion franchise in Dallas—announced he would recommend the league place teams in both Dallas and Houston in 1961. Given Halas' stature as one of the original founders of the NFL, "recommend" was equivalent to "mandate."

Hunt reacted swiftly with uncharacteristic anger.

"They have tried the sabotage route in every city we've been interested in," he said. "For instance, they put out a rumor in Seattle that they'll be given a franchise in the NFL.

"It's obvious what they're trying to do, and it conceivably can get them into trouble. I think some congressmen and senators from states where we will have teams are not going to stand for it."

That same day, Hunt had found out the Texans would call the 75,507-seat Cotton Bowl home. The State Fair of Texas, the bowl's operator, had accepted Hunt's application, which had been submitted only days before. At that point, whether the group would have the maintenance strength or dates to host another pro team was unknown.

Despite the NFL's broadside, Hunt needed to focus on luring two other franchises quickly or else the league would not get off the ground. In late October, Ralph Wilson—who had owned a share of the Detroit Lions—signed on to start a franchise in Buffalo. He named it the Bills, the same name of the failed AAFC entry. It looked like the Florida city of Jacksonville would soon be the eighth franchise.

In early November, attorney William Towers there said nearly two dozen people had offered to invest $1,000 to $5,000 in a new franchise. Hunt had met with local businessmen and told them Jacksonville was his top pick as the eighth team, considering its large stadium and rapid growth.

But the AFL's Jacksonville wooing fell apart, leaving the city barren of pro football until the 1990s.

Instead, the Boston Patriots, led by William H. Sullivan, became the eighth and final franchise of the original AFL on November 22. Amazingly, Sullivan was accepted though he and Hunt had never met. Instead, they engaged in hours of conversations on the telephone. Perhaps even more amazing, that same day, the league started its first draft of 33 rounds. It was little more than a farce.

"We were ill-prepared," Hunt said. "We had only three general managers. We appointed them as a committee to conduct the draft…. We were ill-prepared not only to draft these players but also to go out and sign them. We didn't have any employees."

By the dawn of 1960, the AFL faced more trouble. The league withdrew its Minneapolis–St. Paul franchise in January, leaving it unbalanced at seven teams and prompting Hunt to hurl more charges of sabotage against the established league. Minneapolis–St. Paul owners such as E.W. Boyer said they couldn't hire a coach because they couldn't guarantee the NFL wouldn't show up that season with a franchise as well. The owners were refunded their $25,000 stake.

Though Hunt was elected president of the new league on January 26, his new powers couldn't stop what happened two days later: the NFL awarded

Clint Murchison Jr. and Bedford Wynne the expansion Dallas franchise to begin play in 1960 rather than the original suggestion of 1961.

The Dallas news infuriated the AFL brass. Commissioner Joe Foss warned open warfare and congressional investigations might ensue if the NFL moved into Dallas, "the heart of our league." Nearly 50 years after the decision, Ralph Wilson remained impassioned when asked about it.

"He [Lamar] had tried to get a team for Dallas with the NFL. As soon as he started a team in Dallas, the NFL put one in," Wilson recalled. "You talk about antitrust! If we had had a good lawyer, we'd have owned the whole NFL."

They did try. In March, Foss asked the Justice Department to file an antitrust suit against the NFL based on the league's newfound love of expansion. The government agency refused. (That same month, the NFL let the Cardinals transfer to St. Louis, in what must have seemed like another dagger thrown at Hunt, given his efforts to relocate the franchise.) On June 17, tired of all the NFL's moves, the AFL decided to fight on its own through the courts. It filed a $10 million antitrust suit against the NFL, looking for $180,000 in damages while the Texans sought $1.5 million in reparation. That summer, the courts were kind to the fledgling league as it won three challenges among those who had been signed by both leagues: Billy Cannon (Houston), Charley Flowers (Los Angeles), and Johnny Robinson (Dallas).

During the year since the AFL's launch, Hunt rejected offer upon offer to join the NFL. Soon after the original league meeting in Chicago the previous August, Adams and Hunt had gathered with Halas on a secret trip. Halas explained to them how the AAFC had failed and cost both leagues a lot of money. He offered Hunt a franchise in Dallas and Adams one in Houston. They declined.

When Murchison had received approval from the NFL expansion committee, also the previous August, he had tried to dissuade Hunt from starting the AFL. Meeting him at Hunt Oil, Murchison offered his rival a big piece—50 percent—of the franchise. Of course, the deal was based on Hunt getting rid of the Texans. Hunt refused.

"We had made a commitment to our partners," Hunt said. "Each team had put up $25,000 to the league treasury. It would be very bad faith on our part not to go forward."

Rams stockholder Ed Pauley even invited Hunt out to a 49ers-Rams exhibition game at the Los Angeles Memorial Coliseum right on the verge of the start of the AFL season. Again he was offered an NFL franchise. Hunt said he had given his word, and he would not be interested.

As fall beckoned, much needed to be accomplished on and off the field. In early July, the eight teams (Oakland had been awarded an expansion franchise, prompted by Hilton's desire for a California rivalry) launched preseason drills. With 71 players on the roster, the Texans opened camp first at their facility in Rosewall, New Mexico. Quarterback Cotton Davidson was not impressed.

"That first Texans training camp in Roswell, New Mexico, was quite an ordeal," he said. "They had a contract with the school, New Mexico Military, to feed us. And they fed us like a military school. It was the worst food in the world."

Davidson recalled that Hunt—who would turn 28 during the camp—wanted to be in on the action.

"Lamar and Bunker Hunt would get over on a field away from where we were working out, and they'd kick and throw. And after practice, we'd have a kicking contest with Lamar."

By August 23, following four exhibition victories, the Texans had trimmed the roster to 43. After a game against Denver later that week, Hunt moved the players' training digs to Fort Worth for a few days, trying to drum up support there. Former Texas Christian University players such as Sherrill Headrick were a selling point to fans during the time in Fort Worth.

They had to fight the Cowboys, who had signed local SMU star quarterback Don Meredith before their franchise had been officially approved by the NFL and despite Hunt's relationship with him.

"I was naïve enough to think that we couldn't have conversations with Meredith, although I knew him personally from SMU, until after his last college game," Hunt said. "We woke up on the Sunday morning after his last college game, and there was a story in the paper that Clint Murchison of the Cowboys had signed Don Meredith."

On September 2, the Texans ended the exhibition season by pounding the Oilers 24–3 in their first game in the Cotton Bowl. The announced attendance was 51,000, though not all paid. Hunt, in fact, couldn't estimate what percentage of the crowd *did* pay (thousands of bandsmen had entered free, and others enjoyed reduced rates).

Only eight days remained until the American Football League officially kicked off, and a headline about Hunt—"Most Happy Fella"—summed up his optimism.

"I think our position now is real good," Hunt said. "We'll always try to interest our people. When you quit trying to promote your product, you're getting lazy."

Thanks to Hunt's efforts, the Texans had stayed in the news as the season approached, even for seemingly lackluster information. On August 3—a year to the day after the new league was formally announced in Houston—the *Dallas Morning News* reported, in a story in its front section accompanied by a photo, that the Texans and Columbia Pictures had struck a "partnership." Hunt handed an autographed Texans football to Kay Sutton, Queen of the Texans, who passed it on to Columbia executive Rube Jackter, who was thus anointed a Texans goodwill ambassador. Sutton was then informed she could head to Los Angeles in September for a screen test—right when the Texans were slated to play the Chargers.

Hunt tried anything to sell tickets. He even hired a woman named Jayne Murchison—the same last name as Cowboys owner Clint—to peddle them. Murchison thought about countering with radio advertisements featuring a woman named Rosemary Hunt, who would say, "This is Rosemary Hunt. My husband talks football all the time. He's finally got me interested in it too, and so now I have decided that I'm going to see all the Cowboys games this year." But Murchison opted not to.

The Texans would be led into the regular season by coach Hank Stram, a former University of Miami assistant. He was not Hunt's first choice. The AFL founder hoped to hire Tom Landry, whom he interviewed in a friend's small New York apartment without success. (Years later, the friend, Tom Richey, found out from NFL Films' Steve Sabol that the apartment killed the deal; Landry saw it as a reflection of the AFL's prospects.) Ironically, the New York Giants assistant ended up joining the crosstown Cowboys as their head man, where he stayed for 29 seasons. Hunt also tried to woo Oklahoma's Bud Wilkinson over many months. "He had a lot of interest, but he ultimately felt he needed to stay at Oklahoma because this was a pretty flighty operation," Hunt said.

Why did Hunt call his new franchise the Texans? After all, that team of the same name had failed in Dallas only eight years before.

"I was naïve enough to think it was a name people associated with football would remember, and even though it was a bad association, it would mean something positive. I called Giles Miller, who had been the principal owner of the Texans, and asked his permission to use the name. He said, 'Gosh, you're welcome to it. I've been trying to forget about it for more than five years.'"

But for the man labeled "Most Happy Fella," the season to come would not be nirvana.

In Los Angeles, the Texans fell 21–20 in their opener against the Chargers. It was an expensive loss. Because the game was played on a Saturday night and ABC's contract only covered Sunday broadcasts, Hunt spent $10,000 to beam the game back to Dallas. At the midway point, after a defeat of the Broncos, the team stood at 3–4, hardly an inspiring debut. Leaguewide, Hunt offered a grim assessment of franchise finances.

"I feel fairly sure that all of us will lose money this season," he said. "That is to be expected for at least the next two years. They all know what they've got to do—sell more season tickets."

Single-game sales also distressed Hunt. They had traditionally been large at college campuses, such as SMU, since nearby rivals shipped thousands of fans for road games. But with cities such as Los Angeles and New York visiting Dallas, especially in that age of inferior air travel, the visiting team would make little dent in ticket sales.

Hunt suffered through a rapid decline in attendance. While 41,000 entered the stadium for the Texans' home debut against the Chargers, 38,000 came out to see the New York Titans, and only 21,000 appeared when Oakland visited.

During this time, the best news had arrived from a courthouse. In an unexpected move, a federal judge dismissed the AFL's suit against six of the seven Western Division NFL teams (Baltimore was excluded), while letting it stand against the six Eastern Division teams. The problem, according to the judge, was that the suit was filed in Washington, D.C., where Western Division clubs didn't appear. Hunt saw the decision as a victory. "The NFL sought a delaying action, hoping for a ruling that required the AFL to file in 13 cities. Thus, the judge actually ruled in the AFL's favor since one suit can now be filed elsewhere, such as in Baltimore," he said.

As the second half of the season commenced, Hunt made a radical move. He jettisoned general manager Don Rossi, who had been hired less than a year earlier. The owner said he would take over some responsibilities. Rossi did not go quietly, claiming he was owed a salary for 1961 because of the timing of Hunt's decision (his owner did not concur) and pointing out he disagreed with Hunt's policy of giving away thousands of tickets for home games, since it hurt season-ticket holders who had paid in full.

Despite saying he had no one in mind to replace Rossi during a press conference discussing his departure, two days later Hunt hired Jack Steadman. Hindered by a lack of sports experience, Steadman had been a well-regarded employee at Penrod Drilling, part of the Hunts' oil businesses, and had graduated from SMU like Lamar. At the time, Hunt said Steadman wasn't hired for any definite period. Steadman lasted with the franchise until 2007.

A new GM didn't change results on the field right away. The Texans finished with nearly as many exhibition wins (six) as regular-season ones (eight). In its final game, a home affair against Buffalo, the Texan Coaches Club deemed it Lamar Hunt Appreciation Day for all he had done to bring pro football to the city. Hunt was thankful for the gesture—where he received eight signed balls, one from each team, at halftime—and for the result, as the Texans finished the campaign by drubbing Buffalo 24–7.

Others weren't as appreciative. Only 18,000—not even 25 percent capacity—sat in the Cotton Bowl for the game. The tally for season-ticket sales in the massive stadium ended up around 6,300.

Recalling the franchise's first season, *Dallas Morning News* columnist Gary Cartwright compared it to a circus:

> His first general manager was a sporting goods salesman, his first talent scout kept all records on the back of an envelope in his coat pocket, and his first head coach, Hank Stram, had neither experience in pro football nor as a head coach.
>
> When Paul Miller, who was later elected captain of the team, described the whole operation as "Mickey Mouse…Donald Duck…Disneyland," club officials were crushed.

The league itself leaned closer to folly than respect. From coast to coast, a low-budget operation dominated. Films were watched on bedsheets while players sat on milk crates. The New York Titans played in the decrepit Polo Grounds, which coach Sammy Baugh described as "the worst place I ever saw." Players hustled off the field faster than on to try and cash checks as the Titans teetered toward bankruptcy. Denver couldn't afford to outfit its players, so they brought their own practice uniforms.

In fact, at the end of the first season, the financial picture was dismal. The league lost $3.5 million. L.A. led the way with a $900,000 deficit. Houston followed with a $710,000 loss. Hunt's franchise in Dallas didn't release estimates, but sources pegged its losses at $400,000 minimum.

Even H.L. Hunt was dismayed. He responded by canceling an advertising contract worth a few hundred dollars Penrod Drilling had inked with *Oil and Gas Journal.* Why? The account executive learned the following: Lamar's franchise and its losses were under the Penrod name, thus this would help soften the blow.

For Hunt and his squad, perhaps the one shred of good tidings lay in the fact that the Cowboys finished 0–11–1. In spite of a war of words between he and Murchison in the Dallas dailies, the two enjoyed a friendship forged as rivals during war.

At a lunch just before Christmas 1960, Clint surprised Lamar by wearing a bright-red Texans blazer. A week later, Clint had a party at his home. Two friends brought in a six-foot-high gift-wrapped box. Clint unwrapped it and was shocked when a smiling Lamar emerged.

And for the league itself, there were positives amid the financial bloodbath. The rules that owners adopted helped give the AFL a unique identity. Two-point conversions were allowed after touchdowns and names were emblazoned on the backs of jerseys. ABC's innovations also showered the AFL with a special flair. The network let viewers hear the sounds of the game, such as crunching tackles and captains talking during the coin toss. It tried to personalize players by showing what they looked like up close, superimposing their names on the TV screen.

But then came 1961.

A number of investors in the Raiders sold their interests to Ed McGah and Wayne Valley on January 17. Less than a month later, the Chargers bolted Los Angeles—where they had little success battling the entrenched Rams—to become the first major pro sports franchise in San Diego. That spring, after one season of play, the Howsam brothers sold the Broncos.

At the Cotton Bowl that fall, the Texans were mediocre. After starting off 3–1, they suffered six losses in a row, snuffing any championship hopes. One defeat in Boston typified the anything-goes AFL: on the final play, a fan barged into the end zone and deflected a pass as Dallas looked to tie the game. The Texans finished 6–8, good enough for second place in the

Western Division but far from cementing their place in a two-team town. Yet the seeds were planted for a strong 1962. Led by Haynes, who averaged 4.7 yards per carry, the Texans rushed for more yards than anyone in the AFL, gaining 2,183. Despite poor crowds, the games were exciting. About two particular contests, *Dallas Morning News* columnist Bud Shrake wrote, "The crowds were so thin that one press box observer suggested Lamar Hunt buy a few thousand dummies to put in the upper decks. But for uninhibited action, those Texan games were superb."

Despite that newspaper reference, compared to the previous year, Hunt was barely mentioned in the press, save for society items such as being named an Easter Seals trustee-at-large. He would be back in the spotlight in 1962, especially as the AFL's antitrust suit crawled through the legal system. On February 26, Hunt testified for four hours in United States District Court in Baltimore. His main point: the NFL did not announce expansion plans until after he founded the AFL in 1959. AFL attorney Warren E. Baker asked, in addition to the damages, for the NFL to move its Dallas team and for the league to allow exhibition games against its rival, among other requests.

By June, a decision had been reached—and it was a blow to the AFL, especially to Hunt. In the U.S. District Court in Maryland, Judge Roszel Thomsen opined the AFL's monopoly case wouldn't fly, throwing out the $10 million suit. The AFL couldn't show the NFL had a monopoly on players or that the older league could ban the AFL from television outlets. Further, the NFL's decision to place franchises in Dallas and Minneapolis suggested no proof of a monopoly.

Hunt had attended all the court sessions, the only AFL owner to do so. The cost of the case to the AFL was high, estimated at about $200,000—the same amount eight franchises had thrown in not even two years earlier to get the whole gambit started. Wismer, who disliked the suit from the get-go, said, "It has been a most costly lesson."

Hunt remained optimistic about the league, so much so that in June he indicated either New Orleans or Atlanta would probably be granted an expansion franchise that month to start play in 1963. Both groups had offered $25,000 in earnest money, but neither had met the AFL's mandatory requirement of selling 20,000 season tickets. Despite the chairman of the expansion committee's wishes, neither Atlanta nor New Orleans joined the AFL.

But a report a few months later put Hunt on the spot about his own desires. He was forced to deny the Texans would move to New Orleans.

"There's nothing to it," he said. "I wouldn't consider moving the franchise until it became clear that the people in Dallas simply didn't want the club. As I see it, the true Dallas interest hasn't even been tested yet, either by the Texans or the Cowboys. Neither club has had a winning season, so you can't really tell how Dallas fans feel about them."

They would soon find out.

In their opener against Boston, Haynes exploded at the Cotton Bowl. He scored four touchdowns—including two on 25-yard and 30-yard runs. The team's beefy offensive line opened large holes. Rookie Sonny Bishop, a 240-pounder from Fresno State, was an important addition to a young line that also featured 6'6" Ohio State alumnus Jim Tyrer. The Texans thrashed the Patriots 42–28.

Five days later—for the only time on record in his long career as an owner—Hunt meddled in his team's player-personnel affairs, prompting the wrath of Stram. Hunt made sure Cotton Davidson was traded to Oakland (who would become the Chiefs' biggest rival) in September for the Raiders' No. 1 draft pick in 1963. After all, he surmised, the Texans had picked up Dawson. The Raiders contacted Stram about a possible trade, but he wanted too much in return, so they tried Hunt. The newfound wheeler-dealer came out a winner. With the top pick in the entire draft after the Texans left Dallas, the Chiefs drafted Grambling's Junious Buchanan (better known as "Buck"), who became a mainstay on their defensive line for years.

"It worked out pretty well," Hunt said. "But I never made another trade. How could I have topped that?"

Despite his wrath over the trade, Stram was having fun unleashing innovations. During a September 30 game at the Cotton Bowl, a 41–21 throttling of Buffalo that lifted the Texans to 3–0, he installed closed-circuit televisions so coaches and players on the bench could watch plays and learn from them. The picture on the field was ugly to Bills owner Wilson, who recognized a team on the rise. He told Hunt, "You have a fine club. It has talent and leadership and it comes up with the right play at the right time."

After losing its next game, Dallas rolled on, finishing 6–1 at the halfway point. In one victory, Haynes was ejected for punching a Titans player, but not before he had gained more than 200 yards rushing and receiving. To Hunt's pleasure, the AFL also was picking up steam. On the television front, nearly 200 stations were showing games, a jump from 130 in 1961. For the first time, the league notched two sellouts on the same weekend. In Denver, attendance was rising to such heights that Hunt won a $100 bet with the curmudgeonly George Marshall, owner of the Washington Redskins. Before the AFL started, Marshall wagered that the Broncos would never draw more than 10,000 for a home game. But Hunt wrote him that the Broncos had recently attracted more than 34,000 fans for a contest.

Marshall responded with a letter Hunt kept in a scrapbook the rest of his life:

Dear Lamar,

You will have to forgive me because I had forgotten about the bet, as it is more than two years old now. At that time the Denver people were playing in a baseball park and I knew I was safe since it did not seat that many. However, according to your statement, where they are now playing they have a much larger capacity and have exceeded the figure on which we made our bet, so you will find our check for $100 enclosed. I was amazed in looking over the statement that 34,396 paid admissions only derived a net ticket income of $106,467.46. Evidently Denver is very reasonable in its ticket prices.

The looming issue Hunt faced in the AFL involved the floundering Titans. Wismer's TV and radio connections aside (and they were important; the ABC contract he helped generate drew 13 million TV viewers a game and about $200,000 per team in 1962), he had become a financial liability with his franchise. During a game against the Chargers at the Polo Grounds that fall, darkness began to fall during the fourth quarter. Across the Harlem River, lights bathed Yankee Stadium during the Giants game. Yet in the Polo Grounds, the bulbs remained off.

The Chargers complained, and word quickly reached Wismer. No lights were turned on; he didn't want to pay the $250 fee.

On November 8, the AFL told players it would try to facilitate a sale and guarantee their paychecks in the interim. The next day, Wismer was given an ultimatum to sell the New York franchise within a week or lose it to the league. The team's debts were estimated at more than $400,000, which proved to be wildly optimistic. Though Hunt initially had been adamant that the AFL needed a team in New York, he began to believe the league should abandon the Big Apple, especially considering the crumbling Polo Grounds.

Dallas visited the dank Manhattan field in November, soon after the AFL took over the moribund franchise. Led by Haynes and Curtis McClinton, who both rushed for more than 100 yards, they thrashed the Titans 52–31. In fact, during the second half of the season, the Texans continued their march through the league. After dispatching the two-time AFL championship runner-up Chargers 26-17 in the season finale in the Cotton Bowl, the reserved Hunt sipped a Coke in the locker room and couldn't contain his pleasure. "Man, 365 days ago this just didn't seem possible, did it?" he said.

In later years, Hunt would remember that final game in Dallas for one of the few promotion-minded brainstorms that he didn't implement. Since the Texans had clinched a berth in the championship, the game was somewhat meaningless and wasn't expected to draw a big crowd. The night before, Lamar talked with Chargers owner Barron Hilton.

Hunt recalled: "I said, 'Barron, I read somewhere about a game in the 1930s when two owners locked everybody out and sat one on one side of the stadium and one on the other and cheered for their teams. Let's do that tomorrow.'" Though it would have garnered national publicity, the AFL still needed gate receipts, and the idea was scratched.

Two days before the AFL championship, the city of Dallas unveiled Dallas Texans Day to honor the team for winning the Western Division and to send it off to Houston with good luck. After the parade, Hunt drove to the Statler Hilton and parked his car, which was emblazoned with Texans decals. Two youngsters asked him what his name was.

"Hunt," Lamar said.

The kids were excited. "Bobby?" they asked, hoping he was the Texans' rookie defender and would sign an autograph.

When Lamar said he wasn't, they left unhappily.

Those were the last dissatisfied fans Hunt would see for a while. On December 23, 1962, the Texans captured Dallas' first pro football title during the double-overtime thriller in Houston. More than 400 fans, hoisting signs such as "World Champs," waited at Love Field that Sunday night to welcome Hunt and his champions as they walked off their DC-7 plane at Braniff Gate 17. Not all players heard the applause. Haynes and Holub drove back to Dallas, and Brooker—he of the winning kick—headed to Alabama through the night to visit relatives. But those who appeared were mobbed. And Hunt—dismissed by autograph seekers only 48 hours earlier—stood in the terminal, his tie the victim of scissors and his shirtsleeves still drenched from champagne, signing autographs.

In the AFL, few champagne corks were popped in 1963. In the original announcement of the league on August 14, 1959, six cities were given franchises. By the league's fourth season, only half of those cities—Houston, Denver, and New York—still boasted teams. And New York's franchise under Wismer had failed ignominiously and filed for bankruptcy in February with debts approaching $2 million, including some dating from 1960.

"Lamar really held the league together during the early years," Steadman recalled in a documentary about Hunt. "Every league meeting that we had, and we had a lot of them, people would say, 'Well, we're going to the meeting—this will be the last meeting.' And Lamar would go to the meeting, and he would have laid out what the next steps were for the success of the league. And owners who had come to the meeting thinking, *Well, I've had enough. I've spent enough money. I've lost enough money*—they'd leave all enthused about losing another million dollars."

That spring, the AFL let both the Titans and the weak Raiders choose players from other franchises to try to improve their dismal teams. More importantly, David A. "Sonny" Werblin became the Titans' new owner in March. Few foresaw the success he would engender by changing the team's name to the Jets, moving it to the new Shea Stadium—and drafting Joe Willie Namath.

Part of the league's core involved a Houston-Dallas rivalry, which Hunt modeled after the Rams-49ers rivalry that had drawn an NFL-record 102,368 to Los Angeles Memorial Coliseum in 1957 for a game. As Hunt later said, "I went to Bud Adams first because he was the key. If he hadn't been interested, I wouldn't have gone on, and we never would have proceeded."

Yet on May 22, Hunt announced that the Dallas team was moving 500 miles away to Kansas City. The Cowboys were so happy to see their rivals leave town that they not only purchased the Texans' practice facility, they paid $100,000 to the franchise for what were deemed "moving expenses."

Bills owner Ralph Wilson succinctly summed up what happened to Hunt. "He was forced out," Wilson said. "The NFL was well known, and the AFL was not."

But in that short period of time—from the double-overtime championship game in December to the moving vans heading to Kansas City in May—the AFL was made. The exciting title contest had captivated many who watched that dreary December day, drawing new fans to the league and making it a topic of national conversation. Then, Werblin's stake in the Jets in March brought franchise stability to the city most crucial to the league's long-term success. In May, the AFL announced that NBC, not ABC, would broadcast its 1963 championship game, paving the way for the blockbuster $36 million deal with the network that would be signed the next season. And as Hunt and the former Texans departed for Kansas City, they finally basked in a city's attention, from fans to media, all to itself.

That first year, more than four dozen Kansas City companies bought at least 50 season tickets each; in Dallas, the Texans could never persuade more than four. During the Chiefs' first luncheon with the city booster club, more than five times more people appeared than had shown up that first time in Dallas in 1960.

"It feels strange to be in a city that does not suffer from an overpopulation of professional football teams," Hunt said. "But it feels good."

Almost everything was free. The Chiefs paid no rent on a modern office building or the next-door practice field. Municipal Stadium came without charge until the 1965 season. Though the Texans didn't earn a penny of concession profits in the Cotton Bowl, in Kansas City they would earn 50 percent.

The club's uniform was essentially the same, save for the name Chiefs and the helmet logo, which was created by none other than Hunt. On a napkin he sketched an interlocking KC within an arrowhead on the helmet. The state of Texas, obviously, was removed.

Entertaining the fans was crucial. Hunt hired Tony Dipardo—known as Mr. Music in Kansas City—and brought forth Tony Dipardo's Zing band, dressed in red jackets. The mascot horse Warpaint raced around Municipal Stadium after touchdowns, mounted by a rider wearing an American Indian headdress.

"No other team was doing things like that," recalled Jim Schaaf, who began his 22-year career in the Chiefs' front office during their Municipal Stadium days. "Everyone knew and liked Tony. He'd get up there and blow his trumpet. It made the game that [much] more colorful."

Even the field was colorful—groundskeeper George Toma, who became an NFL legend for his immaculate fields, painted the end zones and the center of midfield.

For its first regular-season game as the Kansas City Chiefs, the team flew to Denver to play at Bears Stadium, which had been constructed on the site of a dump. Stram introduced a new I formation for the running game, and the Chiefs notched an AFL record for points scored, demolishing the Broncos 59–7. Aside from shredding the defense with their running, both Haynes and McClinton even tossed passes, the latter's for a touchdown. Hunt watched it all while sitting in the last row of the 34,000-capacity facility (truth be told, Hunt enjoyed sitting in the worst seats for all types of sports events) and knew a special team was blossoming. With their strong play, he was probably little-fazed when later that month, the AFL lost again in its appeal of the $10 million antitrust lawsuit against the NFL. After all, the judge's decision in the U.S. Fourth Circuit Court of Appeals in Baltimore, in a backhanded way, highlighted AFL positives: "It was successfully launched, could stage a full schedule of games in 1960, has competed very successfully for outstanding players, and has obtained advantageous contracts for national television coverage." Who had trouble competing?

In fact, franchise values—at least in the rival NFL—were starting to reflect pro football's popularity. A $1,000 share in the Detroit Lions bought in 1948 was sold for almost $15,000 in 1963. Los Angeles Rams owner Dan Reeves was aghast. "They [franchise prices] are ridiculous. They violate every logical rule of investment on the basis of earnings." But with a small supply and great demand, franchise values were just starting their march upward into the stratosphere.

While the Chiefs started defending their title on a high note, Hunt still lived in Dallas, where he and Rosemary had divorced and where he was now dating Norma Knobel. And because he remained a resident of the Texas town, he, along with his brother Bunker and his father, became embroiled in one of the most traumatic events of the 20th century: the assassination of President John F. Kennedy.

On the morning of November 22, 1963, Kennedy arrived in Dallas with his wife, Jackie, during a quick trip to the city. That day's *Dallas Morning*

News, on page 14 of the front section, featured a full-page ad, bordered in black. Under the headline "Welcome Mr. Kennedy," which stood in all-capital letters, it accused him of ignoring the constitution. A dozen questions were posed to the president, many suggesting communist ties, such as, "Why have you scrapped the Monroe Doctrine in favor of the 'Spirit of Moscow'?" The ad was signed by the American Fact-Finding Committee. Nelson Bunker Hunt was a primary contributor to the ad.

During this time, H.L. Hunt was putting out a newsletter called *Life Line*, which lambasted Kennedy and championed business. Its opinions were also broadcast on numerous radio stations. Since the mid-1950s, Hunt had been increasingly dedicated to right-wing political causes.

And on November 21, a man drove a woman named Connie Trammel to Lamar Hunt's offices in downtown Dallas. His name was Jack Ruby.

Shortly after noon on November 22, Kennedy was assassinated by Lee Harvey Oswald as his motorcade drove through Dallas (H.L. Hunt watched the president pass from his office building). Two days later, Ruby killed Oswald on live television. Among Ruby's possessions when the police wrestled him to the ground was *Life Line* literature he had recently picked up at an exhibit—and during a later search elsewhere, police found the phone number of Lamar Hunt among Ruby's possessions.

For years, conspiracy theorists have tried to implicate the Hunts as being in some way involved with the assassination, but no proof has ever come to light. Regarding Ruby, according to testimony, he was driving Trammel to a job interview at Hunt's offices in the Mercantile National Bank building for a teen club Hunt was starting in a former bowling alley. Ruby told her he had never met Lamar and hoped to. But after escorting her to the lobby, he let Trammel go up to Hunt's offices on her own. He never met Lamar.

After the assassination, given H.L. Hunt's controversial views, the FBI called him that afternoon and asked him to leave town immediately, fearing that he and members of his family might be shot in the ensuing rage over what had happened. Hunt reluctantly agreed. He and his wife, Ruth, departed for Washington, D.C., using false names.

When the Warren Commission began its investigation into the assassination, it interviewed H.L., Bunker, and Lamar. The youngest Hunt appeared first, speaking with Special Agent Lansing P. Logan of the FBI less than a month after the assassination. Lamar said he had never met Ruby and had no idea why his name was listed in Ruby's notebook.

Bunker, for his part, said he contributed a few hundred dollars to the *Dallas Morning News* ad. But he noted he didn't know any of the others who had paid for it, nor did he know Oswald or Ruby.

When the Warren Commission released its hefty report on the Kennedy assassination, none of the Hunts were implicated in any way, nor were there any assertions they had even indirect involvement. Still, magazines and the occasional book continued to make accusations against them for decades.

Amid all this, on the day of the assassination, a sports decision had to be made quickly: would the pro football leagues play their games that Sunday? The NFL chose to and has been vilified for decades for letting the contests go on so soon after a national tragedy. The AFL decided to postpone its games.

A few months later Lamar—who, when he had gotten divorced from his first wife, paid for a newspaper ad in Dallas to announce it since he was a public figure—married Norma Knobel, a 20-something beauty who had once worked in promotions for the Texans. She was a schoolteacher who graduated from North Texas State University with honors. Like her husband, she adored football and attended dozens of games with him during their courtship.

Hunt's honeymoon with Norma lasted far longer than their trip to Innsbruck, Austria, to watch the 1964 Winter Olympics, but Kansas City's romance with its new franchise started to sour early on.

The Chiefs were not the first major pro sports team to make the Missouri town its home. That honor belonged to baseball's Athletics, owned by Charles O. Finley. He would become famous for his eccentric ways once he moved the franchise to Oakland, where his team won three straight world championships in the 1970s. He paid players minuscule wages but offered a bonus for those who grew mustaches, he touted orange baseballs, and he fired second baseman Mike Andrews for making two errors during the 1973 World Series before public outcry forced him to be reinstated.

Finley was no fan of Kansas City from the get-go. When he first met Hunt, he didn't mince words. "This is a shit town," he said. "And no one will ever do any good here."

The Chiefs faced off-the-field woes in a city beset by crime. Guard Ed Budde was beaten in a 1964 bar fight and ended up with a metal plate in his skull. The next year, tight end Fred Arbanas was mugged and lost vision in an eye. Chiefs executive Don Klosterman enraged Kansas City with both derogatory comments and suggestions the team may move to Los Angeles. He was forced to resign.

Near the end of the 1965 season, running back Mack Lee Hill was injured against Buffalo. After surgery on his knee two days later, he died from an embolism, which basically means his bloodflow was blocked. Hunt called Hill's death "the worst shock possible."

Troubles mounted with the fan base. Though the Chiefs sold slightly over 15,000 season tickets their first year, that number dropped to 10,000 in 1964 (when they drew 18,126 to a game at Municipal Stadium) and 9,600 in 1965. In fact, K.C. had become a weakling among AFL teams by its third season in town. That year, the Jets—the formerly bankrupt Titans franchise—sold more than 40,000 season tickets, jump-started by the signing of University of Alabama star quarterback Namath. The Bills surpassed 30,000, and Denver was around 23,000. The Chiefs were trailing their brethren badly.

Hunt was forced to hold a news conference after the 1965 season announcing the Chiefs would not be moving, though he admitted a few AFL owners had suggested they should, especially with the Chicago and Los Angeles markets open. He added that AFL owners could not legally force him to relocate.

While the Chiefs' viability continued to be debated, good news arrived from the oil fields. Placid Oil Company had unearthed a massive find in

Louisiana, adding tens of millions of dollars to the accounts of Lyda's six children. Considering the war for talent among the AFL and NFL that had been unleashed, it was an opportune moment to have money flowing in pro football's pre-salary-cap era.

The Chiefs had not been shy competing for players. Before the team had played a game, Hunt tried to persuade former SMU teammate Forrest Gregg, an offensive lineman for the Green Bay Packers, to join the squad after the 1959 NFL season.

"I was selling cars for Ken Grantham, who had been a running back at SMU. He had a Ford dealership in Irving," Gregg recalled. "He told me one day, 'Forrest, I saw Lamar Hunt today and mentioned you were working for me.' Lamar asked Ken if I'd be interested in playing for his Dallas Texans. I told Ken, 'Yeah, I'd be interested.'

"He talked with Lamar again. I said, 'What would they pay?' Lamar had said, 'We'll give him what he wants.' That got my attention. But that was the first year Vince Lombardi had come to Green Bay. We had a good record [7–5]; we were on track. I was happy in Green Bay and thought they had a chance to win, which was the most important thing to me."

The Texans and Cowboys battled mightily for in-state players. During the 1961 draft, both teams picked Bob Lilly, a defensive standout at Texas Christian University, and E.J. Holub, a tough linebacker from Texas Tech. Joining an established league persuaded Lilly to go with the Cowboys. Holub picked the Texans, mainly because of Hunt.

"The Cowboys wanted me to sign right away. They had some guys out at the East-West Shrine Game," he said. "I told them, 'Leave me alone. I want to play football.'

"Lamar was there, and he said, 'OK. If you promise…we won't bother you anymore.' I told him, 'I will not sign anything or commit myself to anybody.' He left me alone. The Cowboys kept badgering me. I just felt like Lamar was an honorable man, so I went with him.'"

Even after the Texans left Dallas, they still fought for players with the Cowboys. Hunt worked hard to induce Roger Staubach to head to the AFL, offering to pay him during his service in the U.S. Navy. But Dallas matched the Texans' proposal and, like Lilly, Staubach couldn't say no to the NFL.

Subterfuge was common between the leagues. On behalf of struggling Oakland, Hunt called Roman Gabriel and for 30 minutes used his soft-sell approach laced with financial incentives to try to persuade the gunslinger to join the Raiders. Gabriel ended up with the Rams, and Hunt discovered one reason why two years later: he actually had been talking with Rams GM Elroy Hirsch, not Gabriel.

By the time of the 1963 college draft, Hunt and others were working ferociously to keep top choices out of the hands of the NFL.

As *Sports Illustrated* reported, after the annual draft, Hunt got the entire staff going in an effort to sign the team's top choices at once. He also used a couple of lease hounds from his oil operations, who gave up wheedling oil leases out of reluctant farmers long enough to gather signatures from reluctant football players.

When one of the lease hounds knew he would be trying to sign Ed Budde, the big Michigan State tackle, he sent the player's wife two dozen yellow roses of Texas. When he sat down to talk terms with Budde, he had a ready-made ally in Mrs. Budde. The Texans signed three high draft choices that year—Junious Buchanan of Grambling, Budde, and Bobby Bell of Minnesota—almost immediately. Oddly, Hunt himself was the least successful signer, though he offered the fattest contracts.

By the 1965 draft, the stakes had soared. Untested players such as Namath were earning six-figure salaries before taking a snap. Two Chiefs draft choices, Otis Taylor and Gale Sayers, typified the intensity of the battle.

Taylor assumed he would sign with the Chiefs, no matter where he was chosen in the 1965 draft. He watched a Chiefs-Oilers game in Houston and met with team executives along with Lloyd Wells, who scouted for the team and had been Taylor's friend since his teenage years. It seemed to be a fait accompli.

Then the Cowboys invited Taylor to an event for top recruits the next weekend, and the youngster thought, *Why not?* More than a half dozen other recruits were there. As Taylor wrote: "The plan was simple—the Cowboys would keep me 'hidden' until after the AFL's draft that upcoming Saturday, and then they would sign me to an NFL contract instead."

Upon hearing that the Prairie View A&M standout was visiting the Cowboys, Wells flew to the city immediately and started checking hotels for him. Taylor switched hotels three times that weekend. The Cowboys had convinced him he would be teamed up with Olympic gold medalist Bob Hayes, considered the fastest man on the planet.

Though many rumors have flourished around Taylor's time in Dallas—involving sex, bribery of his mother, and other untoward maneuvers—the basic facts follow. Wells discovered which motel in Richardson, Texas, Taylor was staying at; gave $20 to a porter to find Taylor's room; posed as an *Ebony* reporter to gain entrance to his room; then returned in the middle of the night and whisked Taylor to an airport after the recruit had snuck out his bathroom window to avoid NFL security. Within days he had signed with the Chiefs for a $15,000 salary, equivalent bonus, and a new red T-Bird that Wells had promised him at the motel.

Sayers, who attended the University of Kansas, was known as the Kansas Comet for good reason. During his college career, the two-time All-American gained nearly 4,000 all-purpose yards, rushing for 2,675 and also catching passes and returning kickoffs in three varsity seasons. His sophomore year, he averaged a jaw-dropping 7.1 yards per carry and gained 283 yards in a game against Oklahoma State.

With his exciting style of play and his Kansas roots, Hunt became quite interested in Sayers and made sure to meet him his junior year. Sayers came back impressed with the Chiefs owner.

"I liked him very, very much," recalled Sayers, who also was introduced to Hunt's family. "He was very mild-mannered."

The next year, Hunt made his intentions clear.

"He was saying, 'Well, Gale, depending on what you do your senior season, we'd be interested in drafting you,'" Sayers said.

During that 1965 draft in New York City (which actually occurred in November 1964), the Chiefs selected Sayers with their top pick, while the Chicago Bears chose University of Illinois linebacker Dick Butkus first with the third overall NFL pick and Sayers second with the fourth overall choice. When Sayers arrived in New York, Buddy Young, in the employ of the NFL, whisked him away.

"Buddy Young said, 'I've got a car waiting for you.' I chose to go with Buddy Young to the hotel," Sayers said. "Dan Klosterman was the babysitter for the Chiefs. They tried to get me."

Hunt needed to talk with Sayers. Butkus was also in New York at a hotel. He heard a knock on his door.

"It was Lamar Hunt," Butkus noted. "He said "Okay, now we have to try to get Gale with us." Hunt assumed Denver, which had selected Butkus with its top pick, would offer him so much more than the Bears that he would go there. And Hunt wanted Butkus' help to persuade Sayers to join the AFL as well.

Sayers did sit down with Hunt for a 45-minute meeting in Manhattan.

"He was saying that this league was very competitive with the National Football League and hopefully we can sign you," Sayers said. "Lamar said, 'We think we can sign Dick Butkus for the AFL.'"

Both teams offered Sayers a contract. George Halas, leader of the Bears franchise who was famously accused later by tight end Mike Ditka of throwing nickels around like manhole covers, was willing to go as high as $25,000 a year for four years. The Chiefs offered only 10 percent more, $27,500 for four years.

"I really felt that if Lamar and the Chiefs had offered me $50,000 a year for three years, I probably would have gone to the Kansas City Chiefs," Sayers recalled. "I thought that being new in the football business, they wanted to get the best players so they could keep their league together. It seemed like the Bears and Chiefs were in cahoots, because I really thought the Kansas City offer would be $40,000 to $50,000 a year."

To Sayers, the answer was obvious.

"I really felt for me to better myself as a football player, I had to play against the best, and that was in the NFL."

Even those not picked in the upper echelons of the draft were fought over. In 1964 Marty Schottenheimer—the future head coach of the Kansas City Chiefs—played for the University of Pittsburgh Panthers as a starting linebacker. During the 1965 draft, the 6'3", 223-pounder was coveted by two teams. NFL's Baltimore selected him in the fourth round, making him the league's 49th overall pick, while Buffalo tapped him with a seventh-round selection and 56th overall in the AFL.

Both Bills general manager Dick Gallagher and Colts GM Don Kellett wooed Schottenheimer. "I got a call from Dick Gallagher. He said he was at a Holiday Inn, halfway between downtown Pittsburgh and where I lived. I went to meet him, and we reached an agreement," recalled Schottenheimer. "Don had arranged to meet me on the same day at a later time. As soon as I accepted the Buffalo offer, I tried to get hold of Mr. Kellett. This was well before cell phones. I couldn't get hold of him. I went on to my home.

"He came out to my house," Schottenheimer continued. He came up the steps. I said, 'I've been trying to get hold of you for six hours; I signed with Buffalo.' He said 'You didn't sign the contract, did you?' I said I did. He was upset. He had sent his cab back into town. I had to drive him to town to get another cab."

The 1966 draft would be just as brutal. Don Weiss, a former executive director of the NFL who oversaw dozens of Super Bowls, was surprised by what he saw near commissioner Pete Rozelle's office soon after joining the league in 1965. As he noted in his book, *The Making of the Super Bowl*, "It was an incredible sight. Piled high on a 10- to 12-foot-long worktable were more United Airlines tickets than I had ever seen in my life. There had to be hundreds of them, to every conceivable destination in the land.... Airline tickets were critical supplies for the soldiers carrying out a special mission along the front lines of our raging war."

Handing contracts worth hundreds of thousands of dollars to college players simply to keep them out of the hands of the rival leagues threatened the existence of the AFL and NFL.

The idea of a merger had been floated before without anything close to a deal. But in 1965, owners in both leagues turned serious. AFL president Hilton had heard the NFL was interested in merger talks. He appointed Bills owner Wilson and New York Jets owner Werblin to represent the AFL. The NFL appointed Baltimore Colts owner Carroll Rosenbloom.

Decades later Wilson recalled the talks that ensued. "I met with him [Rosenbloom] 10 to 12 times in Miami Beach, where he had a house. We both set out parameters for a merger plan that might work. He said we'll do it after four years. After that, we'll have realignment into one league. He said we'd pool all television money, which was very attractive, being in little old Buffalo.

"I had lunch at the Sea View Hotel with Pete Rozelle and Tex Schramm. We talked about the merger. Tex said, 'In order to merge, we want $50 million.' I said, 'Forget it, Tex. We aren't paying you $50 million.' The thing kind of fell apart in the fall of 1965."

But seeds had been planted. Aside from the dollars being wasted on the draft, the NFL couldn't assume the AFL was going to die; if anything, the rebel league was getting stronger. The new Miami franchise was slated to pay a $7.5 million expansion fee—a huge jump from the $25,000 charge in 1959. The cost would be softened by the $500,000 a year in TV fees it would gather; the established teams were pulling in almost $750,000 a year at that point.

In early April 1966, Hunt took a phone call from Schramm. He wanted to get together on an important matter. Hunt met Schramm at Love Field for about 30 minutes.

"We met at the statue of the Texas Ranger inside Love Field that evening and went out to his car in the parking lot," Hunt said. "It was just a feeling that there would be a little more privacy if we did that. It looked very suspicious to have two guys out in the parking lot in the dark."

Schramm asked if Hunt believed there was an opportunity to merge the leagues, and Hunt said he did. Yet after that secret meeting out of a Cold War spy novel, the leagues started a shooting war that promised to scuttle everything. After a longtime understanding that players wouldn't be raided, the New York Giants and owner Wellington Mara signed soccer-style kicker Pete Gogolak, whose option year had finished, away from the Bills in May. In a record contract for a special-teams player, Gogolak—the second-leading scorer in the AFL—was slated to earn nearly $100,000 for three years. Within the next two weeks, the AFL—now led by a take-no-prisoners commissioner, Al Davis, who had taken over from Joe Foss in April—signed Roman Gabriel and made astounding six-figure offers to other players, including John Brodie.

For Schramm and Hunt, peace talks continued at their Dallas houses. They agreed only to tackle major issues; the rest could be sorted out after a merger was consummated.

Hunt returned to his group of owners amid tension with the NFL. The man who had been with him from the start, Bud Adams, said Hunt's demeanor helped appease some angry individuals.

"The teams on one side of the table had gone out and started signing some of the NFL players, and the other side felt it was more important to stay friendly with them because we were trying to do business," Adams told *SportsBusiness Journal*. "I was on the other side of the table from Lamar, but he was the one who kept us together while the deal with the NFL was getting done. He did a lot to keep peace in the family."

At the end of May, Hunt visited Schramm's house for a final meeting. He wrote down the NFL's offer. A major sticking point: the league wanted $18 million from the AFL over 20 years.

Hunt recalled what happened next.

"My recollection is that there was an AFL meeting in Sonny Werblin's condominium in New York, nine people from the AFL teams at the dining room table," he said. "We had two that were really not favorable to a merger, New York and Oakland. They didn't like the playing conditions for the teams in New York and Oakland. But we continued to try to work those things out."

To Hunt, a merger was obvious. "You couldn't be opposed to the concept of a merger," he said. "I was in favor because teams are businesses. It was important to know in 1966 where everybody was going. At that point we had proved the league could succeed."

Yet Adams and Wayne Valley of Oakland voted against the merger. Werblin, who also cast a dissenting vote against the historic pact, called it "another Munich," adding "Instead of us paying them [$18 million], they should be paying us." But with six owners (including new Miami) voting aye and only a two-thirds majority needed, the AFL passed the merger, as did the NFL (with no dissenting votes).

The major details were historic. Among the main points:

- A common draft in 1967 would end the seven-year bidding war for college athletes.
- A championship game would take place between the two leagues starting in 1967.
- All teams would stay in their present locations. Two new teams would be added by 1968.
- Two networks would continue to broadcast pro football.
- Pete Rozelle would serve as commissioner.
- The merger would be completed in 1970.

The June 8 announcement was followed by a press conference with Hunt, Schramm, and Rozelle. Howard Cosell—soon to be one of the most famous football announcers in history—made Hunt squirm.

Cosell asserted that the AFL had forced the merger by secretly offering huge amounts of money to NFL stars. "You know that it's true," he told Rozelle. Rozelle replied that he knew no such thing. "I know that it's true," Cosell snapped back. He turned to Hunt and demanded a confession. Hunt denied the accusation. "You mean you're negotiating for your league without knowing what your league is doing?" Cosell asked.

"I've tried to answer your question," said Hunt a bit crisply. He then apologized, "I don't mean to be abrupt."

"It's not a question of being abrupt, Lamar," Cosell shot back. "It's a question of being evasive at a time when the American people are entitled to know the truth!"

After they finally agreed to merge, a number of owners, including Hunt, retired to Toots Shor's in New York City for the night.

"The mood? I'd say one of reflection," said Schramm. "It was like two fighters hugging each other at the end of a fight...they're just glad they don't have to fight anymore."

Amid the end of the battle, ironies abounded, especially involving Dallas. Merger talks picked up speed in the city where Hunt launched the AFL's first team. Discussions involved Schramm, whose Cowboys had been the spur that forced Hunt to move his franchise from his beloved hometown to Kansas City. And though Schramm and Hunt lived only a few miles from each other in Dallas and both were top-level executives in pro football, they had only met a handful of times before the Love Field get-together.

Amazingly, given the fact they brokered a peace deal, Schramm was one of the few NFL executives who ever uttered a bad word about Hunt. In a book titled *Tex! The Man Who Built the Dallas Cowboys*, he lambasted his Dallas neighbor, saying, "I see Lamar Hunt as one of the most selfish, commercial people I've ever met in sports. He has been able to sell people on the façade that he creates for himself as being Mr. Nice Guy, just a good ol' boy with money. He has created an image of himself as a person who would unselfishly do anything for the betterment of sports, as a guy who only wanted to see pro football come to his hometown. That's a bunch of bull. He was scheming all along to start his own league, and when he saw a chance to get out of Dallas for a better financial deal, he cut and ran, so I hardly think he was all that interested in his hometown as he led you to believe."

As Hunt often repeated, he had not started a league in hopes of a merger with the stronger NFL; he wanted to run a sound business venture. But the merger represented a U.S. sports coup.

The AFL became the only pro football league from the 20th century to be fully taken in by the NFL. Every pretender after it, from the World Football League to the United States Football League to the XFL, was completely shut out by the NFL. Only a few teams, such as the Cleveland Browns, were swallowed from leagues that preceded the AFC. In fact, in the major U.S. pro sports, only the American League in baseball can also say it merged in full with an older professional entity.

Hunt's role in the merger cannot be overestimated. No other owner in the AFL could garner that amount of trust or respect from NFL owners. AFL commissioner Al Davis, who didn't even know about the merger talks until the day before the announcement, certainly couldn't. Hunt's calm façade and ability to keep a secret were crucial attributes as owners on both sides lost their heads during the final signing salvo.

"He was a very, very respected owner in the league," said Wilson. "The fact he brought football to Oakland and Denver, he was looked upon as a leader, someone who expanded the game of pro football where it hadn't been played."

At the same time, reflecting on his brashness at launching a league to compete with the NFL without even lining up a single stadium, Hunt realized how lucky he was it succeeded.

"I'm appalled at what bad judgment it was on my part to get involved," he said. "We were like blind pigs."

Yet the naïve, bespectacled Hunt had emerged a revolutionary. Think of his impact on the pro sports job market, the ability to let young men pursue their dreams.

"When I graduated from SMU, I really wanted to play professional football, because Doak Walker and the Lions were being televised into Texas," said Raymond Berry. "There weren't many teams then, 12 with 35 men on a squad. There weren't a lot of jobs out there. There were a lot of good players who couldn't make it. He was responsible for many guys being able to play pro football.

"When you stop to think about what it took to make a new football league, you're looking at an inner resolve that had to be considerably powerful."

No doubt Hunt's multimillion-dollar fortune helped save the league.

"Lamar Hunt's deep pockets along with others' put the AFL on a financial footing that could compete with the NFL and sign players," said Rob Baade, president of the International Association of Sports Economists and A.B. Dick professor of economics at Lake Forest College.

The impact of the AFL-NFL merger resonates in the 21st century. It's hard to imagine a bigger move in the economics of sports. Take franchise values, which leaped in part because player expenses could be controlled. After Hunt tossed in $25,000 of seed money in 1959, a half-century later *Forbes* magazine assessed the value of the Kansas City Chiefs at $1 billion, 14th in the NFL. The franchise's value increased 40,000 times. In Dallas, Hunt hawked tickets in a desperate way, but gate receipts at Arrowhead Stadium now exceed $50 million annually. Even H.L. Hunt couldn't bicker with those numbers.

Sonny Werblin, he of the dissenting vote and complaints of $18 million paid to the NFL, eventually understood the benefits of the union. In three years, the $1 million he paid for the Jets had grown to be worth an estimated $12.5 million. The franchise has changed hands since Werblin's death, and in 2009 the Jets were valued by *Forbes* at $1.2 billion.

The AFL popularized pro football and helped garner today's NFL billion-dollar television contracts that are envied by other U.S. pro leagues (and football TV revenue is shared in part because of the AFL's move to do so). Bringing the sounds of the game into the living room was a huge success, along with moving cameras. Simple innovations such as official scoreboard clocks that showed how much time remained pleased fans. Pass-happy football, which is more fun to watch, is the norm now.

And in one of the least recognized contributions of Hunt's brainchild, but just as important as the rest, the AFL believed in equal opportunity from the outset. While the Washington Redskins didn't hire a black player until the 1960s (and only then under order of its hometown federal government), the rebel league welcomed African Americans. And no team helped integrate football more than his Texans/Chiefs franchise.

One of Hunt's scouts, Lloyd Wells—the one who worked frantically to ensure Otis Taylor's commitment to Kansas City—focused on small black colleges, such as Taylor's Prairie View A&M. Grambling's Buck Buchanan, who became a Chiefs superstar, was tapped as the first black No. 1 overall draft choice in 1963. Players from Abner Haynes (North Texas State) to Willie Lanier (Morgan State) were signed by the franchise and became stars.

By the time of Super Bowl IV, the last championship battle between the NFL and AFL, the Chiefs had nearly twice as many black players on their roster as the Vikings.

Bobby Bell, an outside linebacker and defensive end who was enshrined in the Pro Football Hall of Fame in 1983, was drafted 20 years earlier in the seventh round. "That was a time when things changed," said Bell. "We were bringing 'em in from all over. If it hadn't been for Lamar Hunt, a lot of players at black schools [might] still be looking for opportunities."

Though Gale Sayers ended up not playing for Hunt, he could tell during negotiations that a man's color meant nothing to him.

"His main thought in putting together a football team [was] he wanted the best players. He didn't care if they were black, white, blue, or yellow," Sayers said. "If he thought you could play, he would get that player."

Hunt also believed fans should not be segregated, though the Houston Oilers mandated separate seating early on for their black fans. He might have learned a lesson from the previous NFL Dallas Texans, who segregated fans in 1952 and lasted all of one year. In the AFL Texans' inaugural game at the Cotton Bowl, they drew an estimated 6,000 black fans. One report said the Oilers attracted 50 black fans to a home game.

After the merger, the fans in Kansas City of all colors were there to stay. By the end of the 1966 season, the Chiefs sold nearly 260,000 tickets for seven home games, the best in their four seasons, and more than 100,000 beyond their 1965 campaign. Hunt's dedicated efforts had paid off.

And the team responded. It opened the '66 season with three straight routs over Buffalo, Oakland, and Boston. Once the 14-game campaign ended, the Chiefs had posted the best mark in their history at 11–2–1. Their 448 points led the nine-team AFL in scoring. Running back Mike Garrett, a Heisman Trophy winner from the University of Southern California, spearheaded the ground attack with a 5.4-yards-per-carry average. The defense, which allowed fewer than 20 points per game, was sparked by 10 interceptions apiece from Bobby Hunt and Johnny Robinson.

After a two-week break, the Chiefs traveled to Buffalo for a New Year's Day matchup against the Bills. And just as they had in the season opener, Kansas City trampled the Bills, 31-7. The next stop: Los Angeles for Super Bowl I.

Still smarting from the Chiefs' victory, Wilson remembered conferring with Hunt about the first contest ever between the rival leagues.

"I can remember sitting on the grass outside of a hotel with Lamar. We were talking about the game and setting prices for the tickets. I think it was $12 [which was seen as exorbitant by L.A. newspapers]," Wilson said.

Though Super Bowl host cities are picked years in advance today, before the first AFL-NFL Championship Game in Los Angeles, the site was settled only six weeks before the game.

It was a spectacle, though hardly anything compared to the Super Bowl today. Two men in jetpacks lifted off into the Coliseum air as did balloons. The Chiefs, though, were grounded. Their team roared through the AFL season, but they were knocked off handily by Green Bay before 61,946 (leaving about 30,000 empty seats). Ahead only 14–10 after the first half, Green Bay responded with 21 unanswered points in the second half. The famously hungover Green Bay receiver Max McGee caught two touchdown passes from Bart Starr—who captured the MVP award—during the game, and the Packers stormed to a 35–10 win.

There wasn't much Hunt, already displeased that no two-point conversion was allowed, could say.

"I'm proud of this team, and we'll be back next year," he said.

He was also proud of the reception back in Kansas City. About 3,000 fans appeared to cheer for the team, more than seven times the number who had stayed up late to see the champion Texans in the winter of 1962. They waved optimistic banners such as "In Our Hearts, You're Still the Champs" and blunt ones like "We're No. 2. So What?"

Despite their owner's outward placidity, the Chiefs were enraged by the loss to the Packers. That summer, they took out their frustration against one of the NFL's original franchises, the Chicago Bears, to try to prove they belonged in the new league. Before a jammed Municipal Stadium on August 23, they destroyed the Monsters of the Midway 66–24. It was the most points Chicago had given up in any game of its 47-year history, and it's hard to believe an exhibition game has ever been more lopsided.

Bears running back Sayers was stunned. "The little horse they had running around after the scores almost died—they beat us horribly," he said. "They wanted to prove they could beat an NFL team. Lamar Hunt and Hank Stram prepared them so well, it was like they were going to the Super Bowl."

They didn't that season. In 1968 Hunt looked for an edge. He called Schaaf, his public-relations director at the time, and shared his vision.

"He said, 'Jim, I have an idea,' Schaaf recalled. "I've just been to England. You see all the kids there kicking soccer balls. I think we could find a kicker over there. That's what they grew up doing. If you could go there with Coach Stram and hold tryouts in the British Isles, hopefully we could find a kicker.'

"Coach Stram and I went. It was quite an experience. We rented stadiums in London, Wales, Glasgow, Manchester. Hundreds would show up to kick, and we hired people to chart them. We brought three kickers back. One was Bobby Howfield, who could kick right-footed and left-footed. He didn't beat out Jan Stenerud, but he kicked in the NFL for many years."

Though Kansas City fielded a strong team in 1968—when its defense allowed just over 12 points a game—the 1969 squad would become a part of history.

Before the season, Stram sent a letter to each member of the team. Though letting one's freak flag fly was becoming a mantra among hippies and others, Stram not only prohibited hair below the helmet, but he also banned moustaches. Just like his owner, Stram was obsessed with details. The team's offensive huddle was not the standard circle. The five linemen stood in one row, running backs and receivers comprised another, and all 10 had their backs to the ball and were looking at the quarterback. For the national anthem, players didn't wander around the sideline; they lined up in order of their number.

The Chiefs enjoyed a successful campaign in their final AFL season but finished second in the West behind Oakland. In previous years, that meant they'd start the off-season, but an expanded playoff format had been introduced, meaning the Chiefs got in. They knocked off the Super Bowl champion Jets and then beat Oakland to make their second Super Bowl. A blowout like Super Bowl I was expected. H.L.'s friend Jimmy "the Greek" Snyder made the Chiefs 13-point underdogs to the Minnesota Vikings.

Hunt was fired up. Veteran Chiefs broadcaster Bill Grigsby recalled a dinner before the game. "Lamar was telling us about Minnesota, how they had double-crossed the AFL at the last minute and switched to the NFL. He was still upset over that," Grigsby told author Jeff Miller. "In the middle of the conversation, he started pounding on the table and screaming, 'Kill! Kill! Kill!'"

Hunt and his wife, Norma, ran into a stunned Max Winter—who had jettisoned the AFL for the greener pastures of the NFL—and his wife in an elevator that week.

"When we got on, their faces looked like the image of fear," Hunt said. "For a few precious seconds, we were the only people on the elevator. I don't think any words were spoken."

In New Orleans' Tulane Stadium—where Hunt had once hoped to move the Chiefs—more than 80,000 fans appeared despite rain on January 11, 1970. The 13-point underdogs from Kansas City took the field wearing an anniversary patch denoting the league's 10th anniversary. The AFL squad stunned its NFL opponent. Three Jan Stenerud field goals lifted Kansas City to a 9–0 lead in the second quarter. Running back Mike Garrett added a touchdown, and the Chiefs entered halftime ahead 16–0.

Even with quarterback Joe Kapp at the helm, the Vikings couldn't respond. Buchanan and Curley Culp helped shut down the running game; the Vikings mustered only 67 yards on the ground. Meanwhile, the Chiefs racked up more than 150 yards rushing and, combined with Dawson's MVP-worthy 12-of-17 performance, defeated the Vikings 23–7 for Hunt's first—and last—Super Bowl win.

Chiefs backers—carrying banners such as "Go Super Chiefs" and "The Purple Gang Is Now Black + Blue"—were ecstatic inside the stadium. Across the country, the Chiefs-Vikings game attracted the biggest TV crowd for a single sports event at the time, drawing about 60 million U.S. fans.

Hunt accepted the Super Bowl trophy—which, at his urging, would be named after the late Packers coach Vince Lombardi the following year—with a big smile in a moment so overwhelming he couldn't remember it. But he would never forget the victory.

"It was, in a lot of ways, a dream come true. It was wonderful poetic justice to win that last game," he said. "It was the last game that was pure AFL."

Hunt also was pleased that his aging father—now 80 years old and somewhat of an American legend—could see his last son shine.

"One of the proudest remembrances I have is how much Dad enjoyed my relative success," Hunt said. During a dinner celebrating the Chiefs' Super Bowl victory in 1970—featuring Commissioner Pete Rozelle and about 1,000 others—"the biggest hand anybody got that night was when Dad was introduced."

"To do bigger and better things than my dad" was Lamar Hunt's stated goal as a teenager, and in many ways he had succeeded. But how? Who was the man who had engineered a merger with the most powerful entity in U.S. sports, whose franchise had captured the fourth Super Bowl when AFL teams were still considered inferior? How did a 37-year-old who could barely give a speech when he founded an upstart league sit atop the sports world? In a word, who was Lamar Hunt?

CHAPTER 4

GENTLE GIANT

AS AMERICA EMERGED AS A SUPERPOWER after World War II, the state of Texas thrived. The country demanded oil, and discoveries and processing of the commodity brought immense wealth to H.L. Hunt and others.

Travel and television soon brought the United States closer together, and up sprouted the stereotype of the rich Texan: an overweight, cigar-chomping, fast-talking, bourbon-swilling braggart topped by a 10-gallon hat, snapping out $100 bills to get his Cadillac washed. Abroad, he'd stop in Paris and loudly ask where the Lou-ver (Louvre) was and feed the Europeans' conviction in the Ugly American. In every instance, Lamar Hunt was the antithesis of this caricature.

Never fat, Hunt was obsessed with keeping his weight at 180 pounds and below (never easy since he loved desserts). He didn't smoke cigars or cigarettes and, save for a few sips of wine on occasion, shunned alcohol. His words didn't tumble forth; they arrived in a slow, even tone, and his Texas accent seemed mild compared to others'. If he placed anything on his brown hair aside from a comb, it likely was in jest, such as when he received the Bonehead of the Year award (a trophy crowned with a large silver nut) from a Dallas club. And merely the thought of spending money made Lamar shudder; he barely carried $10, much less a billfold bulging with cash.

Most importantly, in contrast to the Texas stereotype, he didn't brag. Modest, gentle, unassuming, quiet—all were adjectives affixed to Hunt.

True, he embraced risk, but his personality—unlike, say, that of George Halas at midcentury or Dallas Cowboys owner Jerry Jones today—remained placid. Not dogmatic in any way, he was also the furthest thing from a snob. A story is told of Lamar visiting a sports executive's house overnight. The next morning, rather than assuming a maid would appear, he moved about his quarters carefully making his bed.

Considering the lofty heights of his life, his humble nature and quiet demeanor seemed at odds. He earned the approval of many (being disliked occurred rarely, except with a few hard-headed NFL owners) in part because he was never coarse, never prickly.

Except when serving as a third-stringer on the SMU football team or listening to a teacher's lecture as a student, Hunt rarely found himself in the position of underling. In charge always, of either franchises or businesses (even of the Hill School football team as quarterback and captain), one might think he'd ignore or dismiss those well below his station, especially when he entered the big league, the NFL. Yet he remained unpretentious.

Ernie Accorsi joined Pete Rozelle's staff of half a dozen employees in New York City in 1975. He met Hunt at the first NFL meeting he attended. "I was told, 'Some of these owners are going to order you around and not remember your name.' I was a nobody," said Accorsi, who eventually served as general manager of the Baltimore Colts, the Cleveland Browns, and the New York Giants. "Lamar always remembered my name. He always said 'Please' if he wanted me to look something up, whereas some owners would say to me, 'Go get this!'

"My first impression was his humility. When someone's that rich and that powerful and had accomplished so much, you expected him to be different. He was so understated."

Andrew Brandt, a vice president of the Green Bay Packers from 1999 to 2008 and president of the *National Football Post*, noted Hunt treated him as if he, not Paul Tagliabue, were commissioner.

"You'd see at meetings owners only socializing with owners; he would want to know the names of your wife and children and never looked past you hoping to talk with someone else," Brandt said. "A lot of the attention goes to the owners who are full of ego and bravado. Mr. Hunt was a shining contrast."

Long before he became an NFL owner, Jerry Jones wanted to purchase a team in the AFL. He never forgot Hunt's welcome.

"When I was 22 and trying to buy the San Diego Chargers, he met me at the airport in Kansas City and treated me like I was the president of the United States," Jones told the *Dallas Morning News*.

Tagliabue—who first met Hunt in 1969 as a lawyer for the North American Soccer League—sat through innumerable meetings with him during his 17-year reign as NFL commissioner. He recalled why Hunt stood out from the pack. "He was a good listener, which is a characteristic of leaders," Tagliabue remembered. "He tried to understand what people wanted to accomplish. He was good with following up with owners after meetings, buttonholing them to find out where they were going with their idea.

"Lamar understood that someone who was disagreeing with others may be right. That was uncommon."

The first player signed by the New York Titans, Don Maynard, became one of the most visible AFL stars in the rebel league. He favored blue jeans and sported long sideburns. Fewer than two dozen players lasted all 10 seasons in the league Hunt founded; Maynard was one.

Though their teams were rivals on the field, Maynard embraced his fellow Hall of Famer off it.

"Lamar Hunt was probably one of the classiest owners that has ever lived," Maynard said. "You could never find anything bad about Lamar Hunt. He could talk to me like we had known each other all of our lives. He always had time for you."

Jim Schaaf joined the Chiefs in 1966, coming over from Charlie Finley's Kansas City Athletics. Working for the low-key Hunt after the flamboyant

Finley was like watching paint dry after a fireworks display. The onetime public relations director, who served as the team's general manager from 1976 until 1988, remembered Hunt's management approach.

"If he had ideas," recalled Schaaf, "he would call you and say, 'Can you research this and get back to me.' He didn't want it in five minutes. He wasn't in there banging the door down. He'd say, 'Let's work on it.' He was always supportive."

Few Chiefs coaches worked more closely with Hunt than Marty Schottenheimer, who served the second-longest tenure of any head man (Hank Stram's 15 seasons tops all) in the franchise's half-century history. Hired in 1989, he compiled a record of 101–58–1 and delivered six straight playoff berths before resigning a decade later.

"He's probably the most wonderful person I've ever known in my life, quite candidly," Schottenheimer began. "He was always available if you needed an issue resolved. The thing that was always evident was he truly cared about people. Lamar had a unique ability to engage people and make you so very comfortable being around him. He was very kind."

Schottenheimer shared a story that he believes is the quintessential one about the man. During the 1993 season, Schottenheimer's fifth with the franchise, the Chiefs put together a stellar 11–5 campaign, which included a 23–7 thrashing of the Buffalo Bills at Arrowhead Stadium. They knocked off their first two playoff opponents and headed to Rich Stadium in Buffalo for the AFC Championship Game in January 1994. A victory would put the Chiefs in their first Super Bowl since Stram had guided them there 24 years earlier.

But Buffalo running back Thurman Thomas scampered at will (finishing with 186 yards) and, in the third quarter, Chiefs quarterback Joe Montana left with a concussion. Though leading only 20–13 at the end of the third quarter, the Bills tacked on 10 points in the fourth as the Chiefs struggled with backup quarterback Dave Krieg. Buffalo won 30–13 to head to its fourth Super Bowl in a row.

After leaving the somber locker room, Schottenheimer headed out of Rich Stadium.

"I went out and sat down on the bus after the game," Schottenheimer recalled. "My wife was there along with Norma [Hunt]. The season's over. A big disappointment.

"Lamar came in and sat down. He didn't say anything for several moments. Then he turned back to me and said, 'How you feel, Marty?' I told him how disappointed I was.

"He said, 'Look at it this way. We beat them worse [earlier in the season] than they beat us.' He didn't really mean the points. He was trying to make me feel better.

"The attitude he had after losing tough games was unique. He was always there to pick you up and support you if you were disappointed. His presence after losses was particularly important to me."

Schaaf said Hunt was just as encouraging with Chiefs players.

"If we lost the game, he'd always go to the locker room and talk with the players. He'd say, 'Well, things didn't work out today, but we'll get them next week.'"

Hunt would never rattle a coach by standing on the sideline during games, but he often appeared on the field during warmups.

"Lamar before games was wonderful," Schottenheimer said. "He loved the energy in the stadium and the fans."

Schottenheimer said Hunt attended practices on occasion, but he wasn't exactly making players rerun routes like an Al Davis.

"He never wanted to get in the way," Schottenheimer said. "That's so unlike the norm in the NFL."

Though he was inclined to stay in the background doesn't mean Hunt was aloof. To anyone with a question, complaint, or comment, he believed in responding.

For 20 years Don Pierson covered the NFL for the *Chicago Tribune*, and he also served as president of the Professional Football Writers of America. In the latter capacity, in the 1990s, he needed to address a major problem for reporters: coaches and players were cutting back access.

"I wrote all the NFL owners to express writers' concerns that league rules on access were being violated," Pierson said. "One of the first guys to reply was Lamar, in his own handwriting."

Pierson still has the letter, composed more than a decade ago. "I thought it was typical of the kind of guy he was," Pierson said. The stationery itself is unostentatious: white paper with "From the desk of Lamar Hunt" gracing the top and "Kansas City Chiefs football club" at the bottom. After acknowledging Pierson's correspondence, Hunt wrote in tight, microscopic letters that are nearly illegible:

Rest assured that the Chiefs as an organization are committed to a concept that our personnel are and will be accessible. You certainly have my personal commitment to be available anytime you or any member of the media desires information.

Famous for his handwritten notes, which were dispatched to executives, assistants, players, and others, Hunt was less well known for his sense of humor. Though sometimes it was so low-key as to risk being missed altogether, he liked quietly making jokes, often at his own expense.

"He had a great sense of humor," recalled Bills owner Wilson. "He wasn't Bob Hope, but he had a dry sense of humor."

One time a reporter called on his house as Hunt watched a tennis tournament on a tiny Sony television set. His wife, Norma, examined an antique bust in another room. She asked her husband, "What are the chances that this is really Henry II?"

Though a lover of antiques, nothing could sway him from a sporting event. Hunt said, "17 percent" and continued watching.

When Hunt was preparing to decorate his Dallas office in Thanksgiving Tower in the 1980s—soon after the silver crash hammered the wealth of brothers Bunker and Herbert and sliced his own fortune—he talked about what mementos would hang on three walls. The first would hold pictures of his favorite places. The second would show a history of Dallas. The third? He called it his "disaster wall," which would be filled with items of things gone wrong, such as horrible losses by the Chiefs.

"And I'll have to put something on that wall to do with silver," he said.

Thom Meredith, an administrative assistant for Hunt in Dallas who also worked for Hunt's Dallas Tornado and World Championship Tennis, recalled another humorous story from that office.

"One Friday afternoon in Dallas, I've got a three-piece suit on. It's hot. A friend of mine asked me to move some stuff. I put on jeans and moved some boxes.

"I laid my shirt and suit on a chair. I go back to the chair later and there's a note from Lamar: 'Dear Clark, Sorry I missed you. We would have had a great time. Love, Lois.'"

Lamar's relationship with money was a source of amusement for others. The story of his father's wealth is well known, but in 1982, Lamar made *Forbes'* inaugural list of the 400 richest people in the United States, landing at No. 8 (preceded by his sisters Margaret and Caroline at No. 4 and No. 5 and followed by his brothers Herbert and Bunker at No. 9 and No. 10).

"I don't have any idea where they come up with those figures," Hunt said. "I think they've confused my debts with my assets."

Despite being worth hundreds of millions of dollars, he walked around with holes in his shoes. From ankle to neck he dressed nicely, favoring a blue blazer and gray flannel pants (known as his uniform) for almost all occasions, but he owned fewer than half a dozen suits. Valet parking? Too pricey. Broken glasses? Hunt tried to fix them himself rather than shell out cash for a new pair.

"I probably basically am a cheapskate," he said. "I hate to spend money on things that, when they're gone, they're gone, and you can never get the money back. Also, I pride myself on being a good businessman, or trying to, but I'm the world's worst when it comes to handling my personal finances. I very seldom have any money in my wallet, and that causes some misunderstandings."

Regarding his tendency to be tight with money, Lamar's mother, Lyda, said long ago everyone should have known that from the beginning. "When he was born, the hospitals were not air-conditioned, so they had 'August specials' to encourage people to have operations in off-season. Lamar waited 'til August to be born so he could take advantage of the cut rate."

Decades after he had discovered the extent of his teammate's riches, Forrest Gregg was still amazed at Hunt's propensity not to spend it. "Lamar was the darnedest guy," Gregg said. "When I was a head coach, it seemed invariably we'd be in Dallas before the league meetings in Arizona or California. I was always involved in scouting, and I'd like to go to schools in the Southwestern Conference like SMU, where our kids were.

"As head coach, they flew us first class. We'd sit down there on our way to the NFL meetings, and Lamar and Norma would come on the plane and [go] back to coach. I just thought to myself, *Here's a guy who couldn't only buy first-class tickets, he could buy this plane and the company that owns the plane*."

Tagliabue recalled meeting Hunt at an Atlanta airport hotel as NASL considered expanding to six teams from five in 1969.

"The meeting was held on the bed of the commissioner of the league," Tagliabue said. "It was typical of Lamar that there was probably a conference room he didn't want to pay for."

Murray Olderman, a syndicated columnist whose work was distributed by Newspaper Enterprise Association for 35 years (and who ended up drawing Hunt's portrait for the Hall of Fame), remembered meeting him in Dallas to write a profile in 1960.

"He wouldn't let me take a cab back to his hotel—he thought it was too expensive," Olderman recalled. "I had known a lot about him, but I played dumb and asked him what else he was involved in besides football. He said, 'We have a little bit of oil. I have a little bit of real estate.'

"We went by a row of apartment complexes. I said, 'Are those yours?' He said, 'No, they're Bunker's.'"

Olderman said Hunt lived in a tract house then, but life soon changed when he married Norma ("She introduced him to some of the finer things"). Though she enjoyed stunning Dallas homes with countless amenities, such as a lighted tennis court, Norma wasn't always able to furnish houses as speedily as she hoped. Tex Schramm walked in one house and noticed the den was barren. Lamar explained that when the Chiefs sold 20,000 season tickets, chairs, tables, and rugs could be purchased. Schramm pointed out the Chiefs *had* sold 20,000 season tickets. Despite Norma's protests, Lamar said, he didn't count sales for kids' tickets.

Married to Hunt for 44 years, Norma understood him better than anyone. And she described him in a unique way. "My husband combines two interesting qualities," she once told *Sports Illustrated*. "He's a hyperactive calm person, if you can imagine. He has tremendous inner calm and no moodiness. His disposition never alters. He's always exactly the same easygoing person, but at the same time he's engaged in constant activity."

Schaaf concurred. In the late 1970s, Hunt invited his general manager and his wife to Dallas to watch the Cotton Bowl and considerately picked them up at the airport. Yet Schaaf didn't find his host relaxing about the house on a Sunday morning. "Lamar always had to be doing things. My wife and I were coming out of the kitchen area to go to Mass. I opened the door, and it banged into a ladder. He was trimming the bushes. I almost knocked him off the ladder."

During Chiefs games, regardless of the score, Hunt remained unflappable, perhaps offering a smile or frown at key moments. Schaaf recalled Hunt's reaction after his ultimate victory, Super Bowl IV.

"I remember the happiness, the glow, that look on his face," Schaaf said. "He was smiling. He was happy for everybody. He wasn't just standing up cheering and yelling."

That's not to say Hunt wasn't competitive—his outward calm masked an unquenchable fire to finish at the top.

"At the end of the day, winning is very important to him," his son Clark Hunt said in a documentary about his father's life. "He just happens to be such a gentleman that it doesn't manifest itself like it does in a lot of other people."

In terms of how he looked, perhaps the most vivid description of Hunt was crafted by *Sports Illustrated*, which published a lengthy profile of the sports wiz in the early 1970s:

Observe the 1953 haircut with the sideburns. Note how he wears his graying brown hair parted to the left and anointed with a touch of greasy kid stuff, like Wayne Morris in Kid Galahad. Observe the dishwater-blue eyes behind the Sunday school teacher-type plastic glasses, and his height—why, he isn't even a 6-footer! Does that look like a magnate of sport and industry? Does that look like a man whose Dun and Bradstreet rating runs clear off the top of the page? Note the undersize ears and undistinguished nose and the unassertive chin. Would you buy a used drilling rig from that man?

In H.L. Hunt's first family, Lamar's oldest brother, Hassie, was the spitting image of his father; Lamar's resemblance wasn't as obvious. But when it came to traits and actions, Lamar and H.L. were as similar as could be.

Both were parsimonious in their personal lives. Famously, the billionaire H.L. Hunt brought his lunch to work (after eating a simple breakfast) in a brown paper bag. Depending on the day, carrots, bread, and a few meat slices rested inside. Though Lamar could dine at any fancy restaurant in Dallas or head over to the Tower Club for a three-course meal (or three-martini lunch if he drank), often he would order a tuna-salad sandwich to be delivered.

Rod Humphries, who worked for Hunt in various capacities for World Championship Tennis, remembered, "He told me he learned to be such a cheapskate from his father. He was driving with his father once, and they saw a guy selling watermelon on the side of the road. It was $3. H.L. got him down to $1, then he didn't even buy it."

Rich enough to own a fleet of Cadillacs, H.L. Hunt purchased drab vehicles made by Oldsmobile, Chevrolet, or Dodge. His son followed suit. The patriarch drove a few blocks out of his way to find cheaper parking in downtown Dallas. Once H.L. reached his office, no crackling fireplaces or marble bathrooms greeted him. A simple wooden desk and armchairs marred with cracked leather stood there instead.

Lamar's quarters were about as spartan. Situated eventually in Thanksgiving Tower in Dallas, his office featured one window, a lectern where he would read material, sports books, and a cigar-store Indian taller than himself. It was far from plush. Said his assistant Meredith, "I had a corner office that was better than his."

At the same time, both father and son would find creative ways to generate revenue, especially Lamar. When the Arrowhead Astroturf was ripped up in the 1990s, he made sure squares were sold as cocktail coasters.

The propensity of father and son to dispatch memos or dictate information was legendary. Any idea that popped into Lamar's head, especially those which would improve a team's finances or a fan's enjoyment, he'd jot down and circulate.

Longtime pro tennis executive Mike Davies—who worked with Hunt as executive director at World Championship Tennis for years—received scores of these memos.

"He was forever sending these little notes. Forever!" Davies recalled. "He was disseminating information all the time.

"He would read a lot of magazines and newspapers on planes. He'd see something about sports, tear it out, and write a note that said, 'This is of interest. Please read.' He'd have three to four names he'd want it circulated to: Jack Steadman of the Chiefs, me, their soccer guy. It could be about the size of a stadium, how many season tickets had been sold, what expenses had been for this or that."

That detail-oriented nature came from his father, who created daily memos for *Life Line* commentators, sometimes emphasizing the smallest items such as the right volume level for the hymns.

Both H.L. and son possessed photographic memories. In the father's case, it proved especially helpful in his many poker games. Meredith remembered being astounded at Lamar's ability to recall long-ago information.

"When he was inducted into the Texas Sports Hall of Fame, I collected all of his memorabilia," Meredith said. "Jean Finn, his secretary of 38 years, saved everything. I found a yellow legal pad. There were the items of contention between the AFL and NFL before the 1966 merger. He recited the 18 items in order. This was 1982, 16 years later. I said, 'There's a phone number on the upper corner of the paper.' He recited the number and said it was Pete Rozelle's private line."

Persistence marked both Hunts. Hounded by lawsuits and unrelenting competitors, they persevered in their chosen professions. H.L. kept pushing to make Hunt Oil a power, and Lamar stuck with pro soccer for decades even though the game never approached any of the four major U.S. sports in popularity. To give up, even when the odds were highest, was anathema.

Their minds were perpetually active. Both would wake up in the middle of the night brimming with ideas. Like his father, Lamar preferred secrecy, and he kept even some of his best ideas to himself, most famously when he came up with a plan for a new football league and told no one for months.

Lamar's father followed offbeat exercise routines. His favorite workout was called "creeping," which he claimed beat running and other activities. He literally crawled around his dining room table at a torrid pace. Lamar's exercise may have been more conventional, but as recalled by Davies, his choice of venue was not. He shared a story of when sports impresario Donald Dell engaged in talks to sign tennis star Arthur Ashe.

"We were down to the nitty-gritty and agreed to meet in Donald's office. We were up all night negotiating," Davies said. "At 1:00 AM, Lamar said, 'Let's take a break, have a chat.' I thought Lamar would have a great idea to break the impasse.

"Lamar said, 'This is getting tiring. I need to do some exercising.' He starts doing pushups. After a while, Donald Dell gets nervous, wondering what we could be talking about. He comes to the door and sees Lamar doing pushups."

Lamar seemed to be able to work out anywhere. Recalled Bob Hermann, a fellow North American Soccer League owner, about meetings in the league commissioner's office, "He used to do pushups and sit-ups during the board meeting while we're talking about how we'll get rid of this bad guy or that bad guy."

Finally, though their businesses were as different as an oil rig is from a cornerback, H.L. and Lamar both wanted to build companies from the foundation up throughout their lives. In his seventies, when many of his peers played golf and relaxed in retirement, H.L. decided to enter the food and drug business. Old enough to collect Social Security, Lamar helped found Major League Soccer and served as an owner-operator of three different franchises.

H.L. acknowledged he and his baby son were similar, though not exactly in any of the ways described above.

"Lamar is something like me," he said. "He's stubborn and knows how to fight."

Though initially skeptical about his son's foray into pro football, H.L. came to admire Lamar's national popularity, which eluded the oilman throughout his life. "Even the pro-Communist writers like him," the elder Hunt said. "Have you ever heard anyone say an unkind word about Lamar?"

H.L.'s opinion was so glowing he touted his son as the best presidential candidate in 1972, when President Richard Nixon faced off against challenger George McGovern. Over and over, Lamar's father tried to persuade him to run, but Lamar refused. Persistent as ever, H.L. asked again. And again. His ever-gentle son, exasperated, sent his father a letter and asked that he "please drop the subject." The *Draft Lamar for President* effort died soon after.

Though Lamar, to H.L.'s chagrin, wasn't elected to the White House, he was inducted into a building far more to his liking: the Pro Football Hall of Fame.

Occurring only two years after the merger was completed, the honor would have been unthinkable a decade before. The AFL's first enshrinee was introduced by New England Patriots owner William H. Sullivan.

"Today we salute a man who can neither kick nor pass nor block nor punt," Sullivan said. "But I humbly submit that the man who is being honored here today served more than any one individual in our time to rewrite the pages of sports history."

Hunt—whose Hall of Fame bust featured his trademark glasses—then offered a short speech that thanked many and pointed out that, at heart, he's truly a fan.

Not even 20 years earlier, Forrest Gregg had been beating Lamar Hunt mercilessly during the Oklahoma Drill at SMU. Now, his former teammate had reached pro football's pinnacle.

"I never will forget when he went into the Hall of Fame," Gregg recalled. "I can't tell you how happy I was for him. He slept professional football.

"A lot of times we'd go places where Raymond Berry would be when he was a coach. We'd be at a meeting. Lamar would always ask, 'Did you wear your Hall of Fame ring?' I said no I didn't. He'd say, 'Next time, wear your ring. I'd like a picture of the three of us with our rings.' We finally did it.

"I thought if anything would change him, being a member of the Hall of Fame would change him. But no way."

That summer of 1972 ended up doubly special for Hunt. The crown jewel of the Chiefs, Arrowhead Stadium, opened in August.

The idea for Arrowhead was hatched in the mid-1960s. Municipal Stadium, built for baseball during the Warren G. Harding administration, accommodated fewer than 50,000 football fans and was deteriorating. Charged with acquiring land and getting funding for a modern stadium, a new body—the Jackson County Sports Complex Authority—went to work.

A multipurpose facility, similar to the ones that had sprung up in St. Louis and Oakland and that would emerge in Philadelphia, Cincinnati, and Pittsburgh, was originally preferred to house baseball's Athletics and the Chiefs. A dome was floated as a possibility, but the idea foundered. In a bold move backed by Hunt, two stadiums were proposed—a 45,000-seat one for baseball and a 75,000-seat facility for football. A rolling roof concocted of steel and fiberglass would cover both, a first for any stadium.

In 1967 Jackson County voters approved $102 million in tax-obligation bonds, which dedicated $43 million to the sports complex. It marked the first time residents there had backed a tax increase through the ballot box since the Great Depression. That fall, Hunt and the Chiefs offered more than $52 million for a 99-year lease on both the proposed football and baseball stadium in Jackson County, along with control over parking and other revenue streams. But the proposal was rejected.

Then, a series of events battered the concept. First, an impatient Charlie Finley fled Kansas City in the fall of 1967, taking his Athletics to Oakland, where a multipurpose stadium had just been built. A strike, mixed with cost overruns and delays, postponed the original projection of a football stadium opening.

But fans remained excited. The Chiefs sold 70,000 season tickets in 1971, a year before Arrowhead debuted—a record for a pro sports franchise at the time.

Finally, in August 1972, the Chiefs played host to the St. Louis Cardinals in the first football game at Arrowhead Stadium—not that the complex was finished. So far behind on construction, the stadium even lacked seats in Hunt's private suite. Guests there sat on folding chairs that entire first year.

Still, the stadium—the largest designed for pro football at that point, with 78,000 seats—elicited admiration. No backless bleachers defiled end zones, and 18,000 seats in Arrowhead were even equipped with armrests. Sightlines were superb.

"That [opening of Arrowhead] was a high point in his life and in the life of the franchise," said Schaaf. "These were nice facilities. That was very important to him. He liked something that was new and improved. He wanted to put on a better show for the fans."

"He was ahead of his time with the whole Arrowhead complex," said International Association of Sports Economists president Baade. "When you look at the financial revolution in pro sports, he anticipated a trend.

Stadiums that accommodated both baseball and football like Municipal Stadium in Cleveland, Wrigley Field in Chicago, that whole idea was rejected on financial grounds. Football and baseball owners wanted to maximize their profit.

"Luxury stadiums—this is where Arrowhead comes into play, as a single-use stadium—contributed more franchise value because they generated more revenues for the team."

Buffalo's Wilson, whose team has played at his eponymous football stadium since 1973, knows well the importance of single-use stadiums, though he's no fan of the new breed springing forth in the NFL.

"Football is a game you need to play on your own field. The diamonds make it different," he said. "But they're building all these new stadiums because the owners want more money. I've never heard one fan say, 'We have to have a new stadium.' The fans don't care about drinking a martini in a luxury suite."

Bob Harlan, chairman emeritus and former CEO of the Green Bay Packers who spent 37 years with the organization, knew the problems of playing at a baseball stadium when they used to schedule a few games annually at County Stadium in Milwaukee.

"All we got for revenue was parking and tickets," he said. "We were leaving $2.5 million on the table playing there each year.

"The thing that I admired about Kansas City was to see the way they tailgated. They were smart to build the two stadiums by each other with all the parking. They had the same college atmosphere we had [at Lambeau Field]. It was a tough place to play because of the noise. They did their stadium right."

Fans—the majority bedecked in red—adored the new stadium. Packed houses were common. (During one streak from 1991 to 2009, more than 150 games were sold out. The Chiefs have often led the league in attendance despite playing in one of the league's smallest markets.) Dirt infields didn't disrupt play, nor did teams share sidelines like at Minnesota's Bloomington Stadium.

Always intrigued by ticket sales ("I love working on how do you attract the public to buy tickets," Hunt once said), he even broke down season-ticket holders by state. By 2002 only five states lacked residents with Chiefs tickets.

"To my knowledge, ours is the only organization in the National Football League that knows this, or bothers to find it out," Hunt said.

Unique to Arrowhead among football-only stadiums of the era was a two-story, four-bedroom apartment where the Hunt family could stay on game weekends. The idea of the suite came to Hunt after he visited the Astrodome and saw that Judge Roy Hofheinz enjoyed a similar arrangement.

Known as the Gold Suite, Arrowhead's version featured a football-shaped conference room, complete with football-shaped conference table and chandelier. A game room included one apparatus where, after inserting a coin and squeezing a handle, one endured a small shock. It was a favorite of Clark Hunt's growing up.

"He used to laugh," Lamar Hunt recalled. "He'd get people to do it and not tell them what was going to happen."

Memorabilia oozed out of every corner of the suite: red cowboy boots, seats from Municipal Stadium, jerseys, even paperweights.

"Mostly it's junk I'm too sentimental to get rid of," Hunt said. "I don't want to throw any of it away, so you have to put it somewhere."

But there were more elegant touches. The owner's suite also featured choir stalls from Spain, a fireplace from France, and antiques (including gnomes representing victory and defeat).

In the late 1990s, many new stadiums opening in Tampa Bay, North Carolina, and elsewhere began to make Arrowhead—owned by Jackson County and leased to the Chiefs at $450,000 per year, plus a percentage of revenue—seem a bit tired. More importantly, the others could generate more revenue, primarily through naming-rights deals and from a slew of luxury suites that were rented out to corporations. Even in small markets, new stadiums boasted well over 100 luxury suites; the Chiefs were stuck at 80, which sold for between $34,000 and $104,000 each in 1999.

"Before luxury seating, teams could play an NFL game in a studio and still make money because of the TV package," Baade said. "It used to be that 60 percent of NFL revenue came from TV. It's different today."

Hunt began to think of plans to renovate Arrowhead. Not only was a new stadium judged to be too costly, it would be tough to replicate the popular facility's atmosphere. One attempt at public funding failed. Then, two measures appeared on the ballot for Jackson County voters on April 4, 2006: one to renovate Arrowhead Stadium and Kauffman Stadium and the other to build a rolling roof encompassing both, the same idea that had been jettisoned almost 40 years previously. This time, approval of the latter would ensure an event that wasn't even considered the last time: Kansas City could host a Super Bowl, an idea already approved by NFL owners contingent upon the roof.

Voters approved the 3/8¢ sales tax, which would raise $850 million over 25 years to renovate the Harry S. Truman Sports Complex, but they rejected the rolling-roof concept.

"For my father, whose legacy…he is so closely intertwined with the Super Bowl," Clark Hunt told *SportsBusiness Journal*. "To not be able to bring his baby home for him was a disappointment. But he took it like a gentleman, like he always does."

The revamped Arrowhead—a $400 million project, including $125 million from the Hunts and the Chiefs—is slated to be fully finished in 2010. Wider concourses (club-level ones will be heated and cooled), more concession stands, and the LH Founder's Plaza Club (initiation fee: $795) named after Hunt are expected to greet fans at the home opener. New scoreboards and electronic message boards arrived in 2009. There will also be 19 new luxury suites, including some designed as cabaret-seating-style skyboxes, as Hunt described them, which can host more than 80.

"The NFL spent a lot of years playing in baseball stadiums," Lamar Hunt said, "but now stadium revenues are a very important part of us or any team remaining competitive in the NFL."

Until the end of his life, Lamar treated Arrowhead as he would his own home. He constructed a two-mile jogging path around the stadium by

Interstate 70 and Interstate 435, and he could often be found running on it. He drove a golf cart through the stadium before a game, checking everything from concessions to the toilets (despite his gentle nature, he would tell vendors if the hot-dog roll was not up to par or if the Coke needed to be colder). He charmed the tailgaters.

"He would go around the parking lot, see what the fans were doing," Schaaf recalled. "He'd walk around and ask questions of the tailgaters. It was a low-key visibility."

When Hunt had joined the NFL elite a few years before Arrowhead's debut, he was one of 26 owners who ran what had supplanted baseball as the most popular sport in the U.S. Yet despite his Hall of Fame stature, impressive new stadium, and quick acceptance among the majority of owners as a reasoned, respected voice, Hunt was forced to fight to get what he wanted from the old-boys' club—and many times he fell short.

He focused on making and changing rules for the game and didn't relent for more than two decades. Hunt's passion for rule-making, first witnessed as a boy, had been sparked anew in the American Football League. There, his ideas ranged from the ridiculous (lie-detector tests for game officials and a silent draft) to the entertaining (no fair catches on punts, all kickoffs must be returned, and sudden death for every game). However, in nearly every instance, his vote lost to the seven cast against him. In the NFL, he soldiered on, often a lonely voice in the boardroom.

"They [the Chiefs] always led the league in rule-proposal changes, a million every year," Accorsi said. "You can submit anything to the Competition Committee. Not many of the rules passed. Lamar was usually fighting the battle himself [in the 1970s]. We felt we had a great game and didn't want to change."

Harlan heard a number of Hunt's rule proposals during his tenure.

"He didn't take no for an answer. He was very persistent," Harlan said. "He'd come back the next year with the very same proposal. The commissioner would call on Lamar to describe what he wanted and why he wanted it. He'd always say it was in the best interest of the NFL. It always impressed me that there was nothing selfish in anything that was ever proposed by Lamar."

A few of Hunt's NFL suggestions would almost seem laughable if he weren't so earnest about them. In 1992 he said that the quarterback kneel-down that occasionally takes place at the end of the first half or the game should be outlawed.

"Every NFL team should be required to make a legitimate effort to advance the ball on every play," he argued, pointing out that spectators are paying for as much.

He only mustered five votes as nay-saying owners claimed their coaches didn't like the idea. "The coaches are a suspicious lot," Hunt said afterward.

Other ideas that failed received more scrutiny and would have created a much bigger impact. Though teams pay 53 players per game, they only suit up 45. Hunt wanted at least four more players per team to be able to dress for contests.

"It was a humane thing," Brandt recalled. "He didn't think someone should be told an hour and a half before the game he wouldn't play after he had practiced all week. It also spoke to a concern he had for the morale of teams."

Hunt's attempts to persuade owners to play conference championship games at neutral sites, à la the Super Bowl, fell short, as did his hope that the playoffs would accommodate half the league's teams (16) rather than 12.

When the NFL expanded to the 12-team playoff format in 1990, the league included a playoff bye week for the four best teams (two from each conference). Even 13 years later, Hunt battled to change that decision.

"I can make a very strong case that the bye week is very unfair," Hunt said. "The bye week is contrary to the idea that we try to sell: that in every game, both teams have a fair chance. It's just a tremendous advantage to have a bye, if for no other reason than you're not exposed to losing a game that first week."

From a television standpoint, Hunt thought the bye week was simply ludicrous. "I don't know any business that would say, 'We've got these four best teams, the most attractive teams, with the four best records, and we're not going to put them on television this week. We're going to put them in the freezer for a week and we're going to be televising lesser teams,' which is what it amounts to. That's very unusual.

"Most sports try to feature a Duke or a Kansas or the Lakers or Yankees. And what we're doing is taking our four best teams and saying we're not going to show them on television."

Tagliabue offered another perspective. "In order to keep teams interested late in the season, you have to have some incentive so they'll play competitively and with gusto," Tagliabue said. "The bye week and home-field advantage were the only incentives left at a certain point."

Added Pierson, "Lamar pushed to the end the fact he was against the bye week. We said, 'Lamar, the math doesn't work without it.' He didn't care about the details. He hated the bye week, but he didn't have a plan about how to make it work."

Perhaps no proposal stirred Hunt's blood more than the two-point conversion after touchdowns.

Beginning in March 1971 Hunt introduced the idea (ironically enough, he had voted against the rule in the AFL in 1960). Longtime NFL owners rejected it, and the newly inducted AFL owners supported it; the measure failed. "I'm hopeful it will get in eventually," Hunt said at the time. "I think there's more recognition now that the existing play is meaningless since 90 percent of the conversion kicks are made. I'm not for gimmicks, but there's no suspense when you're going to make 90 percent of plays."

Year after year, Hunt dusted off the same letter—first to Alvin Ray Rozelle and then to Paul Tagliabue—saying he wanted to put the two-point conversion in front of the Competition Committee. Aside from suspense, Hunt saw the benefits in terms of entertainment (after all, has any fan been captivated by an extra-point kick?) and of strategy, though many coaches had no interest in figuring out how to defend a new innovation that could cause defeat.

"He'd always put the two-point conversion into the mix; every year it would get voted down," said Gregg. "Being a coach, I didn't really want something like that to deal with. But Lamar thought it would be good for the league, so I was for it."

On March 22, 1994, at the NFL owners meeting in Orlando, Florida, the two-point conversion was approved—23 years after Hunt first introduced it. In a switch from the AFL, the ball rested at the 2-yard line rather than the 3 to offer more likelihood for a run. That first year, more than 50 percent of attempts succeeded, though numbers dwindled thereafter.

"He was certainly patient," recalled Tagliabue, who heard the proposal again and again. "He seemed to have the sense it [adoption] was inevitable. Some of the resistance was philosophical, some political because of the AFL-NFL conflict. And any rule change involving scoring in sports will always merit resistance."

Aside from championing a handful of rule proposals, Hunt was most insistent on one other item at the league level. He wanted the Thanksgiving Day games, which had been played in Detroit and Dallas seemingly since time immemorial (actually 1934 and 1966, respectively) to rotate among cities.

Around Thanksgiving in 1985, he wrote a letter to then-commissioner Rozelle, complete with articles supporting his point of view.

"I think we have a major scheduling inequity relative to the league's Thanksgiving Day game," he wrote. "It is irrefutable that the every-year scheduling of a home Thanksgiving Day game for the Cowboys has worked to their advantage (.879 winning percentage for Thanksgiving Day and the week after vs. .700 winning percentage in the remainder of the season) and, in my opinion, this is not an advantage that should be permitted."

Hunt further claimed the Cowboys' reputation had been enhanced by being featured annually on Thanksgiving Day.

"Being a popular team is one thing, but to be able to perpetually enhance that popularity by claiming some type of 'Thanksgiving Day franchise' at the expense of others is quite another thing," Hunt wrote.

Hunt offered two suggestions:

1) "All teams who desire to play a home Thanksgiving Day game be permitted to host such a game on a rotating basis."

2) "All 28 teams to be scheduled as a visiting team on Thanksgiving Day on a rotating basis consistent with our Monday night team selection scheduling pattern."

In a three-page reply sent more than two months later, Rozelle defended the Cowboys. Referring to the television contracts that had been approved in October 1977, he wrote, "You may recall that, in the absence of other teams clamoring to play on Thanksgiving, Tex Schramm said that the Cowboys would be willing to play on that Thursday...if it could be an annual game.... When there was no objection to the Cowboys' offer, I stated that it was the League's intention to schedule Thanksgiving Day games in Detroit and Dallas for the length of the new television contracts. The same understanding continued through the five-year television agreements that began with the 1982 season and continue through 1986.

"It would seem ill-advised to do something right now.... Therefore, I urge you to agree not to have these matters listed for discussion at the Annual Meeting next month."

In response to Hunt's articles about the Cowboys' Thanksgiving and post-Thanksgiving success, Rozelle countered, "Detroit, a longer annual host than have been the Cowboys, is just 23–21–2 on Thanksgiving...and the Lions have a losing 20–24–2 record the following week."

Growing up, football and turkey were wedded in Hunt's mind. Important college football games, such as University of Texas vs. Texas A&M, were played that day. Hunt's Chiefs played on Thanksgiving Day for three seasons in the AFL but, like the two-point conversion, his attempts to switch the hidebound NFL's ways were defeated over and over.

"Lamar's proposal had a lot of merit, particularly when a club is down. It's such a big television day," Harlan said. "His point was well taken, but Dallas would argue vehemently that it was tradition for them. Lamar would say it was a home-field advantage. To play a game on a Sunday, then turn around two days later and go to Detroit or Dallas, that's hard."

Finally, Hunt's wish was granted. In 2006, in part to find live programming for the fledgling NFL Network, Kansas City was awarded a Thanksgiving Day game at night in Arrowhead Stadium in addition to, rather than in place of, the two others. But in a sad twist, by that time Hunt—only weeks away from death—could not attend. Even worse, his Dallas hospital's cable system didn't carry the NFL Network. Refusing to give in, Hunt listened to the game against Denver the only way he could: over a telephone. The Chiefs won 19–10.

Still, the Chiefs have never been able to secure a Thanksgiving Day game on a permanent basis.

"It was a big thing to him because Dallas had it," said Rick Gosselin, a *Dallas Morning News* NFL reporter who also covered the Chiefs for the *Kansas City Star* from 1977 to 1989. "I think that hurt him. He really wanted that game. If it had been Dan Rooney or Wellington Mara, they may have gotten it. But Lamar didn't want to one-up anyone. He wanted to be a part of the group."

Another battle Hunt often fought—one he didn't initiate; rather, it was directed at him—involved cross-ownership. Though other NFL owners enjoyed minor business interests outside of football and a handful were involved in other leagues, no one had more money invested in other sports than Hunt. In the 1970s, he owned the Dallas Tornado of the North American Soccer League, World Championship Tennis (which in many ways dominated pro tennis at the time), and a decent stake in the National Basketball Association's Chicago Bulls.

For years the NFL had tiptoed around cross-ownership. A resolution passed in 1967 asked for amendments and bylaws against cross-ownership, but they failed to materialize. Five years later, another resolution called for NFL owners not to buy "operating control of a team in a competing league." Those who did would be required to make a "best effort" to get rid of it.

Then, some owners got mad. For seven of the first eight years in the 1970s, the head of the Philadelphia Eagles, Leonard Tose, lost money. He believed the Philadelphia Atoms of the NASL, a league leader in attendance, hurt his football business.

In 1978, during a league meeting in Palm Springs, California, Hunt's non-NFL interests drew fire. Particularly incensed was Tose. As recounted in *The League: The Rise and the Decline of the NFL*:

[Tose] had read an article in *American Way* magazine about Hunt touting the NASL. "I was glad that my doctor wasn't there to take my blood pressure because I could not believe what I read in the article. What particularly disturbed me...was the fact that Mr. Hunt was quoted as saying soccer is going to replace football."

Hunt had heard similar complaints before and never understood why he was singled out. "I would look around the room and [other cross-ownership violators] wouldn't say a word and wouldn't participate in conversation."

Hunt noted he had tried to divest from both the Chicago Bulls and the Dallas Tornado but, for various reasons, had been unable to. Owners were upset. Old-guard owner Wellington Mara of the New York Giants was blunt: get out of soccer or get out of football. Chuck Sullivan of the Patriots, whose family had passed up opportunities to buy each of Boston's pro sports franchises to abide by the NFL's cross-ownership rules, said, "If Lamar Hunt were to devote more time to the promotion of the Chiefs and less time to the promotion of other sports interests, I think the NFL would significantly benefit. My family made a commitment that we would bring ourselves into compliance with the rules. It cost us $10 million to do that."

Max Winter, the owner of the NFL's Minnesota Vikings who had left Hunt waiting at the altar in the AFL, fretted about competition from the

NASL's Minnesota Kicks. Like Tose, Winter was dismayed about Hunt's backing of the NASL.

"I think I said it to the league, in the room, that I object very much that an American Football Conference President [Hunt] is going to Minneapolis to advance soccer, introduce soccer in my city," Winter said.

In 1978 toothless resolutions were abandoned. An amendment was proposed that would require owners such as Hunt and Miami's Joe Robbie, who operated the NASL Fort Lauderdale team owned by his wife, Elizabeth, to either sell their soccer holdings or leave the NFL. Starting in February 1980, those who didn't comply could face fines starting at $25,000 a month and reaching $75,000 a month. The new wording to amend Article IX of the NFL Constitution and Bylaws read in part: "No person (1) owning a majority interest in a member club, or (2) directly or indirectly having substantial operating control, or substantial influence over the operations, of a member club, or (3) serving as an officer or director of a member club, nor (4) any spouse or minor child of any such person, may directly or indirectly acquire, retain, or possess any interest in another major team sport [including major league baseball, basketball, hockey, and soccer]."

Jay Moyer, the NFL's legal counsel at the time, summed up the league's position. "Because we compete with the other leagues for the entertainment dollar, we feel that cross-ownership is a conflict. You don't see Ford people sitting on the board of General Motors, do you?"

Hunt's position was simple. "I don't think soccer is a threat to the NFL," he said.

Because of the NFL's proposed amendment, the NASL sued the league that fall, sensing grave harm if Hunt and Robbie defected. Hunt was both a proponent of the suit and a defendant.

"Somebody pointed out to me the other day that I can't lose," he said at the time. "But I don't think it's funny. I'm paying 100% of [1/28] of the NFL's legal costs and 90% of [1/24] of the NASL's legal costs."

Letters between Hunt and Rozelle were submitted to show the owner's concern with being forced to sell. Hunt wrote to the commissioner, "The soccer investment of myself and my children (for which I am obviously responsible) is a very substantial one unfortunately, at this point more than I expected. Though the picture looks infinitely brighter for the sport, it is still a long way from reaching fruition for the investors and, in fact, at present there is virtually no market for a going club especially one owned by a 'Hunt.' (We have a historically bad record for selling any business for buyers seem to feel that anything we are selling must really be a 'dog.')"

In 1979, the U.S. District Court in New York stopped the NFL from enacting the cross-ownership ban. A year later, a federal court in New York ruled in favor of the NFL's ban. But on January 27, 1982, a federal appeals court overturned the previous ruling, saying NFL team owners were allowed to have an interest in other pro sports teams. The court ruled the NFL ban was "anticompetitive and violated antitrust law."

The controversy was far from over. Finally, in 1997, the rules governing cross-ownership in the NFL were changed to allow owners such as the Dolphins' Wayne Huizenga to run teams in other sports in their home market (in this case, the Florida Panthers and Florida Marlins) or in cities lacking NFL teams. The rule switch also meant that Portland Trail Blazers owner Paul Allen could buy the Seattle Seahawks. Today, Hunt's son Clark is chairman of the Kansas City Chiefs, is head of Hunt Sports Group (which runs the family's Major League Soccer franchises), and is involved in other sports holdings, such as the family's founding interest in the Chicago Bulls.

Lamar Hunt was engaged in other major NFL moves. As the union voted to strike in 1982, he introduced the idea of replacement players, in hopes football could still be broadcast on television and to tempt players to defy the picket line. Though they weren't used during the two-month strike that year, by 1987 they became a reality (and in many ways, a comedy) for three games.

Hunt opposed instant replay at the outset and, after the league's initial approval of the concept for the 1986 season, it was shelved six years later. But after a long hiatus, Hunt backed the idea with its new twists in 1999 (along with 27 other owners; three voted against it).

"I voted for it this time because I see an opportunity to use improved technology," Hunt said. "I have some misgivings. I still think there are imperfections in the system, but let's see what happens."

Always interested in international ventures, Hunt backed NFL Europe, a league designed to bring American football into the hotbed of soccer.

"The Chiefs were always big supporters of NFL Europe," recalled Tagliabue about the now-disbanded league. "They had examples of players like Christian Okoye that football players could come from everywhere in the world. Aside from bringing the game to fans, NFL Europe was also about introducing the game to athletes."

Hunt always searched for consensus and was careful not to offend. But perhaps his biggest misstep during his 36 years as an NFL owner occurred during the search to replace Pete Rozelle, the NFL's longtime commissioner.

After Rozelle's stunning announcement during the league's annual meeting in 1989 that he was stepping down, Hunt and New York Giants owner Wellington Mara were named cochairmen of the search committee by the departing commissioner. They asked four old-guard owners to join them. When the search commenced, they didn't look far; New Orleans Saints executive Jim Finks, who had previously worked for the Minnesota Vikings and Chicago Bears, was brought forth a few months later as the sole candidate, though the committee interviewed others as well.

During the attempt to nominate Finks as commissioner at a July meeting, 11 owners—including Jerry Jones, who had just bought the Cowboys that year and was attending only his second owners meeting—abstained again and again, refusing to support the 61-year-old candidate. Many had felt left out of the search process on what was arguably the most important decision they would make for years.

Hunt spoke diplomatically afterward while emphasizing his support for the candidate. "All of the 11 said a number of different things," Hunt said. "They didn't focus on any one thing but were upset about the process. Speaking for the committee, they have worked very hard and feel that Jim

104

Finks is very definitely the man for the job. I have never seen that large a number of abstentions in our group. We will get back together and find a way that will make the process acceptable."

A new search committee was created after Finks received only 16 aye votes (19 were needed for approval). Three months later, on October 26, after the 12th total ballot in the lengthy process, Tagliabue became the NFL commissioner, succeeding Rozelle.

Hunt and Tagliabue got along well during the latter's tenure, and there was no ill will over Hunt's initial backing of Finks.

"He was helpful with me, especially on a confidential level," Tagliabue recalled. "He knew how demanding the job of commissioner was."

And by the time Tagliabue announced his retirement, Hunt—though in failing health—was appointed to the next search committee, which appointed NFL veteran Roger Goodell to the post.

During his decades with the NFL, long after people had forgotten which teams had actually played in the AFL, Hunt kept meticulous track of how they fared.

"I still keep up with the rivalry," he said nine years after the AFL had ceased to exist. "I can tell you, for instance, the AFC won the regular-season series in each of the last four years. Four years ago, we won the preseason, the regular season, the Super Bowl, and the Pro Bowl. Also, the AFC crowds were larger than the NFC. It was a clean sweep."

Perhaps the accomplishment Hunt will be most remembered for in the NFL came when he actually was still an AFL owner.

A new championship game arose from the AFL-NFL merger in 1966. Among the many items that needed to be decided: what should the matchup be called?

Like the story of H.L. Hunt saying how many years Lamar could fund the Texans' hefty losses, which has been repeated with varying lengths of time, the story of the naming of the Super Bowl has numerous versions. Not in doubt is the fact that Lamar Hunt coined the term and that Super Balls were bouncing around his house. But accounts vary.

A tribute to Hunt appeared in the nation's newspaper of record, the *New York Times*, after he died. It talked about his daughter, Sharron, bouncing a Super Ball over the house, which prompted her father's idea of the Super Bowl. But in the newspaper's official obituary, it quotes Hunt as saying, "My own feeling is that it probably registered in my head because my daughter, Sharron, and my son Lamar Jr. had a children's toy called a Super Ball, and I probably interchanged the phonetics of 'bowl' and 'ball.'" In a different interview with Hunt, the numbers grew. "My wife had given three small Super Balls to my three children [Sharron, Lamar Jr., and Clark] at the time," Hunt said.

Even after creating the name, Hunt and others dismissed it.

"Nobody ever said, 'Let's make that the name of the game,'" said Hunt. "Far from it, we all agreed it was far too corny."

Yet the newspapers—facing limited headline space and not embracing the lengthy AFL-NFL World Championship Game—latched onto the term *Super Bowl* and promoted it. Only five months after the merger, the *New York Times* already referred to the title game as the Super Bowl in its headlines and text, well before the first one was ever played. Though the AFL and NFL resisted—the first two games, on tickets and programs, were referred to as the AFL-NFL World Championship Game—by the third game, Super Bowl had won.

It was clear the name—with its unorthodox origins—worked. "We had no market research," Hunt recalled. "Had we done market research, we'd still be there 40 years later finding a good name for the game."

Before the Super Bowl, there were a few other sports events that could attract the nation's attention one day a year, such as the Kentucky Derby and the Indianapolis 500. None today, though, come close to equaling the magnitude of Hunt's namesake. More than 90 million viewers in the United States—nearly one-third of the entire country—watch the game each February, and the face value for tickets reached $1,000 for the first time in 2009.

Despite being considered the father of the Super Bowl (he also came up with the idea of affixing Roman numerals to each game), Hunt could also enjoy deflating the event's increasingly serious air. Before Super Bowl XXXIV in Atlanta, he was chosen as a coin-flipper. He received a letter from the NFL discussing what would happen the day before the game, which included a coin-toss press conference, a rehearsal, and a preparation, all before the actual flip in front of the players. Hunt scribbled a note to a friend about the letter: "Do you think we are slightly overprepared? My flipping thumb is already twitching, and I'm only going to be one of ten 'flippers' on January 30th. Thank goodness there are no activities on Saturday so we can rest up!"

One of Hunt's dreams involved procuring a Super Bowl for Kansas City. Though Tagliabue announced Kansas City would host the game in 2015 if Jackson County, Missouri, voters approved a rolling roof during a 2006 referendum, it failed to pass. According to sports economist Baade, who studies the impact of one-time sports events on cities and often believes they're wildly inflated, Kansas City would have enjoyed a bigger boost from the game than a city in the South.

"If you go in February and have a Super Bowl in Miami, you're crowding out those who'd usually go for the weather. You're replacing one group of tourists with another," Baade said. "But in Kansas City, it's not exactly a tourist mecca in early February. It's attractive to argue a Super Bowl in Kansas City would have more impact than in a warm-weather city."

Before he died, Hunt had attended all 40 Super Bowls. He was surprised that, in his lifetime, the Chiefs never reached a Super Bowl as an NFL team. Of course, he realized that more than tripling the number of opponents from the AFL severely weakened one's chances for success. In the 35 full seasons Hunt experienced as part of the older league, his Chiefs made the playoffs again and again (despite a bad drought after Super Bowl IV). But, in an unfortunate irony, they never won the Lamar Hunt Trophy, awarded to the champion of the American Football Conference.

And, after sticking by Stram for the entire stretch of the AFL—the only coach there who survived the full decade—Hunt was much quicker to jettison his head men in the NFL. After the merger was completed, the Chiefs founder agreed to give Stram a 10-year contract, which was finally signed in 1972. Yet two years later, Hunt fired Stram, saying it was necessary to "revitalize our organization and give it a fresh approach." The team's faltering record wasn't the only problem; given Hunt's preoccupation with fans in the seats, the drop in season-ticket sales from almost 73,000 when Arrowhead Stadium opened in 1972 to fewer than 66,000 in 1974 became justification enough.

In typical Hunt fashion, to soften the blow somewhat, he said he'd honor the 10-year deal if Stram didn't get another job; if he did, Hunt would pay the difference in salary.

In came Paul Wiggin. But he was hamstrung by some of Stram's moves in the years following the Super Bowl win over Minnesota. Weak drafts and bad trades—such as sending a No. 1 pick away for over-the-hill defensive lineman George Seals, who lasted all of five games—left Wiggin with a mediocre team.

In the middle of his fourth season in 1978, Wiggin was ousted. Hunt himself delivered the news on Halloween night at the coach's home; suffice to say he didn't receive a treat from Wiggin's wife, Carolynn.

"My wife tore into him," Wiggin told *Sports Illustrated*, "and he didn't handle it at all. He got up, walked away, and left. She just wanted to know why. Simply, the repetitive *why*. 'Why you, Lamar? The guy who put together the AFL. The guy who had the guts to hang in and stick to his principles. Why you?' Lamar didn't say anything."

After Wiggin's ouster, Marv Levy was interviewed for the job.

"We had a two- or three-hour meeting, and I was immediately at ease with Lamar. There wasn't a lot of fluff," Levy said. "That's the way he was. There was no, 'Give me an outline of what you want to do.' He knew all about your background."

During five seasons after his hire, Levy mustered one winning record. He was fired, a move Hunt later referred to as the worst mistake he ever made (Levy went on to take the Buffalo Bills to four Super Bowls).

In 1986, even though the Chiefs had made the playoffs for the first time in 15 years, Hunt fired another coach, former Dallas assistant John Mackovic. Essentially, Hunt and Steadman attended a players' meeting where the players complained about Mackovic, and the owner canned him afterward, saying the team lacked chemistry.

Hunt's nemesis Schramm didn't waste words in assessing the situation.

"It's just typical of Lamar and Jack Steadman. The consistent thing about them is that they keep having losing seasons. They get a guy who finally wins for them, and they fire him because some players are upset. There are always some players upset about something."

Frank Gansz was hired to replace Mackovic. In two years, he mustered an 8–22–1 record. By this time, Chiefs ticket sales were cratering, heading below the 40,000 mark per game after one playoff appearance in 18 years.

Some said Lamar didn't have control of the team, since he was such a fan, and complained that the team was not run like a typical NFL franchise. That changed quickly. Carl Peterson—who boasted an extensive football background, including a stint as the former general manager of the Philadelphia Eagles—was hired as general manager, replacing Schaaf. He sacked Gansz and brought in Schottenhiemer.

That started the Chiefs' best run in the NFL to date. They drafted defensive star Derrick Thomas, offensive line standout Will Shields, and game-changing tight end Tony Gonzalez during Schottenheimer's reign, which included seven playoff berths in 10 years.

The former coach said Hunt was interested in the college draft every year, though he never demanded the Chiefs select any particular player.

"He'd come down and listen as we were preparing for the draft," Schottenheimer said. "He'd share a name he had heard about and wonder how he measured up by standards of our scouting department.

"He encouraged open dialogue. In draft meetings, he would ask about individual players, but he let people do their job. The things Lamar said were always well thought-out. He didn't go winging it."

No matter what, Schottenheimer said Hunt's focus was always on the league as a whole.

"He wanted to do what was best for professional football. That selflessness, if you will, permeated his existence. The league's success was paramount."

In fact, that commitment revealed itself in another sport, one also called football just about everywhere but in the United States. Trying to make pro leagues succeed in that sport—soccer—made establishing the AFL look easy.

CHAPTER 5

THE OTHER FOOTBALL

AS THE 20TH CENTURY DAWNED, pro sports in the United States were not a force to be reckoned with. Games played by paid athletes generated scant interest. One could read about contests in the newspaper, to be sure, but no radio or television carried their drama to the masses. Colleges ruled football; the only sport played professionally that generated decent crowds and that remains popular today is baseball.

In other countries, the story was similar. But one pro sport soon emerged in scores of nations that failed to entice U.S. citizens: soccer, called "football" everywhere else.

The simple game required little equipment (especially compared to U.S. football) and captivated youngsters from South America to Europe. Leagues grew and national teams were formed to play for the World Cup, which began in 1930. Twenty years later, a crowd of 210,000 watched the World Cup final in Rio de Janeiro, more than twice as many people who have ever attended any one Super Bowl game. Today, Manchester United in England is considered the most valuable franchise in all of sports, approaching $2 billion.

In the United States, a few early attempts at pro soccer fizzled. The first one, the American League of Professional Foot Ball in 1894, was created mainly by National League baseball owners to fill their stadiums on off days. It collapsed in less than 12 months. The National Association Foot Ball League (NAFBL), formed the same year, fared better, running 27 years before disbanding.

The first American Soccer League (ASL) was developed in 1921 as the NAFBL was dying (and grabbed some of its teams). The ASL enjoyed success on the East Coast, drawing large crowds. But it folded during the Great Depression; two later incarnations also failed.

By 1960, soccer had become an afterthought in the U.S. But that year, former Philadelphia Phillies owner William Cox created the International Soccer League, which imported teams from France and elsewhere to play in the U.S. Though it lasted only five years, a seed had been planted. In May 1966, a group of investors proclaimed they would start another new pro league in 1967.

Less than two months after that news, the World Cup final appeared live on U.S. televisions for the first time. England beat West Germany 4–2 in an exciting match that appealed to American fans' passion for scoring (and thus was an atypical soccer contest). Perhaps the most important U.S. viewer that day was the same man who, when watching pro football's championship game in 1958, realized that sport's potential: Lamar Hunt.

"The first meaningful image I had was the 1966 World Cup final," Hunt recalled. "I was able to see the game on the international level, and I was attracted by the crowds and their enthusiasm."

A month before the World Cup broadcast from Wembley Stadium, Hunt had been approached in New York City—at the time he helped announce the AFL-NFL merger—to gauge his interest in investing in the North American Soccer League (soon to be called the United Soccer Association). Given his commitment to one of the biggest sports deals of all time, he demurred initially but didn't forget the idea. And soon enough, he was in.

On January 29, 1967, the *Dallas Morning News* reported that Hunt confirmed a Dallas franchise would begin that spring in the North American Soccer League. Hunt said he would be the biggest stockholder.

Why would a man already running the Kansas City Chiefs and engaged in other interests gamble his reputation on a sport little loved in the United States, one he himself had never played?

"I think the internationalism is one big thing," Hunt said later on about his attraction to soccer. "The crowd noise, the crowd's involvement is another. When you see it in person you really see it's the world's game."

Added Ted Howard, a longtime North American Soccer League hand who served in posts from director of operations to executive director, "He'd say, 'We have all the world champions for sports in the United States, but they're not really *world* champions.' He loved the competitive aspect."

"It was his love of potential and experiments," said Temple Pouncey, who covered pro soccer for years at the *Dallas Morning News*. "He thought that even though it may not become as big here as in the rest of the world, it could get a lot of interest."

Despite his passion for the game and stake in its success, Hunt knew football paled on the world stage next to soccer.

"We had the biggest television audience in United States sports history for the Super Bowl game, 65 million viewers," Hunt said soon after Super Bowl I, "but do you know how many people all over the world watched the [1966] World Cup soccer matches via Telestar? Four hundred million, and that included about 12 million in this country. And the game came on here at 10:00 in the morning."

Hunt estimated 8,000 to 12,000 tickets sold per game would allow teams to break even financially and conceded losses were expected the first few years. Of the dozen cities designated, he admitted Dallas would be one of the tougher markets to crack.

"I'm sure it will take at least four or five years to sell the sport here," he said.

About two weeks later, as Hunt jetted to Africa to dedicate a new pipeline run by Hunt Oil, Ed Fries, 31, was named GM. Next, the fledgling franchise chose a name. Hunt and his staff looked over more than 1,000 entries in a name-the-club contest. Rejecting ones such as Hunt's Headaches, the soccer entrepreneur settled on Tornado, a singular term to adhere to the international tradition.

In fact, that first year, all NASL teams were slated to be represented by foreign squads, since there was no time to recruit American players. For the Tornado, its proxy would be Dundee United of Scotland, who would play six home games at the Cotton Bowl. Tickets were priced reasonably, up to $3 for a reserved seat to 75¢ for a children's general admission seat.

As with every sports venture he assumed, Lamar envisioned success.

"I only paid $25,000 for a franchise," he recalled afterward. "There were no promotional dollars, the operating cost was low."

Hunt's involvement was a masterstroke for the new entity.

"He was such a huge name for the league because of what he had done to bring about the merger of the NFL and the AFL," said Howard. "He was so incredibly well connected. How important he was to opening doors. People wanted to be associated with Lamar Hunt. Otherwise, who the heck was the NASL?"

Despite the excitement of starting a new league, drawbacks were manifold. Just like when Hunt started the AFL, a competitor existed. In this case it wasn't the entrenched NFL but another new entity, the National Professional Soccer League (NPSL).

Its origins were informal. Recalled NPSL President Bob Hermann, "Four of us were having lunch in New York. The other three were involved in pro sports in football and baseball. They said, 'We don't have soccer in the United States—we should start a league.' I went to the men's room. When I came back, they said, 'You're the only one of us not involved in pro sports. You're the chairman.'"

Though it lacked the approval of FIFA, the international governing body of soccer (which NASL had earned; any league without it was deemed an outlaw), NPSL President Hermann procured something almost as important. He met with the three broadcast networks and, unlike NPSL's rival, secured national television coverage.

"I got a 10-year contract—cancelable after any one year—with CBS," he recalled.

Both leagues featured its share of big-name sports owners, such as Jack Kent Cooke and Dan Reeves, but everyone feared to ask if they could explain basic soccer terms, such as a corner kick. Early in 1967, Dick Walsh was named commissioner of the North American Soccer League. His qualifications were hidden at best.

"I don't know the difference between a soccer ball and a billiard ball," Walsh proclaimed. If that weren't bad enough, the former Los Angeles Dodgers executive recruited with a five-year deal added, "I don't even know how many men there are on a soccer team."

A few weeks later, Hunt ensured the verbal missteps would not be repeated. "Oh, he's been educated since then," he said.

In retrospect, the idea of two professional soccer leagues debuting the same year when demand for the sport barely exceeded that of curling (the term *soccer mom* was still decades away from being coined) was preposterous. From zero pro teams in 1966, America found nearly two dozen swarming about its cities a year later.

The Dallas–Fort Worth area—one of the top 15 television markets in the nation—boasted a minuscule immigrant population, the group where soccer flourished at the time. Years later Bill McNutt, co-owner of the Tornado, still seemed stunned he and Hunt tried to foist soccer onto a football-crazy town.

"We didn't know what we were doing," he said. "When we started the team, you couldn't find three soccer balls in town, and no one knew anything about soccer. We didn't know what to expect, we were blind, each step was on new ground."

On May 23, 1967, about 200 fans showed up at Love Field to welcome the new Tornado team, who would live at the Beta Theta Pi house at SMU. Bagpipes played and signs were hoisted as Dundee United disembarked after nearly a full day getting to Dallas. Norma Hunt joined the welcoming committee and held a souvenir soccer ball marked *Dundee*, which her husband had brought back from Scotland and given to their son Clark.

In a symbol of how far soccer needed to go in the U.S., the new Tornado coach Jerry Kerr eyed it with reservation.

"I'm looking for something 'United,'" he said. "That [Dundee] is our opposition team!"

On a Saturday night in June at the Cotton Bowl, 16,421—more than attended some Texans games—entered to watch Dallas and Houston play to a scoreless tie in their United Soccer Association opener.

Though Hunt realized the crowds would dwindle once the initial excitement passed, he applauded the fans' passion.

"The biggest surprise for me was the crowd response and the fact that they reacted so favorably in a prejudiced, hometown manner," he said. "I was afraid the crowds this year might react to the games as an exhibition. That wasn't true at all."

But Dundee United soon proved to be overmatched on U.S. soil. By mid-July, the 3–9 season ended mercifully as Dallas' summer temperatures soared, which caused players to bake in their blue and orange satin jerseys that did not absorb sweat.

Looking back on the foreign invasion, Hunt realized it was doomed.

"That was a big mistake," he said. "We should have just waited and started fresh in 1968 with our own teams. None of the fans could identify at all with the foreign teams. It was a bad concept to begin with."

Hunt soon introduced a coach for the actual Tornado, Bob Kap, at a press conference. A smiling Hunt placed a Texas-style hat on Kap's head; unfortunately, it was backward. Kap, a Yugoslavian, took it in stride, uttering "Howdy, partner," to his new boss.

Yet the challenges in trying to acclimate a foreign-born soccer coach to Dallas were many. Any football coach who mispronounced the words "Cotton Bowl" would be run out of town; though Kap uttered the word "cotton" correctly, he thought "bowl" rhymed with "owl." In a phrase that probably stunned Hunt (who had recently said "Frankly, I'm in this for financial gain"), Kap was asked about monetary returns in soccer.

"I couldn't care less," he said.

In true Hunt fashion, he endeavored to make a splash with his new franchise. In early September, with 15 players under contract, the Tornado announced it would soon embark on a 25,000-mile tour—going just about everywhere save Antarctica and the Arctic, where soccer fields were as rare as sunbathers. After hitting Iran, India, and other spots, the tour would finish in South America in March.

What was the point? Hunt saw two reasons for what he called the most extensive (and expensive) tour ever by a U.S. sports team.

"We feel that it not only will give our young players invaluable experience at the international soccer level but also will serve as a great goodwill instrument for both Dallas and the United States," Hunt said.

About a month later, readers who picked up the Sunday paper may have been startled to see a new byline at the top of the sports page: Lamar Hunt. Having returned from the team's training camp in Spain, he offered his written impressions for the *Dallas Morning News*.

Hunt noted athletes Kap had recruited were taller than Dundee United players and that they had been so drilled in manners that "meal-time finds myself as the only one with elbows on the table."

He also showed a surprising unfamiliarity (or a charming innocence, depending on one's perspective) with the sport, given the millions of dollars he had begun to dedicate to it, writing, "After seeing a direct shot goal shooting drill, I must conclude that playing goal keeper is as rough as and takes as much nerve as any position in sports. The soccer ball travels at an astonishing speed and the keeper, using his hands and body, is in effect a last sacrifice to defend his team's scoreboard."

Right around Hunt's sojourn, it was expected the United Soccer Association and the National Professional Soccer League would announce a merger. On September 7, 1967, the *New York Times* reported the deal was imminent, quoting NPSL commissioner Ken Macker as saying an agreement had been worked out.

What happened a few days later was the filing of an $18 million lawsuit by the NPSL against the USA, the USSFA, and FIFA, charging them with conspiracy to drive the NPSL out of existence and with violation of federal antitrust law.

Despite the unexpected setback, the flailing leagues resolved their differences and came together to become the North American Soccer League (United Soccer Association's original name) for play in 1968. Seventeen teams survived, including the Tornado.

When the leagues merged, the NASL executive committee included Hunt and Hermann, who served as chairman. To generate publicity, they decided to meet once a month in the hometown of each franchise.

"We'd go to these cities, and the reporters all hung around Lamar," Hermann recalled. "I thought, *Why didn't they hang around me? I'm the chairman*, but they all knew who Lamar was."

Bill Bartholomay, former owner and now chairman emeritus of the Atlanta Braves, invested in the Atlanta Chiefs when they started in the NPSL. He got to know Hunt during the formation of the NASL (the Chiefs captured the league's first title in 1968). What impressed Bartholomay about his fellow owner was his global vision.

"He thought we should internationalize the U.S. soccer game," Bartholomay said. "As much as we could he wanted to bring in star players from around the world for exhibition games. He was right on that. We had Pelé down in Atlanta for an exhibition."

When the '68 regular season started, Tornado players would have preferred to play exhibitions. They were exhausted from the worldwide tour, which included more than 40 matches. What had started with high hopes was marred by a stoning in Singapore and troubles crossing borders. And the Tornado flopped in the merged league, winning only two of 30 matches as attendance dipped below 3,000 per contest from more than 9,000 previously.

Around this time, Butch Buchholz, one of the tennis players marketed among the Handsome Eight who had just signed with Hunt's World Championship Tennis, heard a remark Hunt made about pro soccer. He remembered it clearly more than 40 years after the fact. "We were in Evansville, Indiana. It was an odd place for him to show up, but he had been at a pro soccer meeting," Buchholz said. "I'll never forget him saying about pro soccer, 'You've heard about people taking a bath? This is going to be a long swim.'"

The 1968 season turned into a boondoggle for the merged league. Later, Hunt bristled at the memory of money thrown away. "We went to a big-budget operation [in 1968]," he said. "Owners getting into the league had money but made the mistake of wanting to go major league right away. It took us five years to overcome the setbacks caused by that type of operation. Yes, that was my low point...I did think about getting out."

Despite the massive problems, Hunt soldiered on. He led the league's move to a minimized-budget operation with only five teams in 1969 as franchises folded in droves.

NASL looked for any sort of boost. As head of its executive committee, Hermann recalled flying to Switzerland around that time and trying to persuade FIFA head Sir Stanley Rous to Americanize the game by increasing opportunities for goals.

"I said, 'Gentlemen, we have a sport in the U.S. called baseball. The average score is high," Hermann began. "In basketball, it's 125–110. In football, it's 24–16. Yet the average score in soccer is 0–0. If you made the goal one foot taller and one foot wider, the average score would be 7-3.'

"I stopped and waited. Sir Stanley Rous said, 'Is there anything else?' I said no. He said 'Thank you very much.' I got back on the plane. They never discussed it after that."

Even Lamar's brother Bunker—an investor in the NASL—soon opined on the limitations of the sport.

"It would be easier to take American football to Europe than bring soccer here," he said. "Soccer doesn't fit the American personality. The game doesn't have enough climaxes. In baseball you have three strikes, three outs, and so forth, and in football you have first downs. In soccer you're just out there kicking the ball around."

The Tornado moved into P.C. Cobb Stadium, a high school field with concrete bleachers. Though the atmosphere improved over the cavernous Cotton Bowl, the crowds didn't. During an exhibition match between the Tornado and an English team that featured players from the 1966 World Cup champions, fewer than 800 fans showed up. The team was on its third coach, Ron Newman. Again, European teams were imported to play regular-season contests on behalf of the U.S. squads.

In Dallas, three seasons of pro soccer had meant little.

"The market [for soccer] was pretty scant," recalled Pouncey. "Most people didn't know there was still a team. It was about as small-time as a professional sport could get."

Thanks to the hire of Newman, the Tornado improved in 1970, posting an 8–4–12 mark. Though not good enough to make the playoffs, a foundation had been set with new imports such as goalie Kenny Cooper, defender Bobby Moffat, and sweeper Dick Hall.

Still, attendance sagged, reaching an all-time low of a shade over 2,200 per game. And the Tornado remained a shoestring operation.

"When they were going to play on a Saturday night, [coach] Ron Newman would go out to Central Expressway with little signs saying 'Soccer Game Tonight' and go back after the game to retrieve them," Pouncey said. "None of the players considered themselves full-time. They had other jobs. They shared apartments.

"Lamar, with all of the money he had, could have popped tremendous sums into them if he was inclined. But he felt the league needed to grow as a group."

Moffat remembered how team expenses were minimized.

"We'd fly the red eye," he recalled. "If we played a game in Rochester or in Montreal, we'd fly there the day of the game and fly back the same day [so there were no hotel costs]."

Hunt, as was his wont, hired good people and let them run the operation with little interference. But his voice came through clearly on points he felt strongly about.

"He was a great detail man," Moffat said. "When the national anthem was played, players jumped up and down like they did in Europe. It was passed down to me [from Lamar] that I didn't stand still enough during the anthem."

Hunt promoted soccer everywhere, even at World Championship Tennis events. One time, at SMU's Moody Coliseum before about 10,000 tennis fans, Tornado players walked onto the court to play a game called soccer tennis.

"There were two of us on each side," Moffat said. "You play tennis rules with a soccer ball. I'd stand behind the service line and kick the ball over the net on the service side. They'd have to play one bounce and kick it back.

"Martina Navratilova and Ken Rosewall, I believe, came over and said 'We'll have a game.' The crowd went mad. I thought, *What if Martina hurts her knee?* But it was amazing how that connection helped with our attendance."

Creative promotions such as soccer tennis couldn't lessen financial woes. Spartan as the operation was, the Tornado still lost hundreds of thousands of dollars a year. As 1971 beckoned, the league and team in Dallas faced the possibility it could be the last.

In perhaps the lowlight of the Tornado's run in Dallas, the city threatened to force the team out of its newest high school stadium, Franklin Field, citing a code violation. The embarrassing publicity showed that even with Hunt's backing, the Tornado had little leverage in its hometown.

Yet Hunt's importance to the future of pro soccer—in Dallas and nationwide—became critical in the early 1970s.

"Lamar was very instrumental in holding together what little we had left because he was committed to it," Howard said. "He wouldn't let the league die."

Howard said Hunt's input in league meetings was crucial to helping steer the entity the right way.

"He was always there to make sure people had a conscience and were doing things that made sense," Howard said. "He was always there to give [commissioner] Phil Woosnam directions and advice. He was never a quiet voice in league meetings because people would always turn to him and say, "What do you think, Lamar?" because of his stature.

"He always found the time and energy to say, 'This is something else we should try.' He was not a naysayer about others' ideas unless they were too extravagant, too expensive."

Then, for the first time, in 1971, the Tornado made the playoffs. It dispatched Rochester in the semifinals (one game of the best-of-three series was the longest in pro soccer to that date, running nearly three hours in playing time and finishing about midnight). The team faced Atlanta for the championship. In the best-of-three final, the Tornado emerged triumphant two games to one, capturing Dallas' first pro soccer title.

That's not to say the city responded with a standing ovation. The lone match in Dallas on September 15 attracted fewer than 6,500 fans, and there was no parade for the champions. The championship itself didn't even make the front sports page of the *Dallas Morning News*. What everyone in the organization, along with their spouses, earned was a poolside party at Hunt's estate.

Pouncey was there, and he'll never forget what he saw. "One of the people who came was Verne Lundquist," he began. "He was the only one on the TV side to give the Tornado publicity. One of the players, Tony McLaughlin—who had come over to the team to replace Brian Harvey—with the connivance of a Channel 8 cameraman, threw Verne fully clothed into the pool. Verne was angry. He had to go do the 10:00 PM sports broadcast that night.

"The players wondered what would happen to Tony. Lamar walked up to the tables where players were sitting. He said, 'Do you think Brian Harvey's still available?' They couldn't believe he was able to make a joke of it."

The joke was on McLaughlin, who never wore a Tornado uniform again.

In early March of the following year, the champions were as disorganized as ever. The Tornado had not secured a home field, sold a ticket, or even completed a schedule, though the first game loomed eight weeks away. NASL had reduced the season to 14 games, despite Hunt's opposition, to save on player salaries and other expenses. To make matters worse, Major League Baseball placed its first franchise near Dallas, as the Washington Senators moved to Arlington. The new Rangers would dominate the summer's sports pages and wrest what little attention there was away from the Tornado.

Fortunately, Hunt soon struck a deal to move into Texas Stadium, the new home of the Dallas Cowboys in Irving. Even though ticket prices rose to $4 for a reserved seat and $3 general admission, attendance increased for three years straight, topping 8,000 per game during the 1974 season.

Slowly rising from its depths, NASL even launched indoor soccer that winter, and Hunt, ever the enthusiast, saw great promise in the game often compared to pinball. During one exhibition at Cow Palace in San Francisco before more than 11,000 fans, he remarked, "The atmosphere was incredible, electric. It was like the seventh game of some competition that has been going on for 40 years."

But outdoors, the atmosphere was somnolent. And the Tornado still hadn't made much of an imprint in Dallas.

"We must prove we're major league," Hunt said before the 1975 season. "We had the Moscow Dynamo here and drew 20,000. We have the Denver Dynamo here and people say, ho-hum. We have a selling job to do."

In 1975, during a 9–13 campaign, attendance floundered. Hunt knew the selling job needed a jolt.

In September Hunt hired Dick Berg, a promoter extraordinaire, as general manager from the San Francisco Earthquakes. Berg promised dancing girls and fire trucks at games, anything to get people's attention.

"We have to create a fun, positive atmosphere," he said. "And that can't be generated at Texas Stadium. Lamar agrees."

Soon enough, the Tornado moved into Ownby Stadium on the SMU campus—the same spot, ironically enough, that the college football team had moved out of decades before because Doak Walker's popularity made it too small. But the intimate size (about 23,000 capacity) appealed more to a soccer crowd than did a massive football stadium. And Berg, with Lamar's blessing, quickly implemented ideas to entertain the fans. From dropping the game ball from an airplane to letting dogs roam the field to catch Frisbees to throwing a Halter Top Night, where women paraded on the field in their sultry ware, the soccer atmosphere had changed in Dallas.

"The promotions that Berg did [were] the stuff of legends," said Moffat. "One time $40,000 was spread out on the soccer field during halftime to see how much people could get in a 90-second period. It was in $100s, $50s, all the way down to dollar bills. Four couples ran out—some were chosen at the game. One couple [who had been chosen ahead of time] had even been practicing picking up money out on a soccer field.

"After halftime, they had a Brinks truck come out that sucked up all the extra money. We [the players] had gone out there after halftime hoping to pick up some of it."

Pouncey recalled a time when at least one player, rather than rushing onto the field hoping to pocket cash, would have preferred to be locked inside the locker room.

"There was a guy in Dallas who had a lion," Pouncey said. "They had one game where the lion was supposed to bring the ball to midfield, which he did. After the game started, he sat near the south goal. One of the Tornado strikers didn't even attempt a shot—he was so scared of the lion and that it would run out after him."

At the same time, Hunt wanted players to promote the game in their spare moments. Moffat became the team's publications director in 1975 and its marketing director a year later, all while playing (he had also enjoyed a stint with Hunt Oil early in his career). Two other Tornado players joined the front office around the same time.

"I distributed 50,000 *Soccer Surge* [monthly] newspapers throughout the community," Moffat recalled. "The paper said any time, people could phone up and request a player. We were out in public all the time, doing clinics in the snow, juggling competitions, going to shopping malls. We'd have contests for persons who could head the ball the most."

In 1975 the New York Cosmos lured Pelé out of retirement to the United States, and they started to bring in crowds that packed football stadiums. New franchises had been added since the pitiful low of five that endured the 1969 season. The NASL now featured 20 teams.

Boosted by Berg's creative experiments and the promotion of home-grown talent such as Kyle Rote Jr., son of the football legend who had played at SMU and for the New York Giants, Tornado attendance sky-rocketed. For the first time, in 1976, it reached five figures a game. The next year, a new record was set—more than 16,500 a game. And they were attracting an enviable demographic that would appeal to potential sponsors. More than a third of Tornado fans earned more than $25,000 a year.

There was even talk Hunt's franchise would end up in the black after a decade of mounting losses. And why not? Though foreign-born superstars such as Pelé and Franz Beckenbauer pulled in six-figure salaries, NASL rookies earned only a few thousand dollars per year. As Berg pointed out, pro soccer expenses were cheap, especially compared to his stint in the NFL.

"When I was with the San Francisco 49ers, our medical bills, insurance, and all would run $300,000 some years. Last year the Tornado medical bill was $3,000, and we had a lot of injuries. Also, we can outfit a whole team for the price of helmets in the NFL."

Hunt was heartened by the seemingly sudden groundswell for pro soccer.

"I was in a motel room in Tyler, Texas, when Pelé played his first game in the States, and as I watched on television, I thought, *Well, we've made it. It was worth the agony, the lean years.*

"You can take nothing away from what Pelé's done for the NASL, but I'm sure he'd agree with me when I say that Minnesota, averaging 33,000 in a city where they walked in cold against pro baseball and football, is the real success story. To make it in a major sports market, not pushing anybody out of the way but filling a gap—that's what we're all about. That's success!"

But it was all somewhat illusory.

"They frequently filled Ownby Stadium," Pouncey said of the Tornado at that time. "But the average they got per ticket was 85¢. They were papering North Dallas with free tickets."

Before the 1978 season began, Hunt dismissed Berg.

"Dick sort of wore out his welcome," Pouncey said. "Financially, they were doing terrible. So they went back to a more normal type of marketing. The next year, they went from giving tickets away to being full price. That jarred a number of people."

At the same time, the league started to unravel.

"Everybody was losing a million bucks a year," recalled Hermann, who owned the St. Louis Stars. "We drew 8,000 fans a game in St. Louis when we needed 16,000 to break even. I moved my team to Anaheim Stadium [to become the California Surf]. There were a lot of kids playing soccer there, but we still lost a million a year."

Without a salary cap to limit player salaries, too many teams tried to pay big bucks to what were perceived as name players with the public. And the players struck before the 1979 season, as the salary gap between the superstars and rookies grew ever wider.

Hunt started going against his instincts and followed the free-spending trend. He shelled out about $650,000 in transfer fees for three foreign players, none of whom were likely to captivate the Dallas market. To top it off, in 1980, Klaus Toppmoller was signed for about $1 million.

The next year, it was all over. Five NASL franchises were unable to post a 12-month $150,000 performance bond and were removed from the league—including Dallas. The team's assets, such as player contracts, were transferred to Tampa Bay.

Many factors can be cited to explain why the Tornado disintegrated after a 14-year run. The franchise had to educate a city that knew nothing about soccer; it constantly switched stadiums; except for Ron Newman, coaches and general managers were employed for short spells.

Through it all, Hunt gained immense respect from his players, many of whom had never been to the United States before he launched the Tornado.

"We were all blessed that Lamar was somewhat of a father figure," said goalie Kenny Cooper. "We left our families overseas. Most of the guys were single at the time. Thanks to Lamar, a lot of the guys married American girls."

"I played for the man for nine years, and we never missed a paycheck," Moffat said. "Lamar was a very nice person, always extremely polite. The fact that most people who worked for him, including players, called him 'Lamar' showed a lot. I knew of no one who had anything bad to say about him."

Pouncey echoed Moffat's impression of Lamar's down-home manner. "His standard greeting to anyone was, 'Hey, fill in the name, what do you say?' Always a big smile and a handshake," Pouncey said. "It didn't matter if it was a lowly sportswriter or the head of tennis in Germany. It was all genuine."

Thom Meredith, who had joined the Tornado from the Tampa Bay Buccaneers to work in public relations, was especially impressed by Hunt's keen mind.

"He would sit in a meeting for two hours, and he wouldn't say a word. We'd be packing and ready to leave, happy the old man hadn't said anything. Then he'd raise his hand and say, 'Can I ask a question?' He's been writing 16 letters. Then he would ask an incisive question that we all missed. He was multitasking before anyone had heard of the word."

Marty Rotberg, vice president of marketing services for the NASL, recalled a meeting with owners, general managers, and others at the Waldorf-Astoria in New York in 1980. There, Hunt's inclination not to be a bother to anyone became almost comical.

"We were in a big meeting room that was cold. The air-conditioning was on," he said. "People were putting their jackets on. Lamar has two linen table napkins draped over his shoulders and around his neck. He didn't say, 'Will you check with the building manager to do something with the room?' He didn't demand at all."

Howard appreciated Hunt's commitment to the league, which was steadfast even in the darkest of times. But even he knew one man couldn't turn around NASL, which folded for good in 1984.

"The league expanded too quickly to people who weren't committed," Howard said. "Pelé was selling out stadiums everywhere, but he was also a problem because everyone wanted a Pelé. Owners paid a lot of money to second- and third-division players.

"No matter what Lamar did or could have done, the NASL wouldn't have succeeded. The people who ran NASL were ahead of the development curve. They got great players from Europe, but no one knew who they were."

Pouncey shared a story that sums up not only Hunt's love for soccer during the NASL years but also his imperturbable demeanor. In 1973 he asked a handful of people to fly with him on a Hunt Oil jet to Monterrey, Mexico, to watch a soccer match for the day.

"It was so hot, the front wheel had sunk into the asphalt. It took several hours to fix it," Pouncey recalled. "But Lamar persevered. He continued to say, 'We're going to have fun.'

"We got there and we barely made it for kickoff. On the plane back to Dallas that night, everyone was exhausted. He did paperwork, as he always did. Then he laid down on the floorboard of the plane so someone else could lie on the couch."

Unfortunately, the NASL collapse also left Hunt prostrate; he had lost an estimated $20 million. No one would have been surprised—despite his legendary persistence—if he vowed never to get involved in pro soccer again. Not that he didn't love the game. He enjoyed watching his sons Clark and Dan play (Clark served as cocaptain of an SMU team). And, save for

1978 and 2006, he attended every World Cup from the formation of the NASL until he died.

In fact, Hunt's eventual decision that pro soccer was worth a second shot can in part be attributed to the quadrennial event. For the first 60 years of the World Cup, the United States had never played host. Hunt helped ensure his home country would not be denied forever.

"His influence with FIFA to bring the Cup here was so important," said Hank Steinbrecher, former secretary general of the U.S. Soccer Federation. "He was so quietly powerful. No one knew what was going on behind the scenes, but there was the orchestra leader.

"How did we pick Dallas as a venue? It wasn't by accident."

Once the Cup arrived on the shores in 1994, Hunt was passionate about attending games and enjoying the spectacle. He was pleased to see Americans embrace international soccer, packing football-sized stadiums—and talking about the sport like it mattered.

"The World Cup had been very, very successful here, which gave him a renewed sense of confidence that it may be soccer's time in this country," said Clark Hunt.

No doubt the announcement that the whole event was profitable— organizers said it made $50 million, an amount that even Peter Ueberroth, who had headed the extremely successful 1984 Summer Olympics in Los Angeles, called "stunning"—also encouraged Hunt.

The formation of MLS had been announced in late 1993, but it wasn't until the following November that the first investors were introduced. Along with four other not-so-recognizable names from across the country, there was Hunt, this time joined by his son Clark in running the operation.

The father was no passive investor. Determined not to repeat the mistakes of the NASL, Hunt let his attention to detail take over.

Sunil Gulati, head of the U.S. Soccer Federation and president of MLS's New England Revolution, talked with Lamar often during his second venture into pro soccer.

"He looked at the first business plan and sent it back with many red-lined comments," Gulati recalled. "He knew our ally—and enemy—was time. We needed to last. If we could last, he thought we would have a chance.

"He came from an NFL model with strong constraints on player expenditures. But it wasn't just players—it was spending on everything. It was a cautious approach to building the business."

How hard was it to convince him to invest in pro soccer after he had been burned once?

"That part is never easy," Gulati said. "But soccer was a love. He always had a soft spot for the sport. He could talk about MLS, the business side, any part of the game."

Don Garber was hired as MLS commissioner in 1999 (replacing Doug Logan) mainly because of Hunt, who got to know the former NFL executive during their many years together in football.

"He was very, very, very intimately involved in the formation of the league and assuring that we had the right labor situation, ensuring we hired the right people to sell tickets and to operate our games, and thinking hard about how our games would be broadcast," Garber said in a documentary about Hunt.

Designed as a single-entity structure—which means that investors, aside from owning a stake in the team, also own one in the league—the operation has some advantages over NASL. Because it's a single entity, the league possesses power over trades and other aspects in an attempt to control expenses. At the outset a $1.3 million salary cap was instituted. Free agency did not exist. Players soon filed a lawsuit against the single-entity structure but lost.

"The single entity is the right way for any league to go in the long run," Hunt said. "You've got to have some control over labor costs."

On April 6, 1996, MLS began with a roar. More than 31,000 watched San Jose defeat D.C. United at Spartan Stadium, and hundreds of thousands more watched the game on ESPN. The next year, MLS announced expansion plans to quickly field a dozen teams.

Hunt—whose Dallas Tornado had bounced from stadium to stadium during its rocky run—knew one factor was essential to MLS's success: soccer-specific stadiums, a phrase he coined.

Back in the 1970s—when it is said Hunt asked Clint Murchison Jr. to build Texas Stadium with soccer specifications but was refused—Pouncey and others talked with Hunt ad nauseam about the importance of stadiums devoted to soccer.

"Lamar would graciously receive the advice and say it would work one day, but it's not financially viable now," Pouncey said.

Recalled Howard, "In 1984, when NASL folded, I wrote down a bunch of things that would have made it successful. At the top of the list was stadiums. You can't be the third team in a stadium."

Yet when MLS started, it depended, much like NASL had, on grabbing open dates at football stadiums (including Giants Stadium, where the Cosmos had played and spectacularly failed).

Focusing on his franchise in Columbus, which played in the mammoth Ohio Stadium also used by the Ohio State Buckeyes' football squad, Hunt helped put the matter before voters twice, hoping they'd finance a soccer stadium with tax dollars. They refused, even though the Crew represented the only pro sports franchise playing in town at the time.

Steeled by the memories of the NASL, Hunt decided to privately finance the first pro soccer–specific stadium in the country, dedicating $28 million to its construction. On May 15, 1999, after only nine months of work, Crew Stadium, a 22,555-seat facility, opened for business.

"Lamar decided, 'We're going to build the first soccer-specific stadium in Columbus,'" Clark Hunt recalled. "His advisors said, 'Well, that's not a good idea, it probably doesn't make financial sense.' And he said, 'You know what? We're going to do it anyhow.'"

As expected, Lamar didn't simply approve an architect's plans and move on to other matters. "He was very involved in the design and the construction," Crew president and general manager Mark McCullers said. "Lamar's background is in geology, and when they started to build the stadium they unearthed these huge boulders, and he quickly identified them as glacial boulders that had moved down during the last ice age into central Ohio.

"So he saved all these boulders. They were getting ready to throw them all away—but no, no, no, no, he saved all these boulders and placed them around the stadium as part of the landscape design."

Hunt's brainchild in Columbus sparked not only an attendance boom (the Crew led MLS in attendance the first year it opened) but a stadium-building revolution. By the 2010 season, 10 MLS teams were playing in soccer-specific stadiums.

"He didn't take no for an answer after two failed referendums in Columbus," Gulati said. "That stadium gave an extraordinary signal that MLS was here to stay. Investors wouldn't build stadiums if they didn't believe in the league long-term. When he plunked down money for the building, it gave the impetus for the Home Depot Center [in Los Angeles] and other soccer stadiums."

"I was involved in the project in Columbus and was there opening day," said Steinbrecher, who helped guarantee that a number of national games would be played there if Hunt built it. "In true Lamar fashion, the Columbus stadium is the most spartan one in MLS."

Hunt was fanatical about inspecting other stadiums, trying to assess the best aspects to incorporate into his own. Howard recalls riding with him in the back of the U.S. national team fan bus at the 2002 World Cup in Korea and Japan, before Hunt Sports Group bought what was then called the Dallas Burn.

"Lamar had this notepad with him," Howard said. "He went to every single stadium in that tournament to see what it took [to create great soccer stadiums]."

In 2005 FC Dallas—the new name of Hunt's MLS team—opened a new $65 million soccer-specific stadium in Frisco, Texas. Aside from the main pitch, 17 additional fields ring the stadium for high school teams and youth leagues. Unlike in Columbus, Hunt attracted partners in the venture, including the Frisco Independent School District.

Four organizers of the new American Professional Football League get together in Beverly Hills on September 12, 1959, as the league owners opened a two-day meeting. Clockwise from left are: Barron Hilton (Los Angeles), Bud Adams (Houston), Harry Wismer (New York), and Lamar Hunt. Photo courtesy of AP Images.

Representatives of the embryonic American Football League pose in a football-like formation in New York City on Oct. 28, 1959. Posing in the front row, from left, are: Robert L. Howsam (Denver), Max Winter (Minneapolis), Lamar Hunt, and K.S. Adams Jr. (Houston). In the back row, from left, are: Barron Hilton (Los Angeles), Ralph C. Wilson Jr. (Buffalo), and Harry Wismer (New York). Photo courtesy of AP Images.

Lamar stands with his new bride, the former Norma Knobel of Richardson, Texas. After their wedding at Norma's parents' home on January 22, 1964, the couple honeymooned in Austria for the Winter Olympics. Photo courtesy of AP Images.

The Hunt women. From left: Mrs. Lamar (Norma) Hunt, Mrs. H.L. (Ruth) Hunt, Mrs. Herbert (Nancy) Hunt, Mrs. Nelson (Caroline) Hunt, and Mary Hunt (daughter of Nelson and Caroline Hunt). Photo courtesy of AP Images.

Lamar and Norma stand in front of their home in Dallas, Texas, on June 1, 1970. Photo courtesy of AP Images.

Lamar holds a football for his 5-year-old son Clark to kick in the family backyard on June 1, 1970 in Dallas. Behind them are Hunt's children by a former marriage, Lamar Jr. (13) and Sharon (12). His wife, Norma, joins in the fun. Photo courtesy of AP Images.

President of the Dallas Texans Lamar Hunt celebrates with his team after they defeated the Houston Oilers in a 20–17 overtime win in the 1962 AFL Championship Game on December 23, 1962 at Jeppesen Stadium in Houston, Texas. Photo courtesy of AP Images.

Lamar visits the Green Bay Packers' locker room and congratulates Max McGee, right, who scored two touchdowns for the Packers in their 35–10 victory over the Kansas City Chiefs in Super Bowl I on January 15, 1967. Photo courtesy of AP Images.

Lamar poses with Kansas City Chiefs coach Hank Stram, center, and Commissioner Pete Rozelle prior to the Super Bowl in New Orleans on January 11, 1970. Photo courtesy of AP Images.

George Halas, left, Pete Rozelle, and Lamar talk during the annual meeting of the National Football League in Palm Beach, Florida, on March 22, 1971. Photo courtesy of AP Images.

Former Texas Governor John Connally, center, enjoys the sun at the opening ceremonies of the inaugural St. Regis World Junior Invitational Tennis tournament on July 9, 1979, at Forest Hills, New York. Connally is flanked by Lamar on the left and ball boy Steve Nadaka on the right. Photo courtesy of AP Images.

Famous television commentator Howard Cosell sweeps the court while Lamar and World Championship Tennis COO Rod Humphries look on at Cerromar Beach, Puerto Rico, in 1979. Photo courtesy of Russ Adams.

Lamar enjoys a game of pool at a World Championship Tennis party at his Dallas home in 1980. Photo courtesy of Russ Adams.

Lamar is on hand to present Miami Dolphins linebacker John Offerdahl the Old Spice Rookie of the Year Award during the Denver Broncos 23–20 overtime victory over the Cleveland Browns in the 1986 AFC Championship Game on January 11, 1987, at Cleveland Municipal Stadium in Cleveland, Ohio. Photo courtesy of Getty Images.

Lamar Hunt attends Super Bowl XXVIII, a 30–13 Dallas Cowboys victory over the Buffalo Bills on January 30, 1994, at the Georgia Dome in Atlanta, Georgia. Photo courtesy of AP Images.

Lamar Hunt is excited as he talks to the media after NFL commissioner Paul Tagliabue announced that Kansas City, Missouri, was selected to host a Super Bowl. Photo courtesy of AP Images.

Securing a naming-rights sponsor was important to him. For the 21,000-seat stadium in Frisco, he went cold-calling in his 70s. Stopping at Pizza Hut International and getting an unscheduled audience with a top executive, he discussed the growth of soccer, branding opportunities, and other enticements. After an hour, the executive demurred; finally, Lamar said he planned to fly to Chicago and visit Little Caesars.

"Pizza Hut Park sounds a lot nicer than Little Caesars Park," Lamar pointed out.

The executive agreed, and Pizza Hut signed on for a reported $25 million for 20 years.

Even during the excitement of the stadium's inauguration, as usual, Hunt let nothing get past his eye for perfection.

"On the day of the opening of Pizza Hut Park, he was out there picking up paper," Moffat said.

Aside from being appealing to fans—who were closer to the action and who could create a festive atmosphere similar to soccer stadiums world-wide—Hunt's vision helped ensure MLS's survival. Because the league controlled revenues from top to bottom, it controlled its destiny.

But many obstacles had needed to be surmounted before the stadium boom. Investors poured $100 million into the league with no return in its first seasons. For years MLS suffered a dearth of investors, as Hunt, Philip Anschutz, and Robert Kraft bore the load well into the 21st century.

Hunt found particular problems, surprisingly enough, in Kansas City, where one would have thought his success with the Chiefs alone would have helped sell the game of soccer. But in 2000, despite ending up as MLS champions, the Wizards finished with the second-lowest attendance in the league, averaging just over 9,000 fans per game in Arrowhead Stadium. Previous years had been equally grim luring crowds compared to other franchises.

Few items upset Hunt more than poor ticket sales. By 2003 he personally led an effort to attract fans by selling corporate season tickets. He succeeded; the franchise unloaded about 160 for prices as high as $11,500.

Before the season began, the Wizards had also sold more than 6,000 season tickets, shattering its previous mark by almost 50 percent.

Still, Hunt wasn't satisfied. He hoped to break the MLS mark of about 7,300 set by one of the other teams at the time, the Crew. Aside from the appeal of a new soccer-specific stadium, Hunt had launched the Crew Chiefs in Columbus, season-ticket holders who worked to recruit new ones. A similar model had worked with the Kansas City Chiefs.

But Hunt knew attracting people to a soccer stadium wasn't enough.

"I remember we were at a match," Steinbrecher recalled. "People were saying, 'We've got to put butts in the seats.' Lamar said, 'No it's the opposite. We've got to get butts *out* of the seats.' He knew they needed for people to stand up, get excited."

After six seasons, MLS's survival was far from guaranteed. It suffered its lowest regular-season TV ratings ever in 2001, the same year it postponed expansion plans. And it failed again to find new investors.

"Can we have a business that succeeds?" Hunt asked at the time. "Our expenses are still bigger than our revenues. The AFL theoretically came to a faster level of success, but it wasn't dealing in a pioneering effort. I think MLS has made some good progress, but it has a long, long way to go."

Soon after, though, moves were made to help ensure long-term viability. Two teams were contracted before the 2002 season, a painful decision that seemed like a public-relations bomb at the time, but the league was no longer saddled with those money-losing franchises in weak markets. Then Soccer United Marketing was created, which dealt with the World Cup television rights MLS had purchased for 2002 and 2006. New investors appeared, taking pressure off of Hunt Sports Group (which, unable to secure a taxpayer-funded stadium, sold the Wizards to a Kansas City consortium in 2004). Sponsorship, always a bright spot, continued to grow. By the time of Hunt's death, MLS—though no threat to any of the four traditional major sports leagues—also clearly wasn't about to fizzle out.

And Hunt's role in assuring the league's stability is unmatched. "If it wasn't for him, the league wouldn't be in existence today. Period,"

Steinbrecher said. "The theory is, the game inside the white lines is what's important. But it's the owners' relationships with the union, the TV negotiations, the game outside the white lines that's really important. He played that game better than anyone.

"This was a man who had incredible vision but who was a consummate gentleman. If he disagreed, he was never disagreeable. He was such a voice of wisdom."

Gulati recalled how that voice was received at MLS headquarters.

"When he spoke in the boardroom, it was like an E.F. Hutton commercial," Gulati said. "There's no one who's been in the boardroom of MLS with that respect, whether he was talking about finances or about the playoff format. He followed the sport internationally and on the youth level with his sons.

"He looked at things from the big perspective. It was always about longevity—not just if the Hunt family had the resources, but if other partners had the resources too. He wasn't a proponent of the designated-player rule [where players such as David Beckham could be signed], but he knew we had to do that, so he backed it."

Gulati remembered a story that showed Hunt could enliven staid MLS discussions.

"An MLS referee from overseas had tossed a number of players out of games. At a board meeting, someone mentioned that the referee had had the reputation in Scotland as 'the Terminator.' Someone else said that maybe we should find out the backgrounds of referees before they come to MLS.

"Lamar said, 'Maybe we could just find out their nicknames.' He was smiling from ear to ear."

A little-realized ancillary benefit generated by Hunt's devotion to the sport involved youth soccer. In Dallas alone, the city McNutt surmised once housed three soccer balls, the game exploded among the young. United States Youth Soccer Association, based in Frisco, Texas, now counts more than 3 million players after starting with only about 100,000 during the NASL days.

Gulati said, "Lamar, better than anyone, understood the links between connecting youth soccer to the success of the league to getting the World Cup."

Meredith noted, "Kenny Cooper often said if Lamar Hunt had done for sport in England what he had done in the United States, he would have been knighted by the Queen of England."

And in 1999 Hunt's dedication to the sport was honored in heroic fashion. For 85 years, the U.S. Open Cup had been handed to the national soccer champion. Just before the new century, it was renamed the Lamar Hunt U.S. Open Cup.

"The best property the U.S. Soccer Federation has is the Open Cup, other than the national team," said Steinbrecher when asked to assess Hunt's importance to the sport. "It's named the Lamar Hunt U.S. Open Cup for a reason."

It wasn't just Hunt's longtime investment in the game; his zeal as a fan also played a part. Steinbrecher shared a story that is vintage Lamar. He recounted, "For the French World Cup, I got a phone call from Lamar. He said, 'I have some personal tickets. I can't use them. Make sure you put them to good use.

"I'm thinking, *Hot dog. Since these are Lamar's personal seats, maybe we can get a sponsor [out of it].* I get the tickets. They are Category 3, some of the worst seats in the house. What he preferred was being with people, sitting with the crowd."

For an issue of a national soccer magazine, Meredith said, Hunt was asked to come up with his favorite soccer moment. Instead of one, he filed 10. Each reveals his passion for the sport in a different way. Many show his true nature as a fan—meeting Pelé with Norma and Clark, watching the excitement of French fans in the Champs Elysees after France won the 1998 World Cup. Others indicate his love of stadiums—the opening of the one in Columbus and those he toured in Korea and Japan. And, as always, he expressed his joy of counting the house—one of his most memorable experiences occurred when the MLS Cup drew 56,000 in

RFK Stadium the same day the Washington Redskins were playing only seven miles away.

By 2002, after seeing the last World Cup he would attend in Korea and Japan, Hunt had been involved in pro soccer for 35 years. Despite many setbacks, he remained optimistic, echoing in a way William Faulkner's Nobel Prize acceptance speech more than a half century earlier; soccer would not merely endure, it would prevail.

"I have no doubts that it will be a major sport in the United States," Hunt said. "I'm probably not going to live to see that day because Americans are a little afraid of getting interested in something at which they're not very good…. But I have no question that we're going to see the sport become a major success in the United States."

During his lifetime, Hunt did see major success and stunning transformation in another sport. Yes, his name is emblazoned on the historic U.S. Open Cup in soccer; but in tennis, the term U.S. Open didn't even exist until Hunt took a swing at the centuries-old game.

CHAPTER 6

OPEN MIND

IF THERE WERE A PROFESSIONAL SPORT in the United States in the mid-1960s that drew more yawns and less respect than soccer, it was tennis. And of all of Hunt's big sports ventures, none would engender stronger opposition than his embrace of the pro game. Even the NFL's blows against his upstart entity looked Lilliputian in comparison—at least Hunt struck a deal with the established league after six years of battle. The entire world of tennis, from Australia to England to Europe to his own country, fought to block his desires—not just at the outset, but for decades.

The sport can be traced back many centuries to Europe, when it was played by monks (with their hand in lieu of a racquet) and eventually by kings of France in their courtyards. That game—called real tennis, royal tennis, or court tennis (depending on the country) and featuring hand-sewn balls and a low-slung net—is still played by a dedicated band, but it's a small group compared to the lawn-tennis version that sprang up in the 1800s. Soon after tennis developed on grass, three of the Grand Slam tournaments—Wimbledon, the U.S. Open, and the French Open—were born; the latecomer, the Australian Open, arrived in 1905.

As the years passed—and airplanes were invented, atom bombs exploded, and satellites were thrust into the sky—tennis' traditions barely budged. In the major tournaments, white players donned white attire and struck white balls. And they always played as amateurs. When Big Bill

Tilden, the best player of the 1920s, was paid to write newspaper articles, the United States Lawn Tennis Association quickly banned the practice among its athletes. Paying players in any manner, opined the pooh-bahs, sullied the sport.

Attempts were made to start professional tours, the first by C.C. Pyle (around the same time he tried to take on the NFL with a rival football league. Perhaps he was an early version of Lamar Hunt). In 1926, his players barnstormed the U.S. and drew good crowds, but he abandoned the idea the next year. It wasn't until Jack Kramer turned pro after winning the 1947 U.S. championships and started his own tour that the non-amateur game slowly started to gain attention. At one point that year, Kramer's entourage attracted more than 15,000 to Madison Square Garden during a blizzard.

The idea of open play began to pick up ground. In 1959 Wimbledon chairman Herman David proposed to the International Lawn Tennis Federation (ILTF)—the governing body of tennis around the world—that Wimbledon should allow professionals to compete. The following year, the ILTF rejected the proposal.

As the 1960s moved forward, the pros remained a minor-league operation; the power lay with the amateurs and their governing bodies, such as the ILTF.

"The state of pro tennis was a mess," said Mike Davies, at one time the No. 1–ranked player in Great Britain, who today is president and CEO of Pilot Pen Tennis. "The International Tennis Association made all the rules and decided what was amateur and what was professional."

When Davies turned pro in 1960, the former Wimbledon doubles champion was stunned by the drop-off in his accommodations during his first match in Marseilles.

"We were shown to a room to change clothes. A storeroom. I couldn't believe it. I turned around to Trabe [Tony Trabert]. 'Where's the dressing room? Where are the coat hangers? He looked at me blankly. He went into his bag, took out a hammer and a nail, smacked it into the wall, and hung his coat on it.

"He shook his head like I was a dummy. 'You're not an amateur anymore. You're a pro now. You carry your dressing room with you.'"

It seemed like an upside-down world. The pros—Rod Laver, Ken Rosewall, Pancho Gonzales, and others—were the best players, but they were shut out of the top tournaments. One would think they'd make more money than amateurs, who theoretically weren't earning a dime. But in fact, many amateurs were paid thousands of dollars annually under the table. Meanwhile, the pros' biggest tournament payday as late as 1966 consisted of a $15,000 pot at the Longwood Cricket Club in Boston.

While the Kramer Tour puttered along, a man named David Dixon in New Orleans—the same one who had tried to lure Lamar Hunt's Texans to the bayou—believed another pro tennis circuit could succeed. In 1967 he created World Championship Tennis (WCT). In August of that year, he met with Hunt at the Ambassador East Hotel in Los Angeles and introduced his idea of showcasing pro tennis. Hunt returned to Dallas and shared Dixon's thoughts with his brother-in-law Al Hill Sr. and his nephew Al Hill Jr., who had starred in tennis at Trinity University in San Antonio. All embraced the concept and agreed to invest.

"Most people in the tennis world had never heard of him [Hunt]," said Bud Collins, a longtime NBC tennis announcer who has written a number of books about tennis. "But when I saw [David] Dixon had him as a partner, I was so pleased inside. It meant it wouldn't be a flop."

Hunt had watched his first tennis matches in the late 1950s—which featured pros such as Ken Rosewall and Pancho Gonzales—at SMU's Perkins Gymnasium, where a canvas court covered the basketball floor. His next vivid memory of the sport occurred at the Dallas Country Club, which was hosting a made-for-TV tennis special. Far from being in the crowd, Hunt strolled about the golf course, where his unexpected marksmanship caused a stir.

"The tee to the 14th green was situated beside the makeshift tennis stadium," Hunt wrote. "When my wild iron shot hit the green and rolled in for a hole-in-one, the noise caused by the merriment of our foursome was loud enough to cause a brief disruption in the tennis."

Many aspects of pro tennis appealed to the businessman in Hunt. He did not need to buy a franchise and be weighed by worries about its expenses and win-loss record. Tennis players had rarely earned living wages, so they could be paid modestly. He also saw a unique opportunity in an overlooked brand.

"I think he saw the chance to change the face of the sport," said Rod Humphries, a *Sydney Morning Herald* sports columnist who covered tennis at the time and who eventually became the chief operating officer of WCT. "He knew they were the best players playing in the worst conditions."

But just like in soccer, Hunt's timing was off. George MacCall, a U.S. Davis Cup captain, also decided to organize a pro tennis tour the same year. It would start in earnest in 1968, just as WCT had planned.

At the beginning of that year, WCT signed Australia's John Newcombe, 23, and Tony Roche, 22, to two of the biggest contracts in pro tennis history. Newcombe and Roche would receive more than $100,000 in guaranteed money each year and compete for more than $1 million in prize money in 1968. Joining six other WCT hires—Nikola Pilić of Yugoslavia, Butch Buchholz and Dennis Ralston of the United States, Pierre Barthes of France, Cliff Drysdale of South Africa, and Roger Taylor of Great Britain—the group would be dubbed, in a master stroke of marketing, the Handsome Eight (or, as some joked, the Handsome Seven and Tony Roche).

The players were thrilled. And why not? Newcombe, the 1967 Wimbledon champion, later said he made $15,000 as the No. 1 amateur that year—in 1968, he earned $55,000 with WCT.

In early February—after a stop in Sydney, where the court was set up in a television station's parking lot and temporary scaffolding housed the crowd—World Championship Tennis launched in the United States in Kansas City, home of Hunt's Chiefs. The problem was, the Municipal Auditorium downtown was booked with a sportsman and boat show.

Writing for *Sports Illustrated*, Frank Deford depicted the grim scene at little-regarded American Royal Arena: "It was a dark and forbidding haunted house of a building, its shabby doors fastened shut with twine. Pigeons flapped through the rafters, fleeing, perhaps, from the tart odors that an ill wind blew over from the slaughterhouse next door. With all America to choose from, professional tennis had managed to open its newest tour and its quest for a sharp, modern image in a primitive animal exhibition hall in the stockyards of Kansas City, MO."

That was the least of the players' problems. Buchholz—a former Davis Cup player who once competed on the Kramer Tour—recalled the danger of playing on the Astroturf green court that didn't fully cover an ice rink.

"Dennis Ralston ran for a ball and hit the ice, and the racqet went one way and he went the other," Buchholz said. "He hit the linesman's chair, and the linesman went one way and Ralston went the other."

At Hunt's invitation, Collins attended the Kansas City opener.

"Ralston nearly killed himself in that fall," Collins recalled. "He went into one of the stalls afterward, slammed the door, and it fell off. These guys were disgruntled; they found out life wasn't all like Wimbledon."

In Kansas City, fewer than 5,000 people total watched WCT that weekend, including 387 on a Friday afternoon. In comparison, a high school basketball game in town that evening attracted 2,500. And the event at Municipal Auditorium? More than 12,000 showed up that Friday.

Of course Hunt, ever with an eye toward entertainment and pleasing the fans (especially in Kansas City), made sure the tiny crowd enjoyed itself by implementing some of Dixon's innovations. Dancers took to the court and belted out songs like "Serving You My Love" and "Do the Serve." Fans were encouraged to cheer during points; some won cologne or perfume if "their" player prevailed.

Entertaining as well were the players' clothes. Dixon jettisoned all-white attire to liven up the look on the court (and because it would appear better on television); Newcombe played his first pro match in a green shirt and brown shorts provided by Sears.

"We were all pretty frustrated wearing color clothes," Buchholz said. "They didn't fit. Pierre Barthes [of France] would come in saying, "I look like a cloon, I look like a cloon [clown]." Regardless, fines were soon implemented for those who refused to wear color clothes, ranging from $50 to $100.

After the Kansas City debacle, World Championship Tennis marched on. In St. Louis, an 18,000-seat arena sat nearly empty for three days of tournament play. WCT lost $30,000.

Buchholz recalled the next stops. "We were going to play in Shreveport, and the court didn't show up. They made more from insurance off of that than they would have from the gate. In Miami, the ceiling was too low, and lobs would hit it. I ended up winning the tournament there because players couldn't lob.

"Dave Dixon and the eight of us got together in a hotel room. We said, 'Dave, you need to bring tennis people in here.' It was pretty clear this thing got off to a shaky start."

By March, disarray—and debt—were rampant. Already, losses exceeded $100,000.

Davies soon attended a summit meeting with Dixon, Hunt, Hill, and the eight players at Hill's house in Dallas. "The question was: Should they close the company down or would Lamar listen to the potential and take over the responsibility?" Davies recalled.

A number of changes were crafted. Dixon was out as president and left the tour, replaced by Al Hill Jr. Davies—filling the role as the tennis person the players requested—came aboard to handle sponsorships, ticket sales, and marketing; he would soon become WCT's executive director. Hunt took over Dixon's 50 percent stake, and he and Hill now owned the fledgling circuit, whose headquarters would move to Dallas.

Hunt stayed optimistic. "I put a five-year timetable on soccer," he said, "but I think tennis can do it in three."

Always honest about past misjudgments, Hunt talked about WCT's bad start. "Probably the gravest error we made was trying to do too much in too short a time," he explained. "The concept was two tournaments a week for 40 weeks. That was demanding not only on the players but also on the staff needed to set it up.

"We made mistake on top of mistake. We had it figured out where we could net $17,000 a week, but we never came close. We were just doing everything wrong."

Yet the fact they were doing anything at all scared the rulers of amateur tennis. With Hunt's group having locked up eight of the world's best players and MacCall grabbing a few others (including Rod Laver, a Grand Slam winner, for $500,000), Wimbledon announced, for the first time in its history, it would be an open tournament in 1968. Since Hunt had grabbed its 1967 champion, Newcombe, and two of its semifinalists, the venerable All-England Club's hand had been forced. The ILTF also faced what seemed to be a no-win choice. If it stuck with tradition and demanded amateur-only tournaments worldwide, gates would sink. Inviting pros would enrage purists and risk ILTF losing control of the sport.

In a unanimous vote in Paris in late March, the ILTF agreed to open a limited number of tournaments to professionals, including Grand Slam ones that year, following Wimbledon's lead. That vote completely reversed its rejection of the concept a year earlier, when more than 130 votes were cast against open tennis. (At the same time, the governing body offered a new definition of a "registered" player who would be controlled by national associations and thus eligible for the Davis Cup, which set the stage for later problems with WCT.)

Humphries discussed Hunt's role in the unprecedented decisions by Wimbledon and the ILTF, which overturned nearly a century of tennis tradition.

"He forced tennis to go open in 1968," Humphries said. "The amateur game had traditionally lost only one player at a time when it was plundered by the pro ranks. Now Hunt was skimming a number of amateurs in one fell swoop. There was really nobody left to sell a major international event, and Wimbledon and the other national associations had no real choice but to open up the game.

"He certainly sensed the winds of change swirling around the sport and knew his move would have a dramatic effect on the future of the game. It might be said that he delivered the coup de grâce."

Collins added, "The fact that Dixon brought Lamar in, and then WCT signing the Handsome Eight, moved the world toward open tennis. It was Hunt's money that got the Handsome Eight players who were amateurs to turn pro."

Aside from his crucial financial backing, at the outset of WCT Hunt's day-to-day role (officially, his title was vice president after buying Dixon's stake) was minimal. He was still trying to get soccer off the ground and, of course, remained focused on his beloved Chiefs.

"He didn't know as much about tennis at that time," Davies recalled. "He didn't know the people, the politics involved. Lamar started to realize the politics were pretty big. For instance, we'd say to Wimbledon, when it went open, 'If you want our players, you have to pay us, since we have to pay the players.' They balked at that. We did let them play in 1968, but after that, we said we needed to get compensated.

"There was a lot of tension, bad feelings, threats of lawsuits. He had to get involved in the politics of all that."

As the year progressed—and the money spent on WCT television commercials in each town was not buttressing attendance—some wondered why Hunt's World Championship Tennis and MacCall's National Tennis League (NTL) continued to try to make it on their own. As Hunt was well familiar in pro football and pro soccer, when two rival leagues are bleeding money in a fight, a merger is the sensible course. Instead, they continued to operate on different schedules, one playing at Madison Square Garden while the other toured elsewhere.

"Lamar Hunt's group will not produce enough gate revenue to pay off its players, and in effect his tour is being personally subsidized by Hunt," Eugene L. Scott—who eventually founded *Tennis Week* magazine—wrote for the *New York Times*. "Hunt is a deeper pocket than MacCall, and the idea must certainly soon occur to MacCall and his backers that there may be no great return on their initial investment."

WCT survived its first season, despite a loss of $300,000. But more battles loomed for Hunt. As 1969 arrived, there was no guarantee the two circuits would play in open tournaments sanctioned by the United States Lawn Tennis Association. The reason: disputes with the ILTF, which still didn't allow pros under contract to play for the Davis Cup. In February an agreement was signed—for that year only—saying both WCT and NTL players would compete in four opens, including the U.S. Open in Forest Hills.

Bob Briner, the WCT's executive director, said, "This is a truce, not a peace pact, because the International Lawn Tennis Federation still discriminates against our players."

One player at the time was wooed by both groups: Arthur Ashe. Winner of the first U.S. Open in 1968, the rising star was offered $400,000 over five years by MacCall. Ashe demurred, saying he had just gotten out of the U.S. Army and wanted his freedom.

In midsummer, the National Tennis League made a splash, announcing the largest purse in tennis history. To begin in 1970, a tournament called the Tennis Champions $200,000 Classic would last 13 weekends, and a player could earn almost $150,000. Aside from its six touring pros, NTL hoped to lure Newcombe and a few others from WCT to play.

But before that arrived, players competed for the richest purse ever ($137,000) at the 1969 U.S. Open. Attendance soared past 100,000 at the tournament, directed by newly hired South African Owen Williams, who later would run WCT.

The next month, WCT's Briner resigned to take a position as president of Tennis International Inc. He described the chance of a WCT and NTL merger as "very remote...there is a different philosophy now emerging in each group."

One big difference was profit. Reports said Hunt's WCT had broken even in 1969 after its horrendous debut the year before; the NTL still struggled.

By the next summer, George MacCall threw in the towel. Hunt acquired the contracts of six top pros—including Laver and Gonzales—from NTL to significantly expand WCT's influence. Hunt's WCT had survived the war with NTL, poor initial management, and the stifling blockades of international tennis groups to emerge in its strongest position yet.

WCT even endured players such as Buchholz taking on multiple roles that would be unthinkable today.

"In St. Louis one year I was like the tournament director. I sold a sponsorship, I played, I did the scheduling, and I was a referee," said Buchholz, who lived in the Midwestern city. "It was an unusual situation."

With his biggest rival vanquished, Hunt moved to cement WCT's influence. He signed Ashe in a $1.5 million deal and picked up two others as well—Bob Lutz and Charles Pasarell—giving him 27 players. Further, it strengthened him in the seemingly endless battle with the International Lawn Tennis Association, whose convoluted rules on what constituted a pro versus an amateur still generated confusion and anger.

After WCT bought the flailing MacCall group, Davies soon proposed to Hunt the idea of 20 tourneys for a $1 million purse—$50,000 per tournament—with the best ending up in Dallas for the finals. With an expected launch in 1971, it was dubbed the Million Dollar Tour.

"Lamar loved the idea. He could see it was like the Super Bowl," Davies said.

Skeptics weren't as sure. The *New York Times*' tennis guru, Neil Amdur, asked, "Does World Championship Tennis, despite the huge Lamar Hunt fortune, have the logistical manpower to operate effectively an elaborate 20-city, $1 million tour and make money doing it? Has the company overextended itself with large contractual payments to top players?"

The naysayers didn't move Hunt. Pouncey—who covered tennis as well as soccer for the *Dallas Morning News* in the 1970s—remembered Hunt made sure the inaugural event received blanket coverage.

"He was so adamant about getting good publicity. In Philadelphia he got some press people to fly up to watch the first serve of the first game of the first day of the Million Dollar Tour," Pouncey recalled.

Hunt's passion for promotion and for entertainment—he often said he was bitten by a show-business bug—would flourish during the annual Finals in Dallas.

During the first event in November 1971, Hunt introduced festivities designed to entertain people each day and to imbue the finals with a touch of class. A Tuesday black-tie dinner at the Fairmont Hotel featured Charlton Heston as a guest speaker. A turkey dinner at Hunt's house took place Wednesday, the day before Thanksgiving. On the morning of the Friday final between Ken Rosewall and Rod Laver—watched in person by 8,200, including astronaut Neil Armstrong and Miss Texas—a champagne brunch was served. Inside Memorial Auditorium, a color guard appeared and flags of the players' nations were displayed.

"All this was new to tennis. He wanted the pomp and circumstance to create the drama for the event," Davies said. "What Lamar was so good at was he understood the breadth and scope of professional sports, that it was an entertainment industry. Lamar was very big on the show-business side."

As Pouncey recalled, Hunt spared no expense in generating publicity worldwide for the finals.

"They got all of the top tennis writers from Europe and flew them in for the gala and tournament," he recalled. "All the society people from Highland Park [Texas] would be there. It was covered in the sports section and in the society section."

Buchholz—one of the players given a Cadillac for the week with his name embossed on the door with the WCT logo, courtesy of Hunt—said the WCT Finals "was the biggest thing other than a Slam. It helped the boom in tennis. It was fabulous."

Every year, Hunt treated the Dallas event like his own personal Super Bowl. He was deeply involved in its particulars.

"Lamar would go every day to the court before the doors would open," Pouncey said. "He'd check the flower arrangements, the personal seating. He would be in the hospitality rooms, making sure everything was delivered. No detail was too small. He never felt any of that was beneath him."

"I remember Lamar going up to the ball boys," Davies recalled. "He told them their toes had to be toeing the line, not two inches in front of it. He was a stickler for details."

That first year for the WCT Finals, tickets were $75 per box for the six-seat Silver Boxes at courtside and $90 per box for nine-seat Loge Boxes. Nearly three weeks before the finals, all box seats were sold out.

Instead of an anonymous referee, tennis star Tony Trabert made the calls. The *Dallas Morning News* and the Dallas Chamber of Commerce sponsored the event. In just under three hours, Rosewall prevailed 6–4, 1–6, 7–6, 7–6. Laver hurt himself with 10 double faults.

The event was broadcast to a few other countries, a boon for WCT, which again was embroiled in arguments with the ILTF. Despite the obvious success of pro tennis, the governing body didn't stop playing hardball with Hunt. Not until December 1970 was a deal reached between ILTA and WCT so its 32 pros would play at Wimbledon, Forest Hills, and the French Open in 1971. Even when Hunt's players performed at Wimbledon that year, it was reported that Herman David, chairman of the All-England Club, treated Hunt poorly, pointing at him and saying something to the effect of, "This man will not tell us how to run tennis."

Hunt summed up the resistance to his venture.

"Tennis was basically controlled by lily-white European federations," he said. "They had the mentality of the 1920s that it wasn't proper for anyone to profit from tennis. Then we came along and formed World Championship Tennis, organized a professional tour, and started paying players on a contract basis to appear at our games. The powers that be in tennis threw up their hands and said, 'We've got to stop these infidels, these revolutionaries.'"

Soon enough the infidels were again shut out. The worldwide governing body placed a ban on WCT's players in open tournaments starting January 1, 1972.

Why? The group claimed Hunt demanded too much of the gate at Wimbledon as well as other revenue streams (including catering). What probably upset the hidebound ILTF most of all was Hunt wanted his players to don colored shirts. Hunt countered their accusations of money-grubbing by pointing out he was using "up-to-date business methods" and said he only had asked that airfares be paid.

Frustrated by the ILTF's stubbornness about not letting WCT players (including defending champion Newcombe) compete in Wimbledon in 1972, Hunt fought back. WCT lured ILTF's Cliff Richey, its No. 2 player, away as another volley in the growing war. In March, Hunt announced WCT would hold a $50,000 tournament in St. Louis at the same time as Wimbledon.

Al Hill Jr. said, "It wouldn't make any difference now if the ILTF changed its mind. Let's face it. What are our fellows supposed to do, sit around two weeks during Wimbledon and not make any money?"

The Holton Tennis Classic at Dwight Davis Tennis Center in St. Louis took place during the first week of Wimbledon in 1972. Rick Holton, whose father sponsored WCT's St. Louis event for three years through Citizens National Bank, remembered the elegant scene.

"We did everything with geraniums and green bunting and waiters with white gloves serving mint juleps," said Holton, who saw Hunt each year when he would stay over at his parents' house during tournament time. "The first year we had worked with WCT [1970] was very rudimentary. We put players up in people's homes. Dad and Mom had a tennis court at the home, and Newcombe and [Cliff] Drysdale were there drinking beer and playing tennis. Lamar would hang around the pool with the guys."

The same week Hunt announced competition with Wimbledon, WCT filed suit against the USLTA, seeking more than $72,000 for the organization's alleged failure to pay WCT for providing players for the

U.S. Open in 1971 and 1972. WCT claimed it had not been paid enough for 1971's efforts and, since USLTA had banned its players from the 1972 tourney, would not receive the more than $50,000 due from that event.

After a number of meetings in Europe that winter yielded nothing, a breakthrough occurred when WCT suggested it would limit its schedule to a four-month period. The final settlement mandated that WCT tournaments would invite 64 players and run henceforth from January through April, with May playoffs in Dallas. Then, those same players would enter ILTF Grand Prix events—and they could even compete (finally) in the Davis Cup. WCT would also stop signing pro players to contracts and would honor the ones they had struck until they expired, meaning long-term security was cast aside for the players.

As always, Hunt stayed imperturbable despite the hard work needed to achieve what, in retrospect, so obviously benefited tennis.

"I do remember us meeting the ITF president in London," Davies said. "We got there in the morning after an overnight flight. There was no heat in his offices. There we were freezing with our overcoats and gloves on. Lamar would laugh. He took it all in great spirit.

"The politics of tennis is so convoluted," Davies said. "Without Lamar's influence in the game—running the private organization WCT—you might very well still have tennis run by the International Lawn Tennis Federation."

Added Collins, "The ITF didn't want him around despite the obvious improvement for the game. They wanted to see him fail. Lamar was very patient."

Hunt's incessant battles with international tennis honchos were briefly forgotten when good news arrived on the television front. He had struck a deal with NBC to broadcast eight WCT Million Dollar Tour matches live, starting in Toronto in February and culminating with a championship event in May in Dallas in 1972. Outside of Forest Hills and Wimbledon, tennis matches had not received live national broadcast exposure.

Davies recalled that the deal almost fell apart and only survived because of Hunt.

"We wanted eight tournaments, and NBC said they would if we could sell $1 million in sponsorships," Davies said. "We were disappointed, but we went to work getting them. We decided we could put a refrigerator on the court [to promote a refrigerator company] and said Wilson balls had to be kept at a certain temperature. We worked like hell and came up with the million dollars.

"NBC was surprised—they said they had made other plans. I told Lamar that this was really rotten. He called the head of NBC and said, 'This isn't right.' We got on. The end result was Lamar had muscle there. He knew all the sports entities on TV because of football."

The importance of the NBC deal to WTC could not be underestimated. It gave the group substantial name recognition, respectability among the masses, and weekly publicity during the deadest sports period of the year. And the TV pact would pay off royally its first year.

Leading up to the finals in Dallas, known as the World Championship of Tennis, Hunt again pulled out all the stops. A poolside dinner at his estate kicked off festivities on Tuesday night. As the *Dallas Morning News* breathlessly reported in its *Party Line* column, many of the men "sported their natty white WCT club blazers" (for those who sold at least $400 in tickets) while Norma Hunt was "picture pretty, per usual."

On May 14, 1972, Rosewall and Laver—the same two players who had faced off in the first WCT Finals—were opponents again. The match was played in SMU's Moody Coliseum this time, rather than Memorial Auditorium, and SMU alumni were hired as usherettes, bedecked in cowboy boots and short skirts. The back-and-forth battle was unforgettable, particularly the fifth set. Laver saved one match point, down 4–5 in games, by serving an ace. The 12-point tie-breaker (a WCT invention) was deadlocked 5–5. Finally, Rosewall captured the last two points and prevailed 4–6, 6–0, 6–3, 6–7, 7–6 after three hours and 34 minutes. Nearly 8,000 fans cheered; more than 25,000 passed through the turnstiles over four days.

Those spectators were surely important. But of far more significance was the fact that the lengthy finals match exceeded its time parameters (like an NFL overtime playoff game) and spilled over into NBC's primetime programming, which the network postponed in favor of tennis. More than 21 million—the biggest tennis audience to that point—watched Rosewall capture the $50,000 prize.

That epic match helped spark the 1970s tennis boom in the U.S.

"I think you could compare it with the 1958 Giants sudden-death overtime game that ignited the explosion of pro football," Hunt recalled.

Buchholz said, "The tennis boom—indoor courts being built—it was being on television. Lamar and Mike brought tennis to millions of people through television."

In its fifth season, WCT already wielded quite a bit of influence. Its freedom to create rules and events as it pleased, even in the face of opposition, were crucial to its popularity.

"We were able to do things because we didn't have committees, the ATPs, or the Grand Slams to go through," Davies said. "We didn't have to consult with them to make tennis into a professional sport.

"I changed the color of the tennis ball [from white to orange to yellow]. I didn't have to consult with anyone."

Despite its success, the battles were far from over. In September, another tennis war looked likely, as the Association of Tennis Professionals (ATP) was launched by the players and led by Jack Kramer. The former great had started the Grand Prix tour, which eventually earned the ILTF's blessing in 1969.

At the start, though, the ATP worked within WCT's framework.

"We have no quarrel with WCT, since it provides the services to the players we want to see provided," said ATP president Cliff Drysdale. "Almost everything we know, they taught us. WCT started the rise in popularity in tennis because they professionalized it."

As 1973 dawned, WCT was in solid shape. It boasted 64 players—just about everyone of note save U.S. Open champion Ilie Nastase—who would perform in tournaments around the world. Its finals in Dallas featured two new players, Ashe and Stan Smith—the first time two American tennis players had competed in a major finals match in a generation—and a new day and time for the event, Sunday at noon. The finals were sold out more than a week in advance, and the entire event drew a record 37,260 over five sessions. Even with $100,000 in prize money and parties galore, the seven-day final event in Dallas made money for WCT. Not only that, a new line of WCT clothes was being created, and plans had begun to sell WCT tennis supplies in Europe.

As the 1970s progressed, a number of players—Jimmy Connors, Bjorn Borg, John McEnroe, and others—captured the American imagination and brought tennis' popularity to new heights. The bad-boy antics of Connors and McEnroe, especially, captivated youth while drawing the scorn of tennis elders. But WCT faced problems with one of the rising stars. In early 1977, Borg—the defending WCT champion who said his people had signed him up for WCT but that he personally had not signed—announced he would play for the Grand Prix circuit instead. Within days, WCT slapped Borg, his agents, and Grand Prix sponsors with a $5.7 million lawsuit alleging breach of contract, misrepresentation, and contract interference.

But the bigger news occurred later. After years of battling Grand Prix, WCT joined the circuit. The Dallas group agreed to contribute eight of 28 events to the 1978 Grand Prix. The pact, announced in Paris in March, talked of a $10 million supercircuit. WCT was required to drop its contracts with players such as Connors after they expired. The big upside meant all top players would compete against each other in every tournament, player rankings would be unified, and fans would better understand what was going on in the sport.

Hunt was enthused.

"I feel professional tennis now will enter a period of steadily increasing popularity just as we saw happen for years after the merger in American football," Hunt said.

World Championship Tennis became involved with the building of Reunion Arena in Hunt's hometown, which opened in 1980, providing a showcase home for its finals (and for the NBA's Dallas Mavericks). Humphries—WCT's director of public relations at the time, who became tournament director of the finals—traveled with Hunt to the Summit in Houston to figure out what features may be worth adopting for the new arena.

"He wanted to get a feel for the media setup," Humphries recalled. "We stood at the center of the Summit, and he asked me where I would like to have the media sit in the new arena. Not thinking I had a chance, I told him I would like the entire section right behind the court. It was a prime area for high-priced corporate boxes. He did not hesitate. 'It's done,' he said.

"Then he started thinking about what kind of press seats we would build. I told him we ought to have small television monitors at every seat and audio from the floor so that the writers would not miss a replay or a word from the players, especially McEnroe and Connors. Done again. Goodness knows what it would cost, but it didn't matter to Lamar. Promoters and tournament directors before had always taken the press for granted."

WCT was Reunion Arena's first tenant, and on April 28, 1980, the WCT Finals tournament inaugurated the 17,000-seat, $25 million stadium, which featured the most expensive scoreboard in the country. Aside from their fantastic vantage point on the court, the 300-plus media representatives from around the world also enjoyed a hospitality suite nearby and a media/celebrity tennis tournament during their week in Dallas.

That was the first WCT Finals that featured a "Reunion Stars" event, a gathering of tournament greats of yesteryear that helped give birth to the idea of older pros touring. WCT used to ask beaten semifinalists to face off on Saturday afternoons, but the idea was not popular among players or fans.

"He [Hunt] was searching for a meaningful event to fill out the week. He could not stand the fact that there was a hole in his presentation," Humphries said.

Hunt enthusiastically backed the Reunion Stars event. He offered $50,000 in prize money and lured Laver, Rosewall, Newcombe, and Emerson to face off in the first matches.

"It put people in the seats on Saturday," said Humphries (in fact, that 1980 tournament drew a record 117,465 for the week). "Lamar was pleased."

Hunt's involvement in the details always reached a peak during the WCT Finals, and Humphries had learned firsthand of his boss' meticulous nature during their trip to Houston. He received an itinerary explaining the taxi ride from the airport to the Summit would take 14 minutes—yet the return would run three minutes longer because of traffic.

"Then we'd get to the airport on the way back, and he'd say, 'Do you have a dollar for a hot dog?'" laughed Humphries. "Here's one of the richest men in the world, and he needs a dollar for a hot dog!"

During the matches, players were introduced to music Hunt had helped pick out, and he decided where the trophy would be displayed. The black-tie WCT gala the night before the tournament featured a professional audio-visual show of all the tour events leading to the finals in Dallas. The presentation of the Gold Ball Trophy (a 24-carat tennis ball valued at $10,000) for the WCT points winner was carried by two women wearing gold dresses to the tune of "Goldfinger"; Hunt picked out the trophy and its presentation. Before the event, he would read all the introductions to make sure they were just right and would sit with a stopwatch timing submitted speeches.

"He wanted the WCT Finals to be slick and professional without a touch of boredom," Humphries said. "He choreographed everything."

Though Humphries considered himself one of Hunt's favorite sons—"I got away with murder"—in one instance he was dressed down in Hunt's quiet yet stern way after a WCT Finals at Reunion Arena.

Yannick Noah dropped out of the draw at the last minute due to an injured shoulder, and tournament director Humphries scrambled to fill his place. Finally, he persuaded Sammy Giammalva—considered the 16th-best WCT player in a tourney showcasing the top eight players—to head from Houston to Dallas to play that night.

John McEnroe soon stormed in to see Humphries. He demanded a redraw, according to Humphries, since he wanted to play Giammalva.

"He's screaming," Humphries recalled. "I said, 'John, it's a rule'—I made that up on the spot—and I said, 'At this late stage I can't redraw. Anyway, the match is in an hour. Are you ready to play?' He said no and walked out. That night I had the rule printed in the book—a graphics guy from the Hunt Oil company pulled all the strings to get it done overnight—and I showed it to McEnroe the next day.

"At the staff meeting at the end of the tournament I told Lamar the McEnroe story. I didn't expect this, but he dressed me down. He said, 'That's not the way we do business anywhere in my company.' To him that was an infringement on his integrity too. He wouldn't do anything untoward."

Hunt once told an interviewer if he could come back in another life, he would be a gardener. He always enjoyed placing flowers by the court for the WCT Finals. Ironically enough, that was the sole time one of his closer associates, Thom Meredith—who spent 30 years on and off with Hunt—heard him raise his voice. It was at Reunion Arena in the early 1980s.

"Lamar was moving plants in the stadium," Meredith said. "Then someone moved plants that he had already moved. He turned around and said, not so loudly, 'What the hell?' A couple of us stopped and said, 'Did we just hear that?'"

But as long as no one was moving his flowers, Hunt always had fun—and poked fun—during the WCT Finals. Humphries recalled, "I'm sitting in the official box at WCT with Lamar and [Nelson] Bunker. Lamar said, 'Nelson's the guy who has racehorses in France. He doesn't do very well. They put on some races with just Nelson's horses so he can win.'"

Though Reunion Arena became a nice home for WCT, the group's marriage with the Grand Prix tour was faltering. By 1981 WCT had pulled out and was making plans to go on its own again. Hunt hoped to bury the Grand Prix with his deep pockets. WCT tournaments would offer purses of $300,000—rather than the $175,000 standard at the time—and a year-end final would boast a pot of $1.3 million by 1982.

"The reality is professional tennis is part of the entertainment business," Hunt said. "Players will go where they can make the most money."

Around this time, WCT was considered the largest promoter of pro tennis anywhere. It featured its own television network, which distributed tennis highlights across the country and overseas. ESPN had signed on to broadcast 13 events, including the WCT Final, which moved to Monday night. WCT had built the Lakeway World of Tennis Resort outside of Austin, and Fila manufactured WCT clothes and racquets. The organization created a player-management division, WCT Pro Management. Hunt contended tennis' ruling body, which backed Grand Prix, wanted him to disband the player-management arm, which was one reason he decided to go on his own again.

Soon after WCT abandoned Grand Prix, Mike Davies resigned his post as executive director. After being turned down on the phone, Hunt flew to Johannesburg, South Africa, to court Owen Williams, a tennis management veteran who had jump-started attendance when the U.S. Open began.

"I knew him as a decent fellow," said Williams, who was given the title of chief executive officer and handed a budget of $23 million a year. "I saw him as a very good partner." Hunt purchased Williams' South African businesses and brought him to Dallas.

Williams had expected that by joining WCT, the ruling bodies of tennis would mitigate their antipathy toward Hunt.

"I thought that my popularity with this group—we hunted, fished, did everything together—would soften their thoughts toward him," he recalled. "The opposite occurred. They thought Williams plus Hunt meant more [and was more dangerous] than just Hunt."

In fact, Hunt's decision to leave the Grand Prix ignited yet another tennis war. With the Texas tycoon promising a 22-event tour worth nearly $8 million, the Men's International Professional Tennis Council (MIPTC)—a mid-1970s creation of the ITF, ATP, and various tournament directors (including WCT's Williams), which fashioned itself as the men's ruling body—imposed a rule designed to make sure players did not ignore the lesser-paying Grand Prix tour. Pros were forced to agree to a 10-tournament minimum commitment to Grand Prix. (That measure was soon shown to be a bit of a folly. Borg—a five-time Wimbledon champion—only played seven Grand Prix events in 1982 and thus was told he had to qualify for Wimbledon. He refused and missed the tournament.)

With 22 events to fill, Hunt unleashed an intense player-signing war.

"We had meetings late into the night to organize a worldwide blitz on players to sign for WCT," recalled Humphries. "This was a military operation. We actually employed similar tactics that Lamar and his buddies used to sign players to the AFL. We sent more than 25 people behind the old Iron Curtain, to Australia, and to other places around the world to sign players.

"There was no additional monetary enticement we could offer—only the prize money [$7.9 million]. Basically, if a player wanted to play WCT events he had to sign there and then. It rocked the establishment that we signed 57 of the top 64 players in the world."

Though Hunt did lasso nearly five dozen stars, he could not land Borg or Connors, despite their heritage as past WCT champions. By this time, agencies such as International Management Group (IMG) and ProServ were gaining a great deal of power over player decisions. They kept their clients—including Connors and Borg with IMG and Stan Smith and Yannick Noah for ProServ—out of Hunt's orbit.

In 1982 WCT and Grand Prix tournaments collided on an almost weekly basis. When Grand Prix unveiled a $250,000 event in Brussels, WCT offered a $300,000 one in Munich. Where Grand Prix put on a $200,000 Los Angeles tournament, that same weekend WCT countered with a $300,000 purse in Houston. While McEnroe and Connors would play in Philadelphia for Grand Prix, Ivan Lendl and others would compete in Del Ray Beach, Florida, for WCT. Not only that, the circuits promoted two different computer rankings of players, confusing fans to no end as to who was worth watching.

Alan King, who set up a Las Vegas event at Caesars Palace the same weekend as Hunt's cherished Dallas finals that year, said he didn't see how Hunt could "continue to knock heads" with others in the tennis establishment.

"Caesars is taking it as a small challenge," he said. "And Caesars is not exactly a puddle."

Prize money for players had jumped to $25 million from about $14 million the previous year. Charges of paying players illegal appearance guarantees rattled around both circuits. WCT and ATP fought over Lendl, both claiming he had signed up for their tournaments on the same weekend.

WCT's nemeses were enraged. The Association of Tennis Professionals—now run by old WCT hand Davies—the ITF (the Lawn designation had been removed as tournaments moved to clay and hard court), and others viewed Grand Prix as the official tour. By 1983—after WCT lost an estimated $12 million the year before in part because of the endless roadblocks put up by others—Hunt had had enough. WCT filed a lawsuit that encompassed just about everyone in the world of tennis, from the MIPTC to the ITF and the ATP. The complaint alleged antitrust violations—"conspiracy to monopolize," "conspiracy to restrain trade," and other accusations—and requested money damages that were not revealed (as if to buttress WCT's claims, the ITF paid the ATP's legal fees in the suit).

"The ATP–Grand Prix connection is so patently against the antitrust laws, it's ridiculous," Hunt said at the time. "I've always believed in competition, but this is like the NFL Players Association fielding a team in the NFL. The other side is full of baloney. It's chaos, and it's wrong."

The momentum swings Hunt encountered in pro tennis were as jarring in intensity as a McEnroe-Borg finals match. Not only did the lawsuit end up being settled, but WCT rejoined the Grand Prix circuit. But Hunt was working harder than ever to keep his group afloat. In 1983 he estimated 40 percent of his work was dedicated to pro tennis.

"The finances of tennis are insane, and I spend an inordinate amount of time on it," he said.

Meredith recalled, "WCT would send out 8,000 to 9,000 season-ticket renewal requests. He signed every single one."

Marty Rotberg, who ran the WCT's annual New York event at Forest Hills known as the Tournament of Champions and also worked with Hunt in the NASL, remembered how Hunt's embrace of the corporate hospitality village—a rarity in the tennis world at the time—helped generate revenue for the struggling group.

"One of the things he suggested is he wanted me, in the spring of 1983, to go to the French Open, do a site survey, see what they're doing that we hadn't tapped into," Rotberg said. "One idea was corporate hospitality. I got the grand tour of Roland Garros. I came back and said we can do a corporate hospitality village in 1984 and beyond.

"We started to plan and started to sell it. Put a corporate village on the tennis courts that weren't [being] used. A company would have a small tent for 12 to 15 with food and beverage. It was primitive. It wasn't individual tents but one big tent structure that was cordoned off.

"He had the idea, but he didn't tell us how to do it. Yet he was so interested in the details. He was enthused about new ways to make money. It became an important revenue stream. We probably made a $50,000 profit the first year, when we got 15 to 25 companies; the total budget for the event was about $3 million. By the time it was really going, we probably made a couple of hundred thousand dollars a year."

Rotberg recalled Hunt took keen interest in the success of the Forest Hills tourney in the 1980s.

"He would come to the event with eagle eyes," Rotberg said. "He'd look at different parts of the event on a daily basis, and he'd come with his little notepad and he'd write notes. He'd sit across from me and say, 'Hey, Marty, here are some things I noticed.' I'd say, 'We considered that, but it would cost too much this year. We'll consider it for next year.'

"There would be things I wouldn't see or the head of operations wouldn't see—the bunting on the side of the wall wasn't right—he was that meticulous about those kinds of things. He was absolutely interested in the best experience for the fan. It was part of his DNA."

Regardless of what the fans wanted, there were forces out of Hunt's control that kept pecking away at him. After 15 years, it was estimated that WCT had lost $40 million in its existence. Hunt, though, believed it still had the potential to make money.

Williams was more realistic.

"I told him around that time we should fold up our tent or pursue the [Grand Prix] lawsuit to the very end. When we joined the Grand Prix [again], it was the beginning of the end for WCT," he said. "The top players of the era wanted a lot of appearance money. They'd say, 'Unless Lamar pays me a few hundred thousand dollars, I'm not going to play. There are too many tournaments; we can't play them all.'

"Everyone knew the players were holding Lamar for ransom. But he never raised his voice. 'Gosh darn,' which was one of his favorite expressions, was like me tearing my hair out and ranting and raving."

As WCT fought to stay relevant, it slashed the number of events from nearly two dozen to seven. Soon enough, longtime TV partners questioned the wisdom of continuing with the foundering group.

"Lamar was a great believer in tennis and television. He thought it would grow exponentially," Williams recalled. "It didn't. We were all caught with our pants down in the early 1980s when golf began to supplant tennis.

"We started to lose major TV contracts, but I can state unequivocally that we held on for more years than we should have with ABC, CBS, and NBC because of the belief in Lamar Hunt by the top TV executives."

WCT still pulled out all the stops for what was known as the Buick WCT Finals in Dallas. A pamphlet for the 1986 tournament, which featured McEnroe and Lendl among others at Reunion Arena, reveals the glitz pitched to potential sponsors. Aside from the promise of commercials on CBS and cable, along with print advertisements in *World Tennis* and the city's *D* magazine, a three-day weekend for eight included a garden party at Norma and Lamar's house, dancing to live music until 2:00 AM at a gala ball, and an open invitation to the new Trailblazer Club and Champagne Lanson at the Sunday victory party. The package, valued at $130,000 by WCT, could be had that year for $65,000.

The luster of Dallas notwithstanding, as barely a blip on the tennis scene during the mid-1980s with its handful of tournaments every year, WCT faced a death knell. By 1988, the Men's Tennis Council said WCT tournaments would be eliminated in 1990 as it tried to make the Grand Prix tour—which had ballooned to nearly 80 tournaments—more efficient. The last WCT Finals in Dallas—the onetime premier event of the organization—occurred in 1989. Players yawned. Before his first-round match, Mats Wilander admitted, "I have no feel for this tournament. I never really cared if I played it or not. It's just another tournament."

Newcombe, for one, was stunned by the attitude of new players.

"It's a crime the lack of respect the guys today show for Lamar Hunt. They have no idea what he's done, what he's meant to tennis," he said.

But despite WCT's efforts, it couldn't survive another setback. A reorganized ATP tour shunned the Dallas organizations, and WCT's doors were closed.

The International Tennis Hall of Fame—which inducted Hunt in 1993—doesn't mince words about what happened.

"Unfortunately, the Association of Tennis Professionals, in reorganizing the men's tour in 1990, froze WCT out, and Hunt's organization ceased operations after 23 years of raising standards within the professional game," it notes on its website.

"I never heard him say a discouraging word about what happened," Collins said. "It still puzzles me why they threw him out of the game."

McEnroe echoed Collins' thoughts.

"Lamar was a great addition to our sport in the '70s," he told the *Dallas Morning News*. "He brought a lot of attention and money to our game. I was around early enough to know what he meant to the game. It was such a disgrace the way he was sort of pushed out."

Williams estimated WCT lost around $100 million during its lifetime. But in many ways, it was money well spent.

Hunt's impact on pro tennis was enormous. Because of his dedication, the sport—for the first time—held regular tournaments in major stadiums. Players cashed in on the game's newfound popularity as prize money rocketed. In an ironic twist, one of the nation's richest men wrested tennis from the country clubs and brought it to the masses. WCT introduced colored clothing and balls, the tie-breaker, trainers on tour to help with injuries, and other innovations. Corporate sponsors came aboard, and for the first time television covered tennis consistently beyond the Grand Slams.

Above all, Hunt blasted away the doors that prevented pros from playing at the highest levels.

"Open tennis was the most dramatic thing to happen to tennis in the 20th century," Williams opined. "Would Wimbledon have gone open in 1968 without Lamar? No siree. The specter of this fanatical sports enthusiast with piles of dough terrified them.

"Lamar Hunt took the game kicking and screaming into the commercial world. His legacy will be creating the environment where professional management abounds in the game."

Collins said, "He lifted tennis into the big leagues. He gave it a professional touch."

Buchholz, who himself served a stint as executive director of the ATP when it fought WCT and founded the Sony Ericsson Open, added, "What Lamar did and what WCT did was put professional tennis on a business-like basis. We were trying to run tennis on a shoestring [in the 1960s]. It was basically run out of the trunk of somebody's car.

"He improved the conditions for the players. He was certainly concerned about everybody that was under contract with him. He was very fair in terms of money and in his whole attitude of 'I'm not going to take advantage of you.' For one tournament I went and found these sponsors, did all these things. I didn't ask for money, but he sent my wife a check.

"He always looked at the big picture. It had to make financial sense, but it didn't have to make financial sense for that day."

Rotberg recalled Hunt, despite his many critics in the tennis establishment, ran his business the right way.

"Sports owners can take their business success elsewhere and imprint it on their new involvement in the sports business, and that's 100 percent wrong," he said. "Lamar had other business interests, but he had the intelligence and was modest enough to have good people and let them run things.

"The tennis business is parochial. Some people thought he was out to control the game of tennis. Lamar wasn't built that way, to be a kingpin. He wanted to serve the public who wanted to see great players."

Humphries said Hunt did not deserve the ill treatment often inflicted by tennis' ruling class.

"Lamar transformed the entire sport and produced the blueprint for today's pro tour. Yet Lamar was always treated with suspicion by the old guard in tennis everywhere," Humphries said. "He was fighting all the time—that's why the tour dissolved eventually—because they owned the four main events. They used the four events to screw him. They made players play so many events to get into Wimbledon. They placed so many conditions on them."

Sometimes, though, Hunt got the last laugh on his detractors. WCT created a round-robin tournament for television, and Davies would edit the show down to an hour for broadcast on a weekly basis.

"We had an opening for 90 seconds—beauty shots of a seagull landing," Davies recalled. "Every time the show came on each week, you had the same opening. So Lamar was talking with one of the English people at the ITF. The man said he had seen the show a couple of times, and he was amazed we got the seagull to land in the same place each time! Lamar thought it was absolutely hysterical."

Unlike pro football or pro soccer, run by one league at a specific time of year, tennis seemed to reject a set template as offered by WCT. Part of the problem was that players were free agents, independent contractors who could jump from tour to tour or choose made-for-TV tournaments.

Pro golf—the other comparable sport in the U.S. where athletes play for themselves—seemed to figure out a sensible road map by creating the Professional Golfers Association, which has a defined season and which even boasts a commissioner. During Hunt's era, the wars with competing tennis tours and governing bodies could only be settled through the courts. Battling so many factions ended up being too much for WCT. To this day, aside from the Grand Slams, tennis remains a confusing hodgepodge of tournaments.

Amid his immersion in the business of the sport, Hunt did enjoy playing the game itself. His house in Dallas included a tennis court, and he engaged in a few sets from time to time (though he preferred jogging for exercise). One *Sports Illustrated* reporter who watched Hunt hit balls before his 40th birthday wrote, "Lamar Hunt steps on the tennis court, and it becomes immediately apparent that his game lacks the customary middle-age duplicities—the cuts and dinks that older players use to compensate for muscular collapse. He hits the ball flat and level, his body at right angles to the stroke, his feet firmly planted. Usually his return shots fall close to his opponent; his serve is straight and heavy; he does not seem to possess an overhead smash, but he grinds his opponent down with sheer consistency. At the end, he says, with characteristic politesse, 'You're just out of practice.'"

For some men, creating a football league, backing two soccer leagues, and developing pro tennis into a major force would be enough work for a lifetime. Hunt, though, was insatiable in accomplishing as much as possible. He helped launch an NBA expansion franchise, attempted to buy Major League Baseball and National Hockey League teams, and got involved in a professional bowling league. Some of his biggest ventures, surprisingly enough, didn't even involve sports.

CHAPTER 7

A HAND IN EVERYTHING

BUILDER OF STADIUMS, FINANCIER OF PRO FRANCHISES, it's amusing to think that the first sports enterprise pioneered by Lamar Hunt featured chicken-wire fences. And a watermelon stand.

Five years before the American Football League became a vision, Hunt helped launch a sports business with his friend from The Hill School, Tom Richey. Its name was Zima Bat.

Two Zima Bats, both offering a batting cage and miniature golf course, opened in 1954. One sat near a Dallas expressway; the other, off a parking lot of the Dallas Rangers minor-league baseball team, encountered a few difficulties. Fences constructed of chicken wire were set up to try to contain smashed balls. Yet on the day of the grand opening—even with boys hired to catch baseballs in the parking lot—two struck windshields.

As people waited in line for the batting cages, Hunt—part owner and part operator in his inaugural sports undertaking—thought of another idea. Why not set up a pitching game? Thus 10 balls were handed to customers for 25 cents with the goal of hurling them through a hole. At the other Zima Bat, Hunt unveiled a watermelon stand to satiate patrons on steamy summer nights.

Zima Bat did not have the staying power of, say, pro football and eventually faded away. After the AFL was created, what did have staying power was Hunt's reputation as a launcher of leagues. Approached often about starting somewhat offbeat ones, he didn't bite on either the National Karate League or the National Rodeo League (complete with a calf roper draft system). But as a self-described born sports fan, he did invest in the National Bowling League, which featured a Dallas franchise—and was as successful as a gutter ball.

"That's just the nature of business," Hunt later reflected. "Sometimes you lose. Why, I drilled a dry hole just last week. Several dry holes. Sometimes you get a dry hole in the sports-entertainment business, too."

But one venture Hunt invested in during the 1960s eventually struck a gusher. At that time, the National Basketball Association plodded along with nine teams, and the Boston Celtics nearly always won the championship. In Chicago, pro basketball franchises were discarded like aging benchwarmers. The Chicago Stags failed after a few years during the Harry Truman administration. In 1961 the Chicago Packers—later known as the Zephyrs—joined the NBA. Within two seasons, they moved to Baltimore (today they're called the Washington Wizards).

The Windy City seemed to be a graveyard for pro basketball. But with an excess of teams on both coasts and the nation's second-biggest city—the capital of the Midwest—lacking a franchise, the NBA expanded there in 1966. That January, the latest installment was christened the Bulls. Price tag: $1.6 million.

In April, Hunt came aboard as a shareholder, joining Harold M. Mayer of Oscar Mayer and Elmer Rich Jr. of Bacon, Whipple & Co. Introduced during a press luncheon at the Sherman House, where two other investors—Gregson Barker and one referred to only as a "prominent Chicago industrialist"—were announced, Hunt quickly found himself a bit embarrassed. When Bulls president Dick Klein was asked if the three new shareholders each owned 10 percent, he seethed. "The Bulls do not announce the percentage of stock owned by any individual," Klein said.

A chagrined Hunt admitted, "I've already loused that up. I told 'em."

His confession behind him, Hunt explained his interest in a franchise far from his Dallas and Kansas City holdings.

"I'm coming in as a fan; I'm a sports nut," Hunt said. "Still, I regard this as a potentially fine investment. The business of pro sport is booming. Basketball has been slow to follow the book, but I think it's coming. A prime factor in my investment was the fact that Chicago is a major market. The potential is here for attendance and for the TV market."

During the Bulls' first season, they finished 33–48, the best-ever finish for an NBA expansion squad and good for a playoff spot. But playing in the dingy International Amphitheatre—most famous as the site of the soon-to-be riotous 1968 Democratic Convention—the Bulls drew small crowds. Their first three seasons, they averaged about 4,000 fans per contest.

Enter Pat Williams. Not even 30 years of age, he interviewed to become the team's general manager. And one name was repeated over and over.

"I met with the ownership group, those local to Chicago. You kept hearing about 'Lamar, Lamar,'" Williams recalled. "In the course of the season, I did have occasion to meet Lamar. I was intimidated. That was a huge name, and I was just 29. But your immediate reaction was Wally Cox on 'Mr. Peepers.' He was low-key, softspoken."

With attendance floundering, Hunt initiated an experiment during the 1969–70 season under new GM Williams. The Bulls played eight home games at Kansas City Municipal Auditorium, a venue built in 1936. In a way, the Bulls traded one aging arena by the stockyards for another hundreds of miles west. No panacea, fewer than 5,000 attended the first "home" game against Detroit, and roughly the same number watched a strong Los Angeles Lakers' team battle the Bulls.

"He [Lamar] took that on to help the team," Williams recalled. "We worked closely with Jack Steadman on all the details. The Chiefs promoted it in mailings to season-ticket holders, offering them preferred seats for Bulls games. They oversaw advertising and promotion.

"It drew decently in Kansas City, nothing sensational. The media in Chicago viewed it as the first leg out of town."

Aside from the one-year Kansas City hiatus, Hunt's involvement during Williams' tenure (he left in 1973 and now runs the Orlando Magic) was minimal.

"He never got actively engaged with running the team. He never called about draft picks," Williams recalled. "He was truly a silent partner. I think that's a tribute to a man of his means. He knew when to back off. Even if a team's in capable hands, many cannot do that."

The Bulls endured some near-misses in the 1970s. First, they were stymied by Kareem Abdul-Jabbar, who played for division rival Milwaukee. Then, in an epic seven-game series in 1975, they fell to Golden State to miss a chance at playing in their first NBA Finals. By the early 1980s, after some poor drafts of troubled players—such as No. 1 pick Quintin Dailey, who plead guilty to aggravated assault of a University of San Francisco coed—Chicago Stadium sat nearly empty for Bulls games.

One move changed everything. In 1984 the Bulls selected Michael Jordan with the third overall pick in the draft. Soon, the stadium rocked nightly. The next year, Jerry Reinsdorf and a group of investors bought a 56.8 percent share of the team for $9.2 million. While others such as George Steinbrenner unloaded their stock, Hunt decided to remain as a partner; the value of his stake had already grown more than tenfold.

With Jordan's presence, the Bulls won six NBA championships, thanks to the Hall of Famer's heroics. Hunt attended scores of playoff games during the glory years. A family photo shows him grinning wildly while holding a red No. 23 Bulls jersey. Yet despite being the last of the original Bulls investors, one who could have walked into the locker room anytime on a whim, he and Jordan never got together.

"It became a little bit of a family joke that Lamar had never met Michael Jordan," Clark Hunt said. "He decided on his own that it would be bad luck for him to meet Michael and that it might jinx Michael."

Hunt refused to throw his weight around in other respects during the lengthy championship run. Kansas City Chiefs president Carl Peterson told a story to a newspaper about Hunt inviting he and his wife, Lori, to one of the NBA Finals games in the 1990s. After flying from Kansas City to Chicago, he met Hunt at the Hertz Rent-a-Car counter.

"They didn't have his car immediately available," Peterson said. "So, we're there waiting outside taking in all these fumes from the buses. And while we're waiting, limos are coming and going all around us, much to the exasperation of Norma."

Of the five tickets available for the Petersons and Hunts (including son Daniel), four were prime courtside seats. One rested in the rafters. Hunt said he'd take the lone seat; Peterson insisted they at least switch after halftime.

But Hunt didn't appear in the third quarter. So Peterson trudged up the stairs to try to find his boss.

"He was sitting in a Bob Uecker seat, literally in one of the last rows," Peterson said. "He'd taken his coat off and rolled up his sleeves and was a fan sitting in the rafters! Here was Lamar Hunt, a founding owner of the Bulls, and I guarantee you, he was enjoying himself as the consummate fan. It was so typical of Lamar."

Even after Jordan retired, the Bulls sold out every game for years, despite fielding expansion-like teams. In 2009 *Forbes* estimated the value of the franchise at $511 million, meaning Hunt's original investment of $160,000 or so had soared past $50 million.

Lester Crown is the former chairman of General Dynamics, a multi-billion-dollar company with nearly 100,000 employees. He has dealt with CEOs and others in hundreds of transactions. Each time Crown—who once served as the Bulls' chairman of the board and whose family maintains a large stake in the team—met with Hunt, he came away impressed.

"We had some joint agreements that had to be taken care of, and in each case, he was absolutely reasonable. That's the best thing I can say about anyone in a transaction," Crown recalled. "I also always found he was thoroughly fair and smart."

To the casual fan, it looked like Hunt never wanted in sports. Truth is, he was frustrated at his rejection by two major entities, Major League Baseball and the National Hockey League.

In 1964 Hunt and Tommy Mercer bought the Dallas–Fort Worth Spurs, a Double A minor-league baseball team based at Turnpike Stadium in Arlington. The team, affiliated with the Chicago Cubs at the outset, played in the Texas League. Since Dallas–Fort Worth constituted the largest area in the country without a Major League Baseball franchise, the founders believed the move would help launch them into the MLB one day.

Four years later, Hunt and Mercer expected to receive one of two National League expansion franchises being handed out that May in Chicago. In part due to the opposition of Houston Astros owner Roy Hofheinz, a member of the expansion committee who wanted Texas to himself to capitalize on attendance and television rights, they failed. Instead, San Diego and Montreal— which didn't even possess a major-league stadium and which was eventually forced to play in 28,000-seat Jarry Park—paid $10 million apiece to start play in 1969. Dallas joined Milwaukee and Buffalo as bridesmaids.

For the most part, Hunt—who didn't attend the meetings in Chicago— let Mercer vent their disappointment to the press. "Frankly, I don't like it," said Mercer, who estimated he and Hunt spent close to $80,000 on the effort to land a franchise. Knowing well the entrepreneurial past of his partner, Mercer lobbed a threat, saying he and Hunt might consider forming a third major league.

Instead, they fought on within the system, trying to win approval in the majors. In 1969 the expansion Seattle Pilots flopped. They drew only 670,000 fans, and owner William Daley was unable to meet financial obligations after an $800,000 loss. Following the season, Hunt and Mercer made an offer for the Pilots; Daley said he was impressed. A few months later, as the Seattle situation deteriorated, it looked like Hunt and Mercer had their team.

"Dallas–Fort Worth's 10-year campaign to land a Major League Baseball team appeared to have succeeded Thursday when Seattle interests failed to meet an American League financial deadline," trumpeted the *Dallas Morning News* at the top of its sports section on January 23, 1970.

The official American League meeting five days later to certify Seattle's fate was seen as a formality, as Dallas–Fort Worth was reported to have "at least" the nine votes needed to procure the moribund franchise for about $9 million. Undersized Turnpike Stadium was ready to grow to 25,000 seats in 1970 and would double that amount the next year. Hunt—who had first tried to land a major-league franchise back in the 1950s before focusing his attention on pro football—looked like he finally could add the title "MLB owner" to his resume.

But by this time in his career, Hunt had learned to expect the unexpected. First, another Seattle ownership group surprisingly formed and entered the fray. Then, the American League extended the Pilots' deadline to solve its financial woes another 10 days.

While Hunt huffed that the league "is certainly making every effort to avoid moving Seattle," he felt the Dallas–Fort Worth bid had made progress at the AL meetings.

"We received positive encouragement and recognition from many individual owners, something that has never happened before," he said. "This certainly looks good for the future."

But as a decision kept getting postponed, Hunt and Mercer faced a queasy short-term outlook if they did win the franchise. Spring training loomed in a few weeks. There would be little time to orchestrate a television package, promotions, or ticket sales for the regular season, guaranteeing a whopping first-year loss. Not only that, another possible scenario—Seattle moving to the tiny city of Milwaukee—was gaining ground. Though it seemed at the outset to be an underdog, considering its proximity to two other AL teams (the Minnesota Twins and the Chicago White Sox), the contingent led by Bud Selig had nostalgia and sentiment on its side; it had lost the Braves to Atlanta in 1966.

On February 9, during an American League meeting in Chicago, it was reported that the new Seattle group led by Edward Carlson had met the requirements of league owners. "I think we have a deal," Carlson said.

He did. For the 1970 season, the Pilots would play in Seattle, with the American League lending it about $650,000 to help pay expenses. Hunt and Mercer gave up on getting the Pilots, at least for the time being.

But the crazy saga wasn't finished. A month later, the Pilots were faltering again, and AL owners were unsure they wanted to bankroll them; they demanded a quick switch to Milwaukee before the season. But Washington senator Wayne Magnuson threatened to halt baseball's immunity from antitrust laws if such a move occurred. Amid all this, the Pilots' training-camp contract was canceled. On March 31—about a week before Opening Day—a federal bankruptcy court let the Pilots' owners sell their franchise to Milwaukee for $10.8 million.

Hunt wasn't too upset, realizing the deal didn't make much sense from a business standpoint that late in the game. And by the following year, Dallas–Fort Worth had finally landed a Major League Baseball franchise— but Hunt, after all of his efforts, was not the owner.

In September 1971, after drawing crowds that barely exceeded the number of representatives in the U.S. Congress, the American League approved moving the Washington Senators to Arlington, Texas, where they would be named the Texas Rangers. Owned by Bob Short, they began play in 1972 at Turnpike Stadium (renamed Arlington Stadium). Hunt watched the Rangers slowly succeed and build a popular new stadium, The Ballpark at Arlington. Future U.S. president George W. Bush eventually became the face of the franchise.

Hunt patiently waited more than a quarter century before trying to purchase another MLB club. This time, he gunned for the Royals, whose stadium sat right next to Arrowhead. Partnering in a 50/50 bid with Western Resources, a large utility based in Kansas, Hunt looked to take over the franchise in the spring of 1998. Two other bidders expressed interest as well. By August, Hunt withdrew the offer, which was reported to have fallen far short of the $75 million demanded by the team's board. Two years later, one of those board members, David Glass—the Royals' interim CEO after owner Ewing Kauffman's death—bought the team for $96 million.

Many in baseball were dismayed that Hunt didn't join their ranks.

"Baseball was a natural with him because the stadiums are back-to-back out there," said Atlanta Braves chairman emeritus Bill Bartholomay. "I was hoping he'd buy it."

Added Andy McKenna, former chairman of both the Chicago White Sox and the Chicago Cubs, "Certainly he would have been a welcome owner. He was one of those people who was not in it for the headlines."

Foiled at his final attempt to join the majors, around the same time Hunt engaged in a struggle to acquire an NHL expansion franchise.

It had started in late 1996, when Hunt—already the lead investor in MLS's Columbus Crew—signed an application with Columbus businessmen Ron Pizzuti and John H. McConnell. They sent a $100,000 deposit to the NHL to be considered for an expansion franchise.

"Lamar Hunt is so widely respected in the professional sports community that it is very important to have his name on this application," said Pizzuti, part of the group called Columbus Hockey Limited, which included Wolfe Enterprises, Ameritech, and others. Crucial to the venture was passing a .5¢ sales tax increase to fund a new hockey stadium.

Hunt's attempt to get an NHL franchise soon faced obstacles. First, he needed the NFL to switch its policy prohibiting owners from acquiring an interest in an NHL team. That rule (which was being reviewed when Wayne Huizenga entered the NFL in 1994 while owning the Florida Panthers) was altered in March 1997, clearing the way for Hunt to realize his ambitions.

Soon after, he signed a letter of intent to commit Hunt Sports Group money to build a 21,000-seat downtown arena and 35,000-seat stadium in Columbus (for the Crew) in exchange for the right to operate them. His optimism grew.

"Based on my private conversations with the [NHL team] owners, there is no question Columbus will get a team," Hunt said.

The vote on boosting the sales tax to 6.25 percent from 5.75 percent for three years loomed. If the voters approved, Hunt was convinced Columbus would be granted an NHL franchise.

"I feel more confident than ever that they want Columbus to be in the league," he told the *Columbus Dispatch*. "I'd be shocked if we didn't get an expansion team, provided there is a favorable vote."

On May 6, the measure was soundly defeated by Franklin County residents, demoralizing the would-be owner.

"This will make it impossible for the National Hockey League to come to Columbus," Hunt lamented.

Despite his strong words, Hunt was wrong. With the NHL planning to expand by four teams—and with only half a dozen cities considered viable candidates—Columbus remained in the hunt, mainly because a privately financed stadium emerged as a possibility and the fact Columbus remained the largest U.S. city without a major-league sports franchise in the four big leagues

A month later, Columbus mayor Greg Lashutka unveiled a privately financed arena proposal. Hunt had not been informed that the plan for a $125 million complex would be presented to the city council until hours before it was approved. Even worse for the sports impresario, John H. McConnell—an investor in Hunt's original plan to land a franchise—said an NHL committee had approved him, not Hunt, as an owner of an expansion team.

At the council meeting, Lashutka expressed uncertainty about Hunt's future as an investor. Hunt was clearly puzzled by the changes.

"I assume it's still the same group," he said. "All of our names are on the application with the league."

Less than two weeks later, the NHL approved an expansion franchise for Columbus and three other cities. Hunt was not part of the winning group, headed by McConnell and named COLHOC. They paid $80 million to join the league. Amid the cheering on High Street, a flurry of lawsuits ensued.

McConnell and Wolfe Enterprises Inc. filed a suit against Hunt, claiming he "misrepresented the original investment group when it came time to negotiate a lease with the owners of a privately owned arena." In their eyes, this represented a breach of their agreement. They didn't ask for money, just the ability to get out of the original operating pact and buy an NHL team on their own. The lawsuit alleged Hunt had rejected an offer to become part of the new group.

On June 23 Hunt responded by filing court papers asserting McConnell had no right to create a second ownership group. Hunt claimed he and Ameritech would have owned 80 percent of any team and that Ameritech's interest sprouted from Hunt's involvement. As far as money, Hunt's lawsuit asked for projected profits of the arena and the team for a quarter-century.

A few days later, at a press conference, NHL commissioner Gary Bettman offered hope the situation would be resolved.

"The McConnells and the Hunts are amicably talking about it, and I think that, based on the framework being put together, Mr. Hunt may well be joining this franchise as one of the owners," Bettman said.

It wasn't to be. Despite Hunt's decades-long ties to professional sports, his involvement in Columbus with the Crew, and the fact he had led the original NHL investor group, a Franklin County court in Ohio ruled in November that Hunt was out as an owner of the Columbus franchise. A few months later, Hunt struck back, this time in New York. A new lawsuit asked the New York Supreme Court to prevent the NHL from giving McConnell's group a franchise and to hand Hunt $50 million in damages.

In May 1998 a civil trial with jurors opened in Franklin County, Ohio, on Hunt's lawsuit from the previous year. Accusations flew quickly. Attorney John W. Zeiger, working for the COLHOC group, claimed Hunt secretly considered a plan to put a team in Cincinnati. He said Hunt repeatedly turned down the chance to back Nationwide Arena as an NHL deadline approached.

Hunt's attorney, Anthony J. Celebrezze, fought back, saying Hunt— with a wealth of sports experience—believed the lease agreement on the proposed arena constituted a "bad business deal" and that the franchise would lose money during the entire 25-year period. Celebrezze said Hunt "had the rug pulled out from under him" by McConnell as Hunt looked for ways to improve the lease agreement. Hunt's attorneys also derided the idea he harbored a secret plan to put a team in Cincinnati, especially since that city hadn't submitted an NHL application.

Bettman took the stand. He said that during a discussion of a downtown area in April, 1997, Hunt evinced zero interest in a privately financed arena.

"I asked Mr. Hunt in this session, was he prepared to go forward with the franchise and the project if the referendum failed, and his response at the meeting was 'no,'" said Bettman.

"As far as we were concerned in May and June of '97, it was unclear—to say the least—that Mr. Hunt had any desire or intention to go forward with this project and that, in the absence of Mr. McConnell stepping forward with Nationwide, Columbus would not have been granted an expansion franchise. And so as a factual matter, based on what I know, I don't believe that there should be a claim for breach of duty by Mr. McConnell because, to us, it seemed like he was stepping up to do the right thing."

Hunt didn't testify. Nor did the jury hear the case, as both sides asked for the judge to issue a directed verdict. When he did, Judge John P. Bessey cleared McConnell's group of any wrongdoing. Not only that, he eventually ruled Hunt would have to pay $920,000 in legal fees to the Blue Jackets' new owners.

No doubt the NHL experience soured Hunt. He never again tried to land a pro hockey franchise. Closer to home, though, Hunt found solace in college sports. At his alma mater, SMU, he and Norma donated $5.5 million in 1997 to the building of Gerald J. Ford Stadium and Paul B. Loyd Jr. All-Sports Center. In fact, Hunt cochaired the campaign to build Ford Stadium, which cost $58.6 million.

SMU president Dr. R. Gerald Turner recalled the money-raising prowess of Hunt, who also served on an executive committee that raised more than $500 million for SMU.

"He was surprisingly good at raising money. If he believed in a project, he was more than willing to talk about it," said Turner. "He was the initial driving force behind that [Gerald J. Ford] stadium. I wanted to get football out of the Cotton Bowl. I talked with Lamar. He absolutely agreed. But we tried to see if we could just expand the stadium we had.

"When he was traveling, he read that another college was building a new stadium. He tore the article out of that magazine and said, 'See, they're building a new stadium, not renovating.'"

Hunt enjoyed attending all types of sports events at SMU. Turner recalled the Mustang fan wasn't one to paint his face.

"His basketball season tickets were near mine. Basically, he would sit and watch. He'd have words of encouragement, but I never heard him yelling. He's not the guy who's going to be screaming at officials."

As dear to his heart as sports were, Hunt delved into other business ventures. Always involved in oil, thanks to his father's interests (he served as a vice president at Hunt Energy in Dallas at no salary), while checking in on matters at Placid Oil and Penrod Drilling, he also tried to venture out into entertainment. In the early 1960s, he developed the Bronco Bowl, a teenage club in Dallas that welcomed musical acts—including the likes of Bruce Springtseen and David Bowie—for 40 years. Later in the decade, he set his sights on a place many had spent their lives trying to escape: Alcatraz.

Dominated for decades by an infamous prison—where supposedly no one crossed its surrounding waters without either drowning or being captured—the island off of San Francisco featured 12 windswept acres. The prison was dropped from the federal penitentiary system in 1963.

Six years later, San Francisco publicly appealed for development plans on the Rock a mile and a half from its shores. Proposals ranging from a zoo to a casino poured in. In July, Hunt offered his $6 million plan complete with a 66-year lease, in the wake of the Apollo moon landing. A 364-foot "Apollon" tower—the same size as the rocket and capsule that headed toward the moon—would honor the astronauts who had just landed on the lunar surface. Elevators would whisk visitors to the top.

The reaction was swift. San Francisco columnist Dick Nolan editorialized, "Not even Alcatraz deserves anything quite as ugly as the fate planned for it by Lamar Hunt, that go-getting son of a billionaire from Little Ole Texas.... What is proposed? Lamar wants to make us partners. You good folks (says Lamar) just run right out and buy this here island, lay out the cash, a mizzuble couple of million or so, and then I'll come along, see, and rent it from you right away. I'll pay you enough rent (Lamar continues) so that in a few years—say 20, 30, or maybe 50, or how about 90—you'll get everything back."

That was mild compared to what happened next. In September six members of the board of supervisors in San Francisco voted to approve a commercial development on Alcatraz Island. It was Hunt's. Aside from the space monument, he also proposed a reproduction of old-time San Francisco complete with a shopping area, gardens spread across the island, and guided tours of the prison. He estimated the project would take seven years to complete

"Such a stupid plan," sniffed dress manufacturer Alvin Duskin, who had spent $5,000 to purchase full-page advertisements in San Francisco's daily newspapers, the *Chronicle* and the *Examiner*, to lambaste the idea. "Imagine, propagandizing for the space effort in the middle of San Francisco Bay."

Said one enraged critic, "It's just astonishing that they would even think of letting any of that Hunt money in the Bay area."

A month later, with Hunt in attendance, the Board of Supervisors voted 7–4 to shelve the plan for at least six months. Hunt admitted he was "a little stunned" by the turnaround but vowed to go ahead with the plans in hopes of eventual acceptance. A week later, the supervisors voted to rescind approval of the plan altogether. Perhaps it was for the best. Little did Hunt know that before Thanksgiving, a group of American Indians would seize control of the island and demand the federal government relinquish the land to them to build an Indian cultural center. Nearly two years later, the Indians finally were escorted off. Alcatraz eventually became part of the National Park Service (whose guided tours of the prison—originally suggested by Hunt—today draw millions annually). By then, Hunt had moved on to other opportunities.

In 1973, with Jack Steadman, he opened the amusement park Worlds of Fun. Costing more than $300 million, he situated the complex in Kansas City, where he knew his ventures would be better received than in California. Far from being an absentee landlord, Hunt bought a Humpty Dumpty parade float for $4,000 to help decorate the 165-acre grounds. He named rides and was engaged in landscaping. During one trip there in the early 1980s, he dispatched one of his famous memos to park officials. The reason? He wanted more sugar in the lemonade, sold at Lamar's Libations, similar to a lemonade stand he had run as a boy.

"If my name is going to be on the drink stand, then the lemonade can't be too sour," he said at the time, adding with equal parts humor and bottom-line concern about his sugar request, "I probably wrecked the budget."

Jim Schaaf, the former Chiefs general manager who now runs a sports insurance firm in Overland Park, Kansas, recalled the importance of Hunt's amusement park to Kansas City.

"Worlds of Fun was a tremendous thing for the town," he said. "There were no other amusement parks around at that period of time. It brought people in from all over. It made Kansas City a destination place."

In the 1980s, Hunt opened Oceans of Fun next door, considered the largest water park in the world. In 1995 privately held Hunt Midwest Enterprises (a merger of Mid-America Enterprises and Great Midwest Corp., two other Hunt-owned firms, which today oversees limestone mining and real-estate development among other interests) sold Worlds of Fun and Oceans of Fun to Cedar Fair. But that didn't end Hunt's business ventures in Kansas City. For decades he owned SubTropolis, the world's largest underground industrial park featuring office space and warehouses. Storage for boats and automobiles abounds in its 5 million square feet, along with original copies of *The Wizard of Oz* movie and other classics.

"He always wanted to try to make things better for Kansas City," Schaaf said. "He'd say, 'Besides having the football team, what else can we do? How can we give back?'"

Noted Lee Derrough, who served as chairman of Hunt Midwest until retiring at the end of 2009, "I've been a Kansas City guy my whole life. It's a heck of a lot better place because [Lamar] showed up."

Yet despite his yeoman efforts in Kansas City (he was elected to its business hall of fame in 2004), Hunt's business undertakings beyond sports may be remembered by posterity in one word: silver.

Two of Hunt's brothers, Bunker and Herbert, began buying up silver during the inflation-wracked 1970s. By 1979 Bunker, Herbert, and Lamar—who owned a far smaller stake then his older brothers—had compiled tens of million of ounces. Prices had soared from $6 an ounce in 1973 to around $50. Unlike many who buy silver, the Hunts actually collected the metal and paid extraordinary sums to ship it to Switzerland, where it safely sat in vaults.

In 1980, as word flew about that the Hunts were trying to corner the silver market, prices collapsed. In a matter of weeks, they dropped to below $11, tumbling about 80 percent. While sitting on a severely depleted investment, the Hunts also held futures contracts to buy silver at a price above $50; their liabilities became overwhelming. It was one of the greatest speculative disasters in U.S. history. The three brothers were forced to acquire a line of credit exceeding $1 billion to try to pay off their debts. Collateral included Bunker's nearly 70,000 head of cattle, Herbert's collection of Greek statues, and Lamar's art collection.

The sudden loss of untold millions of dollars—combined with the abhorrent publicity—blindsided the youngest Hunt. Somehow, he found the presence of mind to inform employees at his sports properties that all would be OK.

"Lamar calmly sent a comforting letter to all staff at WCT saying that despite all the negative media coverage that it would not affect their positions and that their jobs were safe," recalled WCT's Humphries. "The letter went to everybody right down to the secretarial staff. It was extremely comforting at the time because the Hunts were front-page news across the country for weeks on end. He could easily have ignored the staff, but he took the time to put their minds at rest."

It was tougher for Lamar to find peace. Lawsuits stretched out against the Hunt brothers for much of the decade. In the late 1980s, Lamar and 10 other defendants settled two claims that he had tried to manipulate the silver market. He contributed $2.75 million to the settlement fund "to avoid the inconvenience and the burden of years of further protracted legal expenses." That wasn't all; Hunt also agreed to fork over $17 million to a company in Peru as part of another lawsuit settlement (his brothers paid more than $100 million in that one).

Hunt spoke little publicly about the whole silver ordeal. In one interview, he opened up a bit on the episode's impact on his brothers.

"It was an investment they made, and as it turned out it wasn't a very good investment, was it? They ended up losing money on it. But they've been characterized very unfairly in terms of the investigations and lawsuits; myself to a lesser degree. It was not a happy experience."

Hunt faced other troubles in court in the 1980s. In 1986 he, Bunker, and Herbert filed a lawsuit against Penrod Drilling Co.'s nearly two dozen bank lenders, charging deception and fraud. Many of the banks responded with lawsuits of their own and demanded repayment of overdue loans. The Hunts escalated the fight with yet another lawsuit, charging the banks with trying to create a drilling rig monopoly and looking for $3.4 billion in retribution. A spokesman for Bank of America merely said, "We don't want any oil rigs at Bank of America. We want our $76 million back."

The next year, one of Lamar's trusts—which held Placid Oil and Penrod Drilling among other holdings—filed for bankruptcy-court protection, as did one of Bunker's (Herbert had filed in 1986).

The maneuver occurred to try to stop foreclosure proceedings by all of the bank creditors. At the time, Lamar noted his trust's total liabilities were $783 million; no value was given on the assets.

Worn out from protracted legal battles, Lamar was happy to turn his attention back to sports. And in the 1990s, with the Chiefs engaged in a multiseason playoff run, Major League Soccer getting off the ground, and the Chicago Bulls winning repeated championships, there was plenty to please one of the biggest sports financiers of his era. But little did he know his time in the world of games was slowly drawing to an end.

CHAPTER 8

A REVOLUTIONARY IMPACT

LAMAR HUNT COULD TAME the National Football League, a sports juggernaut that approached *him* to secure a merger with the rebel entity he founded. He could plant the flag of pro soccer on U.S. soil when few had ever seen a soccer game—and fewer Americans played it. He could whip the rulers of amateur tennis, who had been entrenched in their game for generations. He could build business complexes under the earth and create amusement parks—in many ways he seemed to be an unstoppable force.

A winner all his life—often against implacable odds—what the boy called Games couldn't beat, despite his best effort, was prostate cancer.

Diagnosed in 1998, he endured treatments and surgeries yet stayed active with his sports empire for the first years of the disease. But the cancer didn't relent as the NFL had. Eventually forced to halt his unmatchable streak of attending Cotton Bowls at 67, Hunt watched the game on television (which didn't even exist when his streak began). Far from a couch potato, Hunt, a lifelong director of the Cotton Bowl, dispatched a letter to Cotton Bowl president Rick Baker critiquing the broadcast.

Around this time, the septuagenarian—whose sports accomplishments prompted his induction into the Pro Football Hall of Fame, the National

Soccer Hall of Fame, and the International Tennis Hall of Fame (the only man to be enshrined in all three)—received one laurel that just about topped the rest.

When a players strike halted the NFL season in 1982, Hunt quickly found work—as a keeper of statistics for the St. Mark's School of Texas football team, where his son Clark played quarterback. During the undefeated season, Hunt created a team scrapbook. Afterward, he developed a highlight film, which included footage he shot, set it to music, and recruited legendary *Monday Night Football* announcer Howard Cosell to intone an introduction. Soon after, Hunt described the stint overall as the "hardest work I've ever done."

Hunt also coached Lamar Jr.'s football team at St. Mark's. He cooked hamburgers on Friday nights before games there and kept time during track meets. For a quarter-century Hunt served on the board of the school, finishing as a lifetime trustee. Eventually, a few people approached Clark and Dan (another St. Mark's graduate), saying they wanted to renovate Bailey Field at St. Mark's and name it after their father. The sons stipulated that Norma be included—after all, she had spent more time there than he because of Lamar's incessant travel schedule.

So the field was revamped. It featured a new synthetic surface surrounded by an expanded track, among other improvements. Somehow the boys kept the dedication a secret, even though scores of people knew about it.

On September 30, 2005, Norma and Lamar were invited to Bailey Field under the ruse that Dan and Clark were being honored. Seated on white folding chairs in the front row, a blue sweater wrapped around Lamar's button-down shirt and Norma resplendent in white blouse and scarf, the couple waited for their sons to be fêted.

Then a St. Mark's flag was removed from a wall and the etching appeared right in front of them: Norma and Lamar Hunt Family Stadium. The sports titan was stunned.

"Lamar, who has a list of honors that is simply almost beyond belief, said that he felt it was the nicest thing that had ever happened to him," Norma said.

By this time, Hunt was noticeably thinner, though still attending Chiefs games and other events. The next summer, however, for the first time since 1978, he missed the World Cup as his health declined. On November 22, 2006, he entered Presbyterian Hospital in Dallas. His family surrounded him. According to a sports trade publication report, Lamar then picked Clark—whom he had groomed for many years and who already served as chairman of the board for the Chiefs—as his successor to run the various Hunt sports properties. He signed the necessary papers, and the family backed the decision. As part of his estate-planning a decade earlier, Hunt had already transferred more than 75 percent of his stake in the Chiefs to help avoid future taxes on the team's appreciation.

Hunt's mind stayed focused even in his hospital bed. After one visit, as the family started to leave, he offered one final comment before they departed: "Go Chiefs."

Visitors came and went. One was Ralph Wilson, who 47 years earlier had signed on as one of the final members of the Foolish Club.

"I was probably the last owner in football to see him," Wilson recalled. "They were wheeling him out of the operating room down in Dallas. I said, 'Hey, Lamar, how did you get me into this mess?' Tears came into his eyes."

On the night of December 13, 2006, Lamar Hunt passed away at age 74 from complications of prostate cancer. His wife, Norma, along with his children Lamar Jr. and Sharron Munson from his first marriage and Clark and Daniel from his second one with Norma, survived him, along with 14 grandchildren. The baby of H.L. Hunt's first family died much younger than four of his five siblings; only Hassie preceded him in death.

As expected, the obituaries—appearing in every major American news-paper—lauded Hunt. Special sections were created by the *Kansas City Star* (the city's mayor requested that flags fly at half-staff to honor the Chiefs founder) and other publications to reminisce about his achievements. In Dallas the *Morning News* penned an editorial praising its hometown hero.

"No one, on or off the playing field, has brought more fundamental change to as many sports as did Lamar Hunt," it said. "Lamar Hunt will be most remembered as the man who pushed professional sports into the big-time and helped make football a must-see Sunday afternoon tradition."

Reflecting on his longtime pal, Wilson said, "He just was a heckuva guy."

During a visitation just after his death, more than 150 people appeared and talked about the larger-than-life figure.

"It's going to be a huge, dark space in my life," said former NFL commissioner Tagliabue.

"There's no way to replace him," Jerry Jones said.

Three days after Hunt passed away, Moody Coliseum—the site of so many WCT Finals and other events dear to Hunt's heart—welcomed mourners for his funeral. The six-page foldout program called it the "Celebration of the Life of Lamar Hunt." A color picture of a kneeling, smiling Lamar—dressed as expected in blue blazer and gray slacks—graced the cover. Two pages were dedicated to his life story.

"Mr. Hunt was a devoted Christian, a loving husband, father and grandfather, who enjoyed a vibrant life filled with many dear friends," it said in part. "He was a man of extraordinary vision, faith and integrity, whose deep sense of humility was one of his most unwavering and most endearing traits."

Thirteen honorary pallbearers, including fellow AFL founders Wilson and Adams along with former Chiefs coaches Schottenheimer and Vermeil, filled the seats along with more than 1,000 others. A singer belted out "Joy to the World." Lamar Jr. played the flute on "The Dance of the Blessed Spirits." Daniel and Sharon spoke during Reflections of the Family. Clark offered his thoughts in the Remembrance.

"As we all know, children are so much more perceptive than we think," Clark said. "A couple of weeks ago, my wife, Tavia, was tucking our seven-year-old daughter Grace into bed and talking about Dad, who the children refer to as Pappy. Grace asked, 'Is there football in heaven?' Grace [answering her own question] replied with a wisdom beyond her years. 'It doesn't really matter,' she said. 'If there isn't football in heaven, Pappy will start his own league.'"

An obviously moved Jack Steadman, who had been Hunt's confidant since the Chiefs were called the Texans, added, "I know and I'm confident that God has welcomed Lamar with open arms and very shortly, Lamar will be organizing games for all the angels in heaven because that's who he was and that's who he is."

Meredith recalled the funeral.

"I knew him intimately," he said. "I only knew of 25 percent of the things he had done based on what I heard that day."

At the reception afterward, the wait for the receiving line stretched for hours.

That wasn't all. At the Community of Christ Auditorium in Independence, Missouri, near Kansas City, a 120-minute memorial service less than a week after Hunt's death drew 2,500. Like a stadium, the doors opened two hours before the proceedings began.

"I must say that towns become cities when someone comes along with the daring of the soul," Emanuel Cleaver, a former mayor of Kansas City, told the crowd during the service. "Make no mistake, before Lamar brought the Chiefs to Kansas City in 1963, this was a town known for its lively stockyards, picturesque boulevards, and the dubious distinction as the home of the Kansas City Athletics.

"When the Chiefs won the Super Bowl, the world had to pay attention."

Carl Peterson, Chiefs president and general manager at the time, remembered Hunt's bond with the fans on game days, where he would say "Hi, I'm Lamar Hunt" while walking around and shaking hands.

"Lamar was an uncommon man who had no pretenses," Peterson said.

Clark discussed a party where guests talked of their favorite places: Nantucket, the French Riviera, and others.

"When it was Dad's turn, he did not hesitate in responding with 'Arrowhead Stadium,'" Clark said. "After a little prodding from the other guests, he went on to explain that no place on earth brought him more joy than the home of the Chiefs."

In fact, though some had badmouthed Kansas City as a rube town best known for its pungent stockyards, Hunt himself always championed the city.

"Kansas City is really a wonderful place," he said. "It amazes me how things happen. One of the blessings of my life was moving the Texans to Kansas City."

During his lifetime, Hunt was not one to embrace new technology. He couldn't navigate the web or even, when daylight savings arrived, change the digital clock in his car. And no one would have been more surprised than Hunt by the outpouring online after he passed away. At his Legacy. com Guest Book, well over 1,000 comments—including ones posted more than three years after his death—have appeared. Some write that they wish they had met him just once; others praise the billionaire's son as a man of the people.

"During the early '90s I worked for the catering company that served the owner's suite at Arrowhead," notes one. "Prior to every game Mr. Hunt would always greet the catering staff in his suite before his morning run in the parking lot. His graciousness, even with part-time employees, always impressed me as a great person who knew how to treat people."

Another writes, "I first met Mr. Hunt in person at a Chiefs rally. He loved to mingle in the crowd. When I spotted him I walked over to him, shook his hand, and said it was an honor to meet him. He thanked me and asked how long I have been a fan."

And finally, another—who obviously flies coach—touches upon her brush with fame.

"As I was leaving a jet bound for Dallas from Kansas City one Sunday afternoon after a Chiefs game, Mr. Hunt offered to remove my luggage from the overhead compartment for me. We had been season-ticket holders for 15 years at that time so I was aware that he was Mr. Hunt. We spoke briefly as we left the plane about the season the Chiefs were having that year and what his hopes were for the remainder. It was a great pleasure to have met such a kind and humble man as Mr. Hunt."

Of course, his family also remembered him fondly, and their recollections were gathered in a different media format. A 90-minute DVD called *Games: Lamar Hunt and the Landscape of American Sports*, produced by Steve Sabol of NFL Films and distributed to Hunt's friends and colleagues in 2007, interviewed sports luminaries and close Hunt associates. It also offered ample time for Hunt's children to share thoughts of their father.

Though all of them had access to the best U.S. sports has to offer—NFL games seen from luxury suites, tickets to Chicago Bulls NBA Finals games—their memories of their dad were common to any U.S. family.

Lamar Hunt Jr.: "My dad coached fifth and sixth grade football at the school I was at. And I remember the painstaking effort he made to cut out the decals on our helmets."

Sharron Hunt Munson: "On the beach, he would draw a court and invent some game. Taking vacations, he would always organize elaborate sporting events that included everybody. Night after night, Ping-Pong tournaments or volleyball tournaments."

Dan Hunt: "I remember getting the socks whipped off of me at checkers. There was no mercy in playing him at checkers, and, if I won, I got a dime."

Clark Hunt also spoke on the DVD, but perhaps his most moving comments appeared in an article published the year his father died. In it, he talked about many times opening a bag of footballs and playing catch with his dad in a quiet Arrowhead Stadium the day before a Chiefs contest. As was his wont, Lamar would create a game—in this case who could boot a perfect spiral right into the hands of the other.

"As a kid, to have the chance to be up there when there wasn't a game going on—wow," Clark said. "It's an extremely special memory. It's something I'll associate forever with my father."

Hunt's impact on his family was profound. His impact on pro sports during his lifetime was revolutionary.

The son of the richest man in the U.S., Hunt could have just kicked back for years—decades, really—and lived off his trust. Most work to survive, but no such incentive motivated Hunt. For appearance's sake, he could have grabbed a sinecure at Hunt Oil and whiled away his days; no one would have complained.

Instead, he jumped into pro sports. It can be argued Hunt was the most important sports executive of the last half of the 20th century. His obvious contributions have been noted—founding a pro football league, coining the term *Super Bowl*, welcoming black football players, getting pro soccer off the ground, opening up tennis tournaments—but they helped spark broader achievements that may not be as apparent.

Consider his impact on cities. To be considered big-league in the United States, one needs a professional sports franchise. Cities such as Oakland, Denver, and Buffalo were barely recognized before the AFL placed franchises there; now, they've attracted professional teams from other sports as well. Whereas residents of those cities once only knew pro sports via their televisions, they now can enjoy it live, in some cases year-round.

Building the first pro-soccer-specific stadium in Columbus helped catapult that Ohio city, often overshadowed by Cleveland and Cincinnati, into sports prominence. But his biggest impact, of course, unfolded in Kansas City. He invested tens of millions of dollars in a little-known town, constructing Arrowhead Stadium and building amusement parks. Though he couldn't persuade the populace to build a stadium for his MLS Wizards, his efforts paved the way for new owners OnGoal, LLC to nab approval for an 18,000-seat soccer stadium in 2010.

Consider his impact on leagues. Hunt's success blazed a trail for other competing leagues in other sports, such as the American Basketball Association and the World Hockey Association, to form and fight their well-heeled rivals. They eventually sent four teams apiece to the stronger NBA and NHL, unable to procure a full merger as the AFL had. On the flip side, to face off against the NFL today is folly. The battlefield is littered with pretenders: from the World Football League in the 1970s to the United States Football League in the 1980s and the XFL for one hapless season in 2001. None could stir up even a hint of interest in their teams from the NFL. Smartly, the new United Football League sees itself as more of a feeder of players to the NFL rather than as a competitor.

Consider his impact on employment. By launching the AFL and its eight teams, he created jobs for thousands of football players through the years who otherwise would have been relegated to making a living as trash haulers or as shoe salesmen.

"When I had heard Lamar and some other guys were putting together a new league, I thought to myself, *That might be a pretty good deal. That gives football players another opportunity,*" Forrest Gregg recalled. "You didn't know from year to year if you'd make the team or not. There was always a new bunch of guys coming from college to compete for your job."

Along with players, hundreds of coaches and general managers wouldn't have been employed had Hunt never envisioned the league. By extension, thousands of workers at football stadiums across the country owe Hunt their gratitude.

And it's not just those employed by original AFL teams. The Dallas Cowboys never would have been created without the threat of Hunt, especially since the original NFL Dallas Texans were such a flop. The NFL handed Minnesota a team only because it didn't want to cede the city to the AFL. New Orleans Saints, winners of the 2010 Super Bowl? They exist only because Hunt agreed to merge with the NFL, and congressional approval of said merger depended on U.S. Representative Hale Boggs and U.S. Senator Russell Long, Louisiana politicians who demanded an expansion franchise as part of the bargain.

Consider his impact on the fan experience. Many owners refuse to mingle with fans; Hunt always wanted to hear their ideas. On Sundays during his tenure, Arrowhead Stadium resembled a college-football stadium, as tailgaters filled the parking lots and fans donned red. In-your-face video boards and music so loud it detracted from the game were not Hunt's style. He was devoted to entertaining his customers by simpler means, and he shook his head in dismay when fellow owners disagreed.

For example, during the 1969 season, Hunt asked an AFL owner if he could bring the Chiefs cheerleaders and mascots (a horse and Indian chief) to an away game, as well as let members of the red-coated booster club cheer the Kansas City players as they ran through the tunnel. He was shot down on all requests.

"I don't think any business can stand still, and I think this is the problem with some teams in pro football today," Hunt said. "The owners are still running their clubs like a hobby."

His impact on pro sports unmistakable, the next question that arises is: How did a mild-mannered Texan revolutionize pro sports? After all, Lamar Hunt didn't set out to shake up the sports world; he was mainly concerned with erecting viable businesses.

Hunt possessed four major traits that forged his ability to transform the sports landscape, along with one bonus factor as essential as the rest:

1. Passion

Hunt's passion for sports was obvious. It resembled that of a little kid, save for the fact Hunt rarely expressed his excitement in the manner common to sports aficionados—jumping up and down, yelling loudly, jawboning into the wee hours. His type of ardor wouldn't electrify "Pardon the Interruption" or sports talk radio. But morning, noon, and night—and when he woke up at 3:00 AM and jotted down ideas—sports consumed him.

Wilson said, "He loved all sports. He was in it for the game. He wasn't in it for the big money."

Pierson, the former president of the Pro Football Writers of America, cited an unquenchable inner motivation for Hunt to refuse to settle only for pro football success.

"There was some need in him," Pierson said. "There was something about the sports industry that drove him, probably to his detriment. He was probably more involved in ownership than winning. He didn't equate success to a won-lost record."

Hunt often suggested some people were born to be oilmen (such as his father) while others were born to follow other pursuits. When Hunt spoke at the funeral of Derrick Thomas, the Chiefs' linebacker who died in a car accident in 2000, he pointed out that Thomas was "just meant to be a Chief"—after all, he was born on the same day the Chiefs beat the Buffalo Bills to clinch a spot in the first Super Bowl.

As well, Hunt noted his own fervor for sports was inherent.

"Some people are very good at playing the violin or trading stocks. One talent that I might have—or, at least, a challenge I enjoy—is trying to sell tickets and build a sports venture," he said.

Building a franchise captivated Hunt. Like an entrepreneur, he wanted to be the first, to create, to get in on the ground floor.

"I really enjoy the challenge of start-up operations," Hunt said. "I think there's more of an appeal to creating things.... That has more of an appeal to it to me than buying the Washington Redskins. The Redskins are already there. Where's the challenge? I like the challenge of making new teams a success. There's a lot of fun to that."

His passion for sports often revealed itself in Hunt's obsession with details. Though he remained hands-off in general—hiring the best people and letting them make decisions—once Hunt's mind latched onto something he wanted to be just right, he pursued it vigorously.

When the Chiefs were poised to celebrate the 40th anniversary of the Dallas Texans' lone championship, Hunt wrote the script for the halftime ceremony, arguably the only NFL owner to ever undertake such an endeavor.

"I enjoy it, foolish as it sounds, and I think it's important," he explained.

Hunt even cared about the sales of souvenirs, soft drinks, and programs around the stadium.

"He told me visually one time about how to sell programs," Meredith recalled. "He said you have to attack the face of the buyer with the program three times from the time they leave the car to the time they get into their seat."

Anyone who heard Hunt's pleas to pass certain NFL rules—and WCT chief Williams, a South African who knew little about American football, often had to listen to his boss drone on about why some rules should be implemented—knew his fervor was genuine. Listen to his detailed argument against the most innocuous play in football, when the quarterback takes a knee near the end of the first half or as the game is finishing.

"No other sport allows you to just hold on to the ball like that," Hunt complained. "In basketball, they have the 10-second rule and the shot clock, plus they are allowed to foul you. In baseball, you still have to keep pitching the ball. In soccer, you can try to keep the ball away, but it takes great skill to do that. But in football, we allow our quarterbacks to just fall to one knee to run out the clock, and I don't think that's good for the sport."

Hunt's attention to detail extended to the workplace. Recalled Humphries, "Secretaries would warn us before he'd come down to our offices, and we'd all clean up our desks. He was meticulous."

When plans went awry during an event, Hunt rushed to fix the problem, rather than let others handle the details.

"We had a storm during one WCT tournament near Austin, Texas," recalled Mike Davies. "He was on the court with a broom sweeping up."

For those who believe passion can be measured by numbers, it's hard to argue with Hunt's dedication to the Chiefs. Even though he never lived in Kansas City, he missed fewer than two dozen games in 47 seasons. Nearly every time he'd forgo a contest, he'd choose a family obligation—such as watching Clark play soccer or being with his wife when Lamar Jr. was born. When that wasn't the case, most likely another of his sports' interests interfered. One time the Wizards appeared in the MLS Championship Game the same day the Chiefs played the despised Raiders.

"Very traumatic," Hunt said of the choice. (He watched the Wizards capture the title.)

Hunt's passion for the Chiefs could sometimes lead to myopia. Gosselin recalled that before each season during the down years of the 1970s and 1980s, Hunt would treat the media to dinner.

"Lamar would have everyone write down what they thought the Chiefs' record would be," Gosselin said. "The media would write down 6–10 or 5–11. He'd always write 10-6. It was comical."

Hunt's overall gentleness and placid manner led some to believe he lacked fire inside. Most knew differently.

"He was always involved in a quiet way, but he was competitive," recalled Bill Bartholomay. "He liked to win."

Said the Cowboys' Jones, "He is very, very aggressive within the rules. I smile when I watch him in meetings because I know how competitive he is. He's very gentlemanly, but yet he is a tremendous competitor."

Bottom line: If Hunt hadn't possessed such inner drive, the sports world would feature a completely different look today.

2. Humility

Hunt's profession teemed with egos, as did his home state. Armed with his humility, he stood out like a fan draped in red on a Sunday afternoon at Oakland-Alameda County Coliseum.

Just like it's counterintuitive to think that by swinging more slowly you can hit a golf ball farther than by trying to crush it, Hunt's modest manner helped him accomplish big dreams in sports better than an unchecked brashness ever could.

Recalled Wilson, "He was a very conservative fellow. Whatever he did, he did for the best of the league. That's why I admired him."

"Lamar was always the guy who kept his temper," said Houston owner Bud Adams, referring to the darkest AFL days along with the league's merger debate. "When things would get out of hand, he would bring everybody back around to making a decision. He was a quiet, quiet force."

The Packers' Harlan said Hunt's humility worked to his benefit.

"I think it helped a great deal. You knew how [whatever he proposed] would be presented," Harlan recalled. "He would make his point in a quiet, gentlemanly voice."

As a Christian man, Hunt modeled the best of the religion's virtues, including self-control and honesty along with humility. Think if he hadn't been around for merger talks. With Hunt, known to be rational and trust-worthy, the negotiations could be pursued in secret, a necessity. The alternative? NFL and AFL owners bellowing their demands, which would have scuttled the deal.

Hunt's humility engendered fierce loyalty among staffers.

"I gave him an idea for the Super Bowl coin toss; I think it was to use [New Orleans Saints kicker] Tom Dempsey as a ceremonial coin-tosser," recalled Meredith. "He addressed a letter to Pete Rozelle and wrote, 'I have an idea from a young man in our office.' He could have taken credit but didn't."

And that humble nature never changed, regardless of how many honors Hunt received or leagues he started. Berry said he was impressed when they would see each other at the Pro Football Hall of Fame each year.

"One of the things that's interesting, when I'd see him in Canton, we'd have coffee together. He never changed any," Berry recalled. "He was just sitting there, the same down-to-earth guy he was 50 years before."

Some questioned if his humility were merely an act, but no doubt it was sincere. At one point, his biography in *Who's Who in America*—once the bible of defining important people in the country before celebrity culture took over—consisted of three lines; Hunt objected to cooperating further. Said his longtime secretary Finn, "He just hated to be put in there."

3. Responsiveness

In Dallas, the mail carrier delivered an endless supply of letters addressed to Hunt at his office. Many asked for money (one, from a self-proclaimed "motion picture coordinator," wanted a mere $180 million to build Cinema City and a parking garage) while others claimed they had the secret to guarantee victories. Here's an unsolicited missive from Inglewood, California, that appeared in his inbox:

"Hey, what's the word, Lamar? What's the line of the day? What's blowing in the wind? What's the reason you can't have a winning season?

"Here's the situation: I want to be a full-time football analyst at my home and talk to you on paper or by phone, if I can call collect. I do not use computers, just my head and what's in it .... I want to spend my time analyzing football to someone who will listen and pay me good for it.

"I can really make your team a winner! What am I worth to you?"

One from Odessa, Texas—which included the line, "When you owners realize that winning is a matter of molecular science and not a race to the swift or a battle to the strong, you will increase your gross profits"—drew this penciled note from Hunt in the left corner: "For your 'not' file! LH."

Another letter from Kansas City ended "Sincerely Yours to Command," which drew a handwritten aside from Hunt: "One of the great lines I've ever read (to close a letter)."

Overall the copy was riddled with typos and included a chart about how best to penetrate the goal line. Absurd as it was, Hunt scribbled a note of response at the top: "Jean, type and send, Dear Mr. Young, Thanks for your letter and the ideas expressed. I appreciate your thinking of us and your continued commitment to the Chiefs."

As much as possible, regardless of the nature of the letter, Hunt answered them all. A typical one arrived in July 1985 from a Kansas City man. Written single-spaced over two pages, it essentially discusses his sports interests—especially in terms of photography—but doesn't ask for a job with the Chiefs or state any other purpose for writing. It seems he just wanted Lamar to know his enthusiasm for football ("I love getting tackled hard, to the point where I want 25 carries per game") and other thoughts.

"Neither the Redskins nor the Raiders is a poorly run NFL team, but I don't like to see either team win," the man wrote. "The Redskins and Raiders play too dirty."

Within a few weeks, Hunt responded on his Kansas City Chiefs Football Club letterhead (featuring a KC helmet), which was telling for a few reasons. Even 15 years after the merger, his stationery noted only teams in the American Football Conference at the bottom. Listed were the years the Chiefs were "American Football League Champions" and "World Champions"—no word of the National Football League or of Super Bowls. Not only that, even though the Oakland Raiders had moved to Los Angeles and the Baltimore Colts had fled in the middle of the night to Indianapolis, they were referred to by their original cities. Hunt was not one to splurge on new stationery whenever a team found greener pastures.

Hunt's response to the query read:

Thank you for your letter of July 20. Please pardon my tardy reply.

Appreciated your comments concerning both collegiate and professional football as well as your interest in photography.

Thanks again for your writing and for your interest in sports.

Sincerely,

Lamar Hunt

One can only imagine the excitement in the fan's household when that simple note touched down in their mailbox. But that scene was replayed thousands of times during Hunt's days running sports franchises. Shunning the description as an owner, Hunt said the fans owned the teams; he was simply the founder. Among sports leaders—ensconced in luxury suites and rarely accommodating to fans—Hunt's style was atypical. He believed in engaging his customers or potential customers.

Though it has always been hard to find, say, George Steinbrenner's name in a New York City phone book, Hunt always listed his home number in Dallas. He wanted to be accessible. Fielding calls in the middle of the night from those eager to complain about his sports teams or begging for a charitable handout, Hunt would listen, as hard as it might be after being jolted from his sports-colored dreams.

Tagliabue said, "He was a person who cared about people, and not just because you had a business relationship with him. He didn't have an ego."

SMU president Turner enjoyed working with Hunt, who served as a trustee at his alma mater beginning in 1997. He said Hunt—who could often be found wearing a "Mustang Maniac" T-shirt at basketball games—always expressed concern about the customer, especially when he raised money to help build Gerald J. Ford Stadium and the Paul B. Loyd Jr. All-Sports Center.

"He was constantly talking about the experience the alumni would have—every seat would be a good seat," Turner recalled. "He was a regular guy. He would sit in the back, even though he had seats reserved in the front. He really liked to be the average fan. That made him such a good communicator about what the average fan wanted."

Hunt's good friend Edward "Buzz" Kemble of Fort Worth—a fellow third-string football player at SMU—saw the fruits of Hunt's outreach during a college basketball game in Kansas City.

"The people who came up to him, it was just unreal," Kemble told the *Dallas Morning News*. "He has got to be the most popular person I ever heard of in Kansas City. And they always called him Lamar."

Sometimes, at first blush, Hunt seemed like the least popular person in the room, like a shunned girl at a teenage dance. While many NFL owners could back-slap their way around a packed stadium, Hunt didn't need to be seen hobnobbing; standing alone at an event was fine with him. That's the way Meredith—who worked for the newly formed Tampa Bay Buccaneers at the time—first met his future boss, during a Pro Bowl party in the mid-1970s.

"No one's talking to him. I went over, and we talked soccer for 30 minutes," Meredith said. "Two years later, because of that conversation, he had someone call to see if I wanted to become p.r. director of the Tornado [a job Meredith accepted]. That guy didn't forget anything."

Hunt's responsiveness spurred loyalty from his players.

"When I was in Dallas, Jerry Jones would introduce himself to a lot of players. And I thought that was really neat," said Kansas City Pro Bowl guard Brian Walters. "Then I come here and find out that the guy here, not only does he meet and greet, he knows everything about every player. He comes in every game, no matter if we win or lose. He shakes your hand, calls you by your name.

"I mean, those things—I was blown away by that."

4. Patience

Hunt's three biggest sports ventures all suffered horrendous—even comical—beginnings. The first few years of the AFL, NASL, and WCT would have tested the sanity of any investor. Hunt's patience saved them all.

Think of the two-point conversion. Its importance is exemplified by its use in a number of recent Super Bowls (including a crucial attempt by the New Orleans Saints in 2010, which gave them a 24–17 lead over Indianapolis, meaning a fourth-quarter Peyton Manning drive could only have tied the game, not won it). When Hunt started his NFL crusade, he hadn't even celebrated his 40th birthday. By the time it passed, he was nearly eligible for Social Security.

"It didn't take that long. Just 24 years," he said, laughing. "But seriously, what's more boring than watching a kicker kick an extra point 99 percent of the time?"

Tagliabue recalled a humorous story during his days offering legal advice to the NASL that is a quintessential example of Hunt's patience (as well, in a way, of his quiet passion). In the late 1970s, boxing promoter Don King proposed an NASL franchise, to be called the Montreal Shuffles. They would play in Olympic Stadium, and King said Muhammad Ali would be his partner. King's interest in launching it? The sport would never gain traction in North America unless it appealed to African Americans in the inner city. And with Ali and himself as the front men, that could be accomplished.

Anyone who has seen King's bluster on television or in person knows his love for talking. He began telling the collected NASL owners about his vision. Paul Tagliabue remember the event clearly.

"Lamar was the one who stuck with that conversation from 10 PM until 5 AM," Tagliabue said. "All the owners had long since fallen asleep. If Don King hadn't fallen asleep before Lamar, they probably would have gone to lunch together."

Though Hunt could listen to Don King for hours without betraying any hint of irritation, his patience did fail him in one setting—the golf course.

"I try not to lose my temper with my little kids or the Chiefs," Hunt said. "The only time I lose my temper is on the golf course. And that's because I'm a bad player."

5. Money

Hunt's Buddha-like patience was emboldened by his fortune. The Texan's deep pockets kept at least four professional entities—the AFL, the NASL, WCT, and MLS—from either folding earlier than they did or from facing severe financial crises. Though WCT was the brainchild of David Dixon, he lasted barely a month because the losses were too deep; Hunt soldiered on for another 22 years, even as losses reached nine figures.

Safe to say Hunt, during his lifetime, didn't make much money on sports. The Chiefs could be counted on to turn an annual profit, save for the 1982 strike season, but his soccer teams and tennis circuit could not. But one day, his descendants will benefit from his toil. The value of his stakes in the Chiefs and the Bulls have soared; when those shares are sold (as is likely later this century, since few successful family businesses endure more than three or four generations), Hunt's heirs will cash in well over $1 billion, even after taxes.

Those four traits, combined with the starting pot of money provided by his father, thrust Hunt into the stratosphere of sport's import. He was also known for other characteristics in his business dealings.

Hunt sometimes exasperated associates with his laborious decision-making process. Rational, deliberate, and never willing to fly by the seat of his pants, Hunt examined every possible angle.

"I was doing a contract with a guy from Los Angeles who wanted four of our events," former WCT CEO Williams recalled. "I drew up a five-page document with our counsel. Lamar showed up at 5 or 6 PM on a Friday. He said, 'Can I have a copy?' He took it home during the weekend. He came back, and it had grown to 25 pages. I said, 'Lamar, I don't even have time to read this.'"

WCT signed one of the first deals with fledgling ESPN to broadcast 14 tournaments. When Williams arrived later and looked it over, he was a little confused by one portion.

"I said, 'How did we get to 14¢ per household?' The ESPN guy said, 'Thank God someone asked. It was three weeks of negotiations with Lamar.'"

No dummy when it came to deals, Hunt was unfailingly patient and never jumped on any of the dozens offered each year.

"He had one great saying when a deal seemed too good to be true: 'The money runs out long before the deals,'" Davies recalled. "He always knew there'd be more deals."

Set aside Hunt's precise manner, and his way of doing business seemed almost folksy, along the lines of Wal-Mart founder Sam Walton. Both unassuming—not ones to point fingers and threaten when they didn't get their way—they were also fearful of ostentation of any sort, though their millions could buy ostentation to outdo anyone in the country.

Hunt saw nothing wrong with driving prospective clients around in a two-door Chrysler Cordoba. Recalled Humphries: "I always had to get in the back; he'd be selling to someone in the front. I would move the seatback to get in, and it would just fall down."

Davies said, "He never had time for a haircut. He'd have to get it at the airport. He never had time to buy clothes."

Added Humphries, "What amused me was that his secretary, Jean Finn, would leave piles of written material on the floor, often like stepping stones, so that he would remember to read them."

A famous story involving Hunt regards the time he was too busy to get both shoes resoled, so he settled for one before returning to a meeting.

Williams remembered when Hunt didn't even find the time to send one to a cobbler.

"He'd love to put his feet up on this antique desk I had from South Africa," Williams said. "There would be these two eyes [holes in soles] staring me down to the socks."

Save for his beautiful home and a few other perks, Hunt simply avoided most of the trappings of the rich and famous. He felt comfortable pursuing a simple, all-American life. Recalled Meredith, "We'd drive back from meetings for Davey O'Brien National Quarterback Award in Fort Worth. He'd say, 'You hungry?' We'd go to the rattiest hamburger place. He'd get a cheeseburger, a Mars bar, and a diet Dr Pepper."

Because of his gentle, everyman nature, Hunt's success rarely generated envy or suspicion. And he always made others feel *he* was the special one to be in their presence.

Harlan recalled when Hunt and good friends of his from the Dallas area traveled to Lambeau Field in the mid-1990s when the Chiefs were slated to play the Packers.

"They wanted to see the Green Bay atmosphere—they walked around the tailgating, he saw our private boxes," he said. "Afterwards, he sent me a letter. I'll never forget that last sentence: 'I'm so proud to be in the same league as the Green Bay Packers.' You can imagine how the Green Bay Packers felt about being in the league with Lamar Hunt.

"Number one with me was his love for the National Football League. Pete Rozelle and Paul Tagliabue could have gone to Lamar and asked about anything. If they said it was for the betterment of the league, Lamar would go for it."

Harlan's son Kevin—now an announcer for CBS Sports—broadcast Chiefs games for a number of years after graduating from the University of Kansas.

"Lamar would make it a point to come up to me at league meetings and tell me how much he enjoyed Kevin and his family and the job he was doing for the Chiefs," Harlan remembered. "He always made that a point for years. He even talked about him when he left. 'We sure miss Kevin.'"

Most know about Hunt's legendary refusal to fly first class. Even when he was uncomfortable in coach—and who hasn't been?—he would not try to better his situation, especially at someone else's expense.

There's a story Kyle Rote Jr.—a star on the Dallas Tornado teams of the 1970s—has shared many times with friends and in speeches.

"I was flying to Kansas City for a Fellowship of Christian Athletes board meeting. Unbeknownst to me, Lamar is on the airplane. There were only two seats on his side of the aisle.

"He ends up sitting next to this lady who's very overweight and she's taking 60 to 70 percent of the space of those seats. I say, 'Hey, Lamar. I think I'm the last one to get on the airplane. I have a totally empty three-seat row so I can do some paperwork. Feel free to come back and we can catch up on Lamar Jr., Clark, Dan, and your new soccer ventures.'

"I sat down and I immediately realized that was not going to happen. Despite his love for talking sports in general and soccer in particular, he was not going to join me. Why? He did not want to embarrass the lady next to him by leaving. You don't find many people at his level of significance who are still sensitive to the feelings of others."

One time, Hunt invited *Dallas Morning News* sportswriter Pouncey to a tennis event in London. Pouncey recalled Hunt bought the sportswriter a first-class ticket; on that same flight, he and Norma sat in coach.

Williams said he'd upgrade Hunt to first class whenever they flew together, getting to the airport early to make sure Hunt couldn't dissuade him from the move ("He was like a kid in a candy store in first class"). One time, Williams wanted to take him to Japan to help negotiate the selling of WCT's Japanese event to Seiko. Though a flying veteran around the U.S. and Europe, Hunt had no interest in such a lengthy trip, even in first class.

"He said, 'Why can't we do this deal in Dallas?' I said, 'To get the maximum amount out of this, we have to eyeball the Japanese, meet with Seiko. If I bring Lamar Hunt, that will cement the deal,'" Williams recalled.

"Dallas to Tokyo is 11 time zones. He started 11 days before we left, switching his clock back, an hour each day. When we landed, he was so screwed up. He had so upset his body clock. We stayed three days and flew back. When he arrived back in Dallas, he didn't know if he was Arthur or Martha."

Many times, others had no idea who Hunt was, despite his fame.

"A group of us were out to lunch in Kansas City," recalled Meredith. "A couple of people had Chiefs stuff on. The waitress started talking. 'That Lamar Hunt is a disgrace. He should get a new coach.' Someone at the table said, 'This is Lamar Hunt.' If she didn't turn eight shades of green."

Even when Hunt was recognized, not everyone knew exactly what he did. In Dallas, people would walk up to him thinking he was the owner of the Cowboys and demand that he fire Tex Schramm.

Hunt would never announce his presence to benefit himself. Davies recounted a humorous story of his boss abroad.

"We went to Paris a few times, and he loved to eat in the top restaurants. He had a list of the top 10 restaurants, and he'd cross them off afterwards. But if we didn't have reservations, and the restaurant was full, he wouldn't go in. He'd never use his influence to get a table.

"We were standing in line once to get a table. A friend of Lamar's started to walk in. He said, 'Hey, Lamar, what are you doing? Tell them who you are.' Lamar said, 'Who should I tell them I am?' 'Tell them you're Bunker Hunt,' his friend said. Then the doorman said, 'You're Bunker Hunt?' He let Lamar right in."

Hunt summed up his attitude on the topic.

"I do detest ostentation, big-dealing, like using your name to get a better hotel reservation or a good seat in a restaurant," he said. "I just can't stand to see people thinking they should get a better table because of some influence they think they might have. I believe in taking your turn. It's only fair."

Even at Arrowhead—a place where all of the 78,000 fans would have gladly let him cut in line—Hunt followed his dictum when yearning for a hot dog.

"Someone would come up to him and say, 'You look just like Lamar Hunt.' They just couldn't believe he was in a concession line," Steadman said.

Though a scrub who hadn't lettered and who caught only a handful of passes at SMU, Hunt was honored when his No. 80 football jersey—the one he wore his senior year—was retired in 2000 during the opening of Gerald J. Ford Stadium, which replaced Ownby Stadium. (Hunt also joined a campaign to sell season tickets that first year; about 10,700 were purchased, the second best in Mustang history.)

Hunt's number was retired along with the likes of Doak Walker, Raymond Berry, and Forrest Gregg, all SMU legends. Embarrassed by the honor, Hunt let others know it. Recalled SMU's Turner: "Lamar got from us the name of every athlete who had worn No. 80. There were 20 or so other players who had worn it. He called them and in his good-natured way said he was sorry they were retiring the number because of him because he was on the bench. He told them he realized he wasn't worthy. They were stunned to get the call from him."

Though passionate about sports and the success of his ventures, Hunt enjoyed hobbies beyond sports. His favorite? Nothing could beat working around the yard, ironic considering his neighbors mainly favored landscape services.

"I try to work in the yard any day I'm in town for an hour or an hour and a half," he said. "And I only do it because it's pure fun. I'm not trying to save money on a yard man.

"The yard is what is really important to me. It is a source of much pride. [It] is my happiest time."

Hunt mowed his own lawn, though he often hired gardeners for minor work. He loved topiary, trimming shrubs and shaping them.

At Hunt's French provincial estate in Dallas in the 1980s, near a small lake, he created bears out of bushes and elephants out of shrubs. The idea sprang when he toured a greenhouse during one of Clark's high school track meets. He ordered mesh frames, and voilà—bears and elephants emerged that were almost lifelike. Hunt also shaped yaupon holly trees, laid out flower beds, bought rocks to scatter about, and embraced other gardening work with gusto. He credited his mother—a plant aficionado—for inspiring his joy in nature.

Meredith saw Hunt's zeal firsthand in the 1980s.

"He got me involved in the Dallas Arboretum. He could tell you Latin names of trees," Meredith recalled. "And one Saturday we planted Japanese beetle trees.

"Four months before he passed away, I get a clipping in the mail from the *Dallas Morning News*. There's a picture of the beetle trees on the 25th anniversary of their planting. He wrote a note. 'Thom, thought you'd want to see how they turned out.' He has more things in his head he needs to remember, but he found time to do that."

Starting in the 1960s Hunt—a stamp and coin collector as a boy—invested in art and antiques, sometimes spurred by Norma. He was a big fan of American landscape artist Thomas Moran. Methodical as ever, he'd study the history of a painting before buying it, often at private sales. He shunned publicity about his hobby and preferred purchasing at auctions through third parties, worried about security problems if word leaked.

Hunt's most famous move involved the purchase of *The Icebergs* by Frederic Edwin Church for $2.5 million in October 1979. After 33 paintings sold quickly at auction at Sotheby Parke Bernet in Manhattan, *The Icebergs* appeared. After starting at $500,000, the painting passed $1 million in bids within half a minute. Reportedly the audience gasped when the price topped $2 million for a canvas described as large and dirty that had been hanging for years in a stairwell in Manchester, England. Its seller had expected $30,000 or so at the most. The final $2.5 million offer by an unnamed telephone bidder nearly tripled the previous highest price paid for an American painting at the time.

At first, for public consumption, Hunt neither admitted nor denied he was the buyer. "I know it sounds funny, since I'm in a business as public as professional sports," he said, "but our collecting is very private. We're probably not too discriminating. We buy things just because we like the way they look in the house."

Once word trickled out that a "Texas oilman" had bought it (Paul Mellon, benefactor of the National Gallery of Art in Washington, D.C., was said to be the next-highest bidder at $2.4 million), the purchase infuriated many in the East Coast media. Huffed *Vogue*, "*Icebergs* was big, rare sentimental, but it wasn't a great picture, and its price reflected more about promotion than anything else."

After the hullabaloo over the purchase, Hunt turned around and offered *The Icebergs* to the Dallas Museum of Fine Arts. *People* magazine reported the painting was too big for the wall the Hunts hoped to hang it on, prompting the donation (the artwork did measure nine feet by five feet and weighed more than 500 pounds). Hunt said otherwise.

"I will say that we're tickled to death that it's in Dallas. I think that something like that is great because works of art become available for great masses of people."

Just as he hoped his name wouldn't get out as the buyer and giver of *The Icebergs*, Hunt preferred to support charitable organizations quietly. He backed the Nelson Atkins Museum of Art and Starlight Theatre in Kansas City, while in Dallas he was a benefactor of the Dallas Museum of Art (formerly the Dallas Museum of Fine Arts) and the Dallas Symphony Orchestra. Little known among his philanthropic endeavors was his support of Heart of a Champion, based in Dallas. It supports character development among middle-school students. His son Clark has also been involved with the group.

In fact, wherever one turns in Dallas, the legacy of Lamar and other Hunts is sure to be within sight. Most recently there's the Margaret Hunt Hill Bridge—with a signature 40-story white arch—stretching across the Trinity River, named after Lamar's sister who passed away in 2007. Downtown there's the Reunion Tower and Hyatt Regency Hotel, created thanks to investment by Lamar's stepbrother Ray Hunt. Thanksgiving

Tower was financed by Lamar, Nelson, and other Hunts in the 1980s and has housed Lamar's offices along with those of Hunt Sports Group.

Though many of his friends were passionate about politics, Hunt was not enamored.

"I'm not interested in politics, which is a weakness of mine," Hunt admitted. "I have absolutely no interest in running for political office, but I really feel badly that I am not more intimately aware of politics."

Despite his protestations, Hunt willingly gave money to candidates and political action committees, nearly $100,000 from the end of Jimmy Carter's presidency until he passed away in 2006. Most contributions were earmarked to the Republicans (former AFL quarterback Jack Kemp was backed by Hunt in his campaigns for the House of Representatives and for president). The rare donation found its way into the pocket of Democrats such as Glenn Sugiyama, who ran for the House of Representatives from Illinois.

And he could discuss politics with ease. Said Bartholomay, "He wasn't one-dimensional like some people in sports. We talked about everything—politics, Texas, you name it."

On the flip side, Hunt's wife, Norma, was far more than just a pretty face at his side.

"Norma was as big a sports fan as he was," Turner said. "She would give you statistics just like Lamar could. They were a real partnership in athletic endeavors. When you were talking football, Norma would be right in the middle of that conversation."

Norma, in fact, is said to be the only female who has attended every Super Bowl game. For Super Bowl XLI, she even participated in the coin flip soon after Lamar passed away.

Of course, Hunt will forever be remembered for creating the name Super Bowl and helping launch what has become the biggest one-day sporting event with the largest television audience in the world. In 2009, the Pro Football Hall of Fame made sure Hunt's contributions would not be forgotten when it unveiled the Lamar Hunt Super Bowl Gallery. The

$2.4 million project, which modernized a previous section of the Hall, features jerseys, helmets, footballs, trophies, and rings from all of the contests. Tucked away in one exhibit is an unopened Super Ball, which prompted Hunt's idea for the name.

That August, around the time of the Hall of Fame game, the Hunt family gathered and—holding scissors almost as long as their arms—snipped the red ribbon to inaugurate the gallery.

"My father was an incredible visionary, and I think he had high expectations for what the Super Bowl could become," Clark said. "But I don't think even he understood how important the game would become to American culture. He was always shocked that the halftime show and commercials became almost as important as the game itself."

As it stands now, Clark—who runs Hunt Sports Group, which oversees the operations of its two Major League Soccer franchises, and who serves as chairman of the board of the Kansas City Chiefs—is the future of the family's sports enterprises. If judged by his past, he's an impressive choice. At St. Mark's School, he served as captain of the football, soccer, and track teams. He earned a degree in business administration at SMU in 1987, where he graduated first in his class and was co-valedictorian. During that time, he lettered all four years on the Mustangs' soccer team.

Capitalizing on his lifelong interest in soccer, Clark helped found MLS with his father in the 1990s and now runs the Columbus Crew and FC Dallas franchises. He holds top positions in MLS, including chairman of the competition committee. On the NFL side, he was appointed by Commissioner Goodell to a number of committees, including the executive committee of the NFL Management Council and the labor committee, where at 43 he became its youngest member (Clark first started attending NFL meetings in his twenties). Heavily involved in the renovation of Arrowhead Stadium—a deal he helped negotiate with the powers that be in Kansas City—Clark has also overseen the development of a new practice facility for the Chiefs. He's maintained the Hunt's interest in the Chicago

Bulls and reports say he has made noises about expanding the family's sports properties into Europe.

No surprise, there are differences between father and son.

"Clark, he is a very, very...focused business person," Steadman, who watched the young Hunt grow up, told *SportsBusiness Journal*. "He is different in that respect from Lamar, who was a visionary, but as far as the business side of the club, that was not where Lamar's focus was."

Clark knows the weight of following in his father's large footsteps (not to mention his grandfather's).

"My dad was the most influential person in my life. Will I ever live up to my dad's reputation? No, that'll be impossible," Clark said.

Despite their wealth, no famous American family—from the Rockefellers to the Mellons—can avoid pain or misbehavior. But Lamar at least passed away knowing his family was united, especially compared to the trials his father endured in his effort to bring together three different branches. It was said the closest H.L. came occurred during a touch football game on the lawn at Mount Vernon, as the sons from his first family battled his sons from the two other branches. H.L. watched the proceedings from the porch.

That game took place in the fall of 1960—just as Lamar was starting to blaze his path in the pro game. And he generated such devotion from his immediate family that, once he constructed his sports empire, he could pass it on to his sons (Dan also works at Hunt Sports Group) knowing it couldn't be in better hands.

Of course, Hunt begat admiration far beyond his family. A sportsman who changed the face of professional games in America, Hunt was so well-regarded that he was fêted and honored during his lifetime, while many are toasted only posthumously. Lamar was alive to see his name etched on both the AFC Championship trophy and the Lamar Hunt Cup. And he enjoyed each of his eight Hall of Fame inductions (two hailed his business acumen, in Texas and in Kansas City) in person.

Many were affected by Hunt during his 74 years. But it wouldn't be a stretch to say that his pro football coach of the Chiefs for a decade, Marty Schottenheimer, is among those with the greatest love for the man.

Now in his late seventies, Schottenheimer—a recent inductee to the Chiefs Hall of Fame—has met thousands of people. As a pro football lifer going back to the old AFL, he's gone to war in hundreds of games with fellow players, coaches, executives, owners. Relationships forged with many of them are strong. When it comes to Hunt, a simple sentence says it all:

"He is the finest person and human being I've ever known," Schottenheimer said.

SOURCES

Author Interviews:

Ernie Accorsi (former general manager of the Baltimore Colts, Cleveland Browns, and New York Giants); Rob Baade (president of the International Association of Sports Economists); Bill Bartholomay (chairman emeritus of the Atlanta Braves, who helped found Atlanta's North American Soccer League team); Raymond Berry (Hall of Fame wide receiver and Hunt's teammate at Southern Methodist University); Andrew Brandt (National Football Post president and Wharton School of Business professor); Butch Buchholz (member of the Handsome Eight and founder of the Sony Ericsson Open); Bud Collins (former NBC announcer and author of numerous tennis books); Lester Crown (Chicago Bulls investor and former chairman of General Dynamics); Mike Davies (former executive director of World Championship Tennis); Rick Gosselin (*Dallas Morning News* sportswriter and former *Kansas City Star* sportswriter); Forrest Gregg (Hall of Fame offensive tackle and Hunt's teammate at Southern Methodist University); Sunil Gulati (U.S. Soccer Federation head and president of Major League Soccer's New England Revolution); Bob Harlan (chairman emeritus of the Green Bay Packers); Bob Hermann (former owner of pro soccer's St. Louis Stars and former chairman of the NASL's executive committee); Rick Holton (whose father helped sponsor Hunt's tennis ventures); Ted Howard (former NASL executive); Rod Humphries (former COO of WCT among other positions there); Don Maynard (played in every American Football League season for New York Jets); Patrick McCaskey (Chicago Bears executive); Andy McKenna (former chairman of the Chicago White Sox and the Chicago Cubs); Thom Meredith (Hunt's one-time administrative assistant who also worked for the Dallas Tornado and WCT); Bobby Moffat (longtime Dallas Tornado player); Murray Olderman (former nationally syndicated columnist who drew Hunt's portrait for the Pro Football Hall of Fame); Don Pierson (former president of Pro Football Writers Association); Temple Pouncey (former *Dallas Morning News* sportswriter who covered soccer and tennis); Marty Rotberg (former NASL and WCT executive); Gale Sayers (drafted No. 1 by the AFL Kansas City Chiefs); Jim Schaaf (Kansas City Chiefs general manager from 1976 to 1988); Marty Schottenheimer (Kansas City Chiefs coach from 1989 to 1998); Hank Steinbrecher (former secretary general of the U.S. Soccer Federation); Paul Tagliabue (former commissioner of the National Football League); R. Gerald Turner (Southern Methodist University president); Owen Williams (former chief executive officer of WCT); Pat Williams (former Chicago Bulls general manager and present Orlando Magic GM); and Ralph Wilson (Buffalo Bills owner and original AFL owner with Hunt).

Books:

DeVito, Carlo. *Wellington: The Maras, the Giants, and the City of New York.* Chicago: Triumph Books, 2006.

Dixon, Dave. *The Saints, the Superdome, and the Scandal: An Insider's Perspective.* Gretna, LA: Pelican Publishing Company, Inc., 2008.

Felser, Larry. *The Birth of the New NFL: How the 1966 NFL/AFL Merger Transformed Pro Football.* Guilford, CT: The Lyons Press, 2008.

Gruver, Ed. *The American Football League: A Year-by-Year History, 1960–1969.* Jefferson, NC: McFarland & Company, Inc., 1997.

Halas, George, with Gwen Morgan and Arthur Veysey. *Halas by Halas.* New York: McGraw-Hill Book Company, 1979.

Harris, David. *The League: The Rise and the Decline of the NFL.* New York: Bantam Books, 1986.

Hill, Margaret Hunt. *H.L. and Lyda: Growing Up in the H.L. Hunt and Lyda Bunker Hunt Family*, as told by their eldest daughter. Little Rock, AK: August House Publishers, Inc., 1994.

Hurt, Harry III. *Texas Rich: The Hunt Dynasty from the Early Oil Days Through the Silver Crash.* New York: W.W. Norton & Company, 1981.

MacCambridge, Michael. *America's Game: The Epic Story of How Pro Football Captured a Nation.* New York: Random House, 2004.

Magee, David. *Playing to Win: Jerry Jones and the Dallas Cowboys.* Chicago: Triumph Books, 2008.

McChesney, Robert W. "Media Made Sport: A History of Sports Coverage in the United States," in *Media, Sports, & Society*, ed. Lawrence A. Wenner. Newbury Park, CA: Sage Publications, 1989.

Miller, Jeff. *Going Long: The Wild 10-Year Saga of the Renegade American Football League in the Words of Those Who Lived It*. New York: McGraw-Hill, 2003.

Richey, Tom. *Lamar Hunt and the Founding of the American Football League*. Rochester, NY: Mercury Print Productions, Inc., 2009.

Ross, Charles K. *Outside the Lines: African-Americans and the Integration of the National Football League*. New York: New York University Press, 1999.

Ryczek, William J. *Crash of the Titans: The Early Years of the New York Jets and the AFL*. Jefferson, NC: McFarland & Company, Inc., 2009.

Sayers, Gale, with Fred Mitchell. *Sayers: My Life and Times*. Chicago: Triumph Books, 2007.

St. John, Bob. *Tex!: The Man Who Built the Dallas Cowboys*. Englewood Cliffs, NJ: Prentice Hall Press, 1988.

Taylor, Otis, and Mark Stallard. *Otis Taylor: The Need to Win*. Champaign, IL: Sports Publishing, LLC, 2003.

Weiss, Don, with Chuck Day. *The Making of the Super Bowl: The Inside Story of the World's Greatest Sporting Event*. New York: McGraw-Hill, 2002.

Magazines:

Badenhausen, Kurt, Michael K. Ozanian, and Christina Settimi. "Recession Tackles NFL Team Values." *Forbes* (September 2, 2009).

Boyar, Jane, and Burt Boyar. "Pressure at Forest Hills." *New York Magazine* (August 31, 1970).

Burrough, Bryan. "Game Changers." *Texas Monthly* (February 2009).

Cope, Myron. "Would You Let This Man Interview You?" *Sports Illustrated* (March 13, 1967).

Deford, Frank. "Now Tennis Goes Mod." *Sports Illustrated* (February 12, 1968).

Ennis, Michael. "Would You Pay $2.5 Million for That Painting?" *Texas Monthly* (April 1980).

Goldman, Bruce. "Open Minded." *Cigar Aficionado* (September/October 1997).

Harvey, Randy. "Talking Football with Lamar Hunt." *Football Digest* (February 1979).

Jares, Joe. "Loser Takes $50,000; Winner, $1 Million." *Sports Illustrated* (December 6, 1971).

Jenkins, Dan. "Too Many Chiefs Made Too Many Touchdowns." *Sports Illustrated* (September 16, 1963).

Kirkpatrick, Curry. "Tuning Up for a New Hunt Ball." *Sports Illustrated* (May 22, 1972).

Kirkpatrick, Curry. "Overloaded with Circuit Breakers." *Sports Illustrated* (May 3, 1982).

Kirkpatrick, Curry. "And Suddenly He's a Man of Clay." *Sports Illustrated* (May 16, 1983).

Maule, Tex. "The Shaky New League." *Sports Illustrated* (January 25, 1960).

Maule, Tex. "Saturation in Dallas." *Sports Illustrated* (October 10, 1960).

Maule, Tex. "Judgment at Baltimore." *Sports Illustrated* (June 4, 1962).

No author listed. "Aw Gee, Guys." *Time* (June 9, 1980).

No author listed. "Fie on the Fees." *Sports Illustrated Scorecard*, edited by Jerry Kirshenbaum (August 7, 1979).

No author listed. "The 100 Most Expensive Homes in Dallas 2007." *D Magazine* (July, 2007).

Olsen, Jack. "The Unhappiest Millionaire." *Sports Illustrated* (April 4, 1960).

Olsen, Jack. "Biggest Cheapskate in Big D." *Sports Illustrated* (June 19, 1972).

Ottum, Bob. "Three Names and a Barrel of Money." *Sports Illustrated* (January 16, 1967).

Peppard, Alan. "Oil in the Family." *Vanity Fair* (June, 2008).

Reed, J.D. "Wallflowers in Bloom." *Sports Illustrated* (August 8, 1977).

Reid, Ron. "Coach, You're Fired!" *Sports Illustrated* (March 13, 1978).

Riffenburgh, Beau. "Chiefs' Hunt: His '59 Dream Changed Game." NFL Properties publication (1987).

Shrake, Edwin. "The Big Daddy of Sport." *Sports Illustrated* (September 7, 1970).

Newspapers:

Australian

Chicago Tribune

Columbus Dispatch

Daily Record (Jacksonville)

Dallas Morning News

Dallas Times Herald

Kansas City Star

Kansas City Times

Los Angeles Times

New York Times
News Tribune (Seattle)
Sun-Sentinel
Toledo Blade
Topeka Capital Journal
USA Today
Wall Street Journal
Washington Post

Television/DVD:

Camarata, Paul, and David Plaut. *Full Color Football: The History of the American Football League.* Showtime Sports, 2009.

Sabol, Steve. *GAMES: Lamar Hunt and the Landscape of American Sports.* Commissioned by the Hunt family, 2007.

Websites:

Banks, Don. "Losing Battle." http://157.166.224.103/inside_game/don_banks/news/2003/03/24/banks_insider/ (accessed March 24, 2003).

Dell'Apa, Frank. "Hunt a Quiet Pioneer of U.S. Soccer." http://soccernet.espn.go.com/columns/story?id=394199&cc=5901 (accessed December 13, 2006).

Forbes.com. "Soccer Team Valuations." http://www.forbes.com/lists/2009/34/soccer-values-09_Manchester-United_340001.html (accessed April 8, 2009).

Forbes.com. "NBA Team Valuations." http://www.forbes.com/lists/2009/32/basketball-values-09_Chicago-Bulls_321267.html (accessed December 9, 2009).

Gretz, Bob. "Album Brings Lamar to Life." http://www2.kcchiefs.com/news/2009/05/25/album_brings_lamar_to_life/ (accessed May 25, 2009).

Kansas City Chiefs. "The Game That Never Was." http://www.kcchiefs.com/news/article-1/THE-GAME-THAT-NEVER-WAS/9508B6ED-429A-4D15-9051-BAAF7770D9ED (accessed September 2009).

Kansas City Chiefs. "The Best Draft Trade in Chiefs History." http://www.kcchiefs.com/news/2009/04/13the_best_draft_trade_in_chiefs_history/ (accessed April 13, 2009).

Kansas City Chiefs. "Chiefs History: Uniforms." http://www.kcchiefs.com/team/chiefs-history/uniform-history.html (accessed October 2009).

Kansas City Chiefs. "Chiefs History: 1960s." http://www.kcchiefs.com/team/chiefs-history/1960s.html (accessed October 2009).

NFL.com. "History: 1951–1960." http://www.nfl.com/history/chronology/1951-1960 (accessed September 2009).

NFL.com. "History: 1961–1970." http://www.nfl.com/history/chronology/1961-1970 (accessed October 2009).

NFL.com. "History: 1991–2000." http://www.nfl.com/history/chronology/1991-2000 (accessed October 2009).

Pro Football Hall of Fame. "Lamar Hunt's Enshrinement Speech Transcript." http://www.profootballhof.com/hof/release.aspx?release_id=2268 (accessed October 2009).

Pro-Football-Reference.com. "Abner Haynes." http://www.pro-football-reference.com/players/H/HaynAb00.htm (accessed September 2009).

Rappaport, Ken. "AFL Opened Doors for Players from the Historically Black Colleges." http://www.nfl.com/news/story?id=09000d5d811dc3f7&template=without-video-with-comments& confirm=true (accessed November 2009).

Sullivan, Jeff. "Going to Kansas City: AFL's Texans Moved from Dallas in 1963." http://www.dallascowboys.com/news/news.cfm?id=3B862531-C242-17D4-EB7E58785A20B5CD (accessed October 2009).

Southern Methodist University Athletics. "90 Greatest Moments in SMU Football History." http://smumustangs.cstv.com/sports/m-footbl/spec-rel/greatest-moments.html (accessed October 2009).

Southern Methodist University Athletics. "Alumnus Lamar Hunt Remembered for His Lifelong Support of SMU." http://smu.edu/newsinfo/releases/06092.asp (accessed November 2009).

Other Sources:

Associated Press

Federal Elections Commission

North American Soccer League v. National Football League case: U.S. District Court, Southern District of New York, 1979.

North American Soccer League v. National Football League case: U.S. Court of Appeals, Second Circuit, 1982.

SportsBusiness Journal

Sports Business Daily

1982 Guide to World Championship Tennis

INDEX